BRING 'EM
BAC~~K ALIVE~~

By

with Ed~~~~

Hart Publishing Company, Inc. • *New York City*

Contents

TO BEGIN WITH . . .

It might be well to state at the outset that my aim is not to write a book that will add one more volume to the world's collection of natural histories or the existing treatises on the habits of wild animals. Whatever I have to say about the peculiarities of different species is incidental to my adventures in the field of collecting.

For eighteen exciting years I have been gathering live animals, reptiles and birds for the zoos, the circuses and the dealers. I have brought back to America thousands of specimens. A great many of these were collected for the New York Zoological Park, the Philadelphia Zoological Garden, the Lincoln Park Zoo in Chicago, the St. Louis Zoological Gardens, the Dallas Zoo, the San Diego Zoological Park, the Milwaukee Zoo and the smaller zoos located in Memphis, Kansas City, San Antonio, Minneapolis and other cities. Many others were absorbed by the Ringling Bros.-Barnum & Bailey Circus, the Al G. Barnes Wild Animal Show, the Sells-Floto Circus, the Christy Brothers Circus, the Hagenbeck-Wallace Circus and other similar organizations. A good percentage of these specimens were sold direct to the zoo authorities and circus owners, the rest through dealers.

I have had more than my share of thrills, including narrow escapes. Yet I am frank to say that these close calls do not represent a love of looking Death in the eye. I am not that kind of adventurer. I take no unnecessary risks. When a man operates on as big a scale as I do he doesn't have to look for trouble. No matter how careful one is, something is bound to go wrong when live animals and reptiles are handled wholesale. It is then that experience counts.

When I listed all the specimens with which I've returned to America since I started bringing 'em back alive I found myself wondering that I hadn't had more anxious moments. There were plenty, as I have indicated, but on the whole I consider my-

self lucky. So many live creatures, if they had tried real hard, could have made much more trouble for me.

Here's the list: 39 elephants; 60 tigers (Royal Bengal, Malayan and Manchurian); 28 spotted leopards; 20 black leopards; 10 clouded leopards; 4 Himalayan snow leopards; 20 hyenas; 52 orang-utans; 31 gibbon apes (white-handed, silvery, agile, Hoolock's and siamang); over 5,000 monkeys of different varieties; 20 tapirs; 120 Asiatic antelope and deer, including black buck, nilgai antelope, Indian gazelle, axis deer, barking deer, hog deer, sambor, etc.; 9 anoas or pigmy water buffalo; 1 sladang or Malayan gaur; 1 babirussa (rarest of wild swine); 2 African cape buffalo; 18 African antelope, including sable, waterbuck and the rare white oryx of the Sudan; 2 giraffes; 40 wild goats and sheep, including Markhor goats, Barbary sheep, Malayan serow and Punjab sheep; 11 camels; 40 kangaroos and wallobies; 2 Indian rhinoceros (the rarest and most valuable wild animals in America as this is written); 40 bears, including Malayan honey bears, Himalayan black bears and Indian sloth bears; 90 large pythons (over twenty feet in length); 1 king cobra (largest ever captured alive); over 100 small snakes, including half-grown pythons, cobras, vipers and other varieties; 5 giant monitor lizards; 15 crocodiles; over 500 small mammals of different species, including civet cats, Asiatic squirrels, binturongs, wild dogs, musangs, porcupines, marble cats, ant-eaters, etc.; over 100,000 birds, ranging all the way from the big ostrich-like cassowaries of the Panpan Islands down to Australian finches as small as humming birds, and including cockatoos, parrots, birds of Paradise, swans, cranes, peafowl, Himalayan song-thrushes, and such rare pheasants as the Impeyan, argus, tragopan, blood, fireback, Bulwar's and Prince of Wales.

There are scientists who have never left the great centers of civilization whose categorical knowledge of animals, reptiles and birds, based on years of delving into all the available records dealing with origin and other phases, exceeds my own. I know a man on the staff of a great museum who by the hour can trace back for centuries the feathered ancestors of birds that I have collected by the thousand for the American pet-shop market and the ancient forefathers of wild animals I have brought back by the score for the zoos and circuses. This man is an authority even though he has never left the United States. He is primarily a student.

I am a student too but in a different way. I have had to make a study of such hard-boiled details of the collecting business as the best way to get a snarling tiger out of a pit into a cage without getting messed up in the process, how to transfer a murderous king cobra from a crude native container to a modern snake box, how to—

But perhaps I'd better launch my story.

Tapir on a Rampage

ALMOST any animal is dangerous when aroused. In 1926 I came close to being killed by a tapir, the meekest of animals.

I was in Sumatra assembling a group of specimens that included some pythons, Sumatra hornbills, langur monkeys, civet cats, porcupines, a siamang gibbon and a tapir.

Normally it would have been safe to bet that the pythons would make more trouble for me than the rest of this collection put together. But this was not a normal situation. It was the tapir that won the Trouble Sweepstakes, breezing in with several lengths to spare.

The experience proved to me all over again how foolish it is to generalize about animals. I've seen two tigers, for instance, animals of the same sex and age and caught at the same time, display utterly different characteristics. One grew so tame that after a few weeks I was putting my hand inside its cage and stroking the back of its neck; the other became more and more vicious, until the process of feeding it involved real danger and required absolute caution.

It isn't much less intelligent to generalize about animals than it is to generalize about people. It's about as sensible to say, "Elephants are kind," or "elephants are mean," or "tapirs can be trusted," or "tapirs can't be trusted," as it is to say flatly that all human beings are noble, or the opposite of that proposition. One finds almost as much variety in animal character as one does in human character.

Of course, there are certain basic things that are true of animals just as there are certain fundamentals that apply to most people but this does not alter the fact that the minute a man starts generalizing about animals he displays his inexperience. Perhaps the nearest one can come to a generalization is to say that most animals are dangerous when they think they're in danger. And, after all, that is less a generalization about animals than it is a basic fact of life, involving human beings and the animal kingdom both.

The tiger that strikes at the man who is feeding him through the bars has decided that this man is an enemy with designs on his life; the gentler tiger has something in his make-up that resigns him to his captivity and tells him he has nothing to fear from the two-legged creature who is looking after him. Eventually the rougher specimen, when he discovers that his keeper is not someone he will one day have to fight for his life, tones down too and becomes manageable.

Of all the animals in the Malayan jungle the tapir is probably the least dangerous. He is much less formidable, for instance, than the wild boar which has tusks that are capable of ripping open an unwary enemy in a fight.

The tapir in addition to having no tusks is also clawless. Each front foot has four hoof-like toes, each back foot three; and these are hardly weapons. He has big powerful teeth but since he is known to be a vegetarian these are feared by neither man nor beast. One is about as conscious of them as one is of the teeth, however capable, of the average horse, cow or deer.

The tapir is a strange creature, in a class by itself. It is the only animal on earth today that has come down the ages in its present form. Evolution has left it untouched. It was as it is today thousands and thousands of years ago when the camel was no bigger than a greyhound and the horse was a four-toed animal the size of a fox terrier. It has always been to my mind such a placid symbol of age and tradition, so perfect an embodiment of the quiet mellowness of the years, that I could have as easily imagined myself being suddenly attacked by the Sphinx as by a tapir.

I couldn't have given less thought to the troublesome possibilities of my specimen if he had been a jack rabbit. The only thing that made me at all conscious of him was the fact that he had a badly barked back.

He was a full grown Malayan tapir, weighing about six hundred pounds. I had secured him to fill an order from an animal dealer in Kansas City who supplies the zoos of the smaller cities. It hardly pays me to round up the scattering orders of the very small zoos and such transactions are usually made through a dealer.

For the full length of the back, along the spine, the skin of this animal was badly barked. He had walked into a trap that was a log-fenced enclosure with a gate that snapped to. (The inside of the trap and the approach to it had been baited with tapioca root, a favorite delicacy of the tapir tribe.) In his frantic efforts to escape he had plunged about blindly and succeeded in scraping whole patches of skin off his spine.

In terms of my business this meant that I had to do a job of healing on that back, for, after all, I had an order for an animal with a whole skin. I wanted to apply some ointment when I first noticed the animal's condition in Sumatra but the conditions were not favorable there nor on the little Dutch boat on which I brought my collection back to Singapore.

On the outskirts of Singapore is the small town of Katong where I maintained a compound. There I instructed Dahlam Ali, the Malay who served me on expeditions in and around the Malayan district—(just as Lal Bahudar assisted me on collecting trips where a knowledge of Hindustani and Hindus was essential)—to build a small pen for the tapir. He and another boy in my employ built one about twenty feet square. They drove posts into the ground and with two-by-four planks built an enclosure about five feet high, a height which the animal could not jump. When three sides were up I drove the animal in from his cramped native cage, and with Ali hastily nailed up the opening while the other boy kept our captive cornered with a pole. Never had I seen a more harmless looking tapir. It seemed as I regarded him that it had been wholly unnecessary to keep him cornered while we nailed him in. He was completely absorbed in the business of contorting himself so that he could scratch his irritated back, which was itching, against the planks of the enclosure.

No gate was made in the pen as this seemed unnecessary labor. The spaces between the planks (through which the animal was fed) provided a good foot-hold and it was a simple matter to climb over. I did so, as casually as if I were entering a cow pasture. In my hand I carried a pound can of zinc ointment.

Ali was with the other boy feeding a great collection of birds which I had stored in a shelter 200 feet away, a collection that included a big cage of hill minas. These are coal black chattering birds with yellow wattles, some members of the species possessing the doubtful gift of gab even to a greater extent than parrots.

I scooped up a handful of the ointment, and, walking over to where this member of the animal kingdom's Oldest Family was scratching himself against a plank, slapped it over his back with as much detachment as if I were a bricklayer slapping some mortar on a brick. Bricks aren't very dangerous (unless heaved at one) and neither are tapirs . . . unless . . .

As I slapped that fistful of ointment over the tapir's spine he started running, I following as best I could, with my hand over his back like a bareback rider preparing to leap aboard his charger. Suddenly the animal whirled around, dropped back a few feet and charged straight at me, burying his head in my stomach and knocking the wind out of me as his six hundred pounds sent me sprawling on my back. I had hardly hit the ground when the Meekest of Animals jumped on me, his front feet bearing down on my chest, his hind feet on the ground.

I started swinging over on one side in an effort to get up. This inspired the jungle's Greatest Example of Humility to hoist his hind legs over my lower end, in the process dealing me a painful and weakening blow in a delicate region. It was a palpable foul but as there was no referee present this pacifist proceeded to stomp up and down all over me, bruising me in a dozen places.

I didn't exactly enjoy what was happening to me but neither did I become alarmed until the animal's six hundred pounds began to feel like a ton. It's hard to take a tapir seriously until something happens that forces you to do so. In all my previous dealings with the species it had lived up to its reputation for harmlessness, so it took me a few minutes to get it through my head that this tapir was more than nettled; that the infuriated creature had murder in his heart.

It's hard to figure out what happened inside that animal's sluggish brain when I applied that first big daub of ointment. The salve doubtless caused some irritation but this hardly could have been enough to convince the beast that he was in the presence of an enemy. . . .

The tapir had me painfully pinned down. I could feel his breath on my face. Not a sound came from him, except his heavy breathing. His eyes had a look that made my flesh creep. I had never seen such hate in a tapir's expression.

My first attempts to whirl around and free myself having failed, I poised myself for a great effort into which I put every ounce of strength I had. In swinging around I succeeded in partly freeing one shoulder, but this accomplished nothing, for the enraged beast pounded me flat again, moving up a few inches closer to my head in the process.

And then I had a moment of horror. Opening his big mouth, the animal bared his powerful teeth and reached to get hold of my face. It didn't take much computing to see that that awful mouth was capable of taking in the width of my head. Once he got my face between those jaws it would be an easy matter to pull the flesh off.

As I looked straight down the throat of this panting brute, I realized my danger and the next thing I knew I was yelling —yelling for all I was worth. I'm not ashamed to admit it. I had no desire to have the meat ripped off my face by this vegetarian on a rampage.

With all the lung power I could summon I fairly shrieked, "Ali! Ali!"—at the same time freeing one leg by a tremendous effort. As the animal strained forward, his teeth coming nearer and nearer, I got my right knee under his lower jaw, and reaching up, got hold of both his ears with my hands. He started furiously swinging his head right and left in an effort to shake me off but I held on for dear life, my knee keeping his teeth and my face apart.

. . . And then the demented creature started dragging me all over the enclosure, jumping off me to make it easier for him to take me for a ride. Every time I made an effort to get up he'd pound me flat against the turf with his front feet.

"Ali! Ali!" I yelled myself hoarse. Why didn't he come running over? Where the hell was he? . . . And then I answered my own question. I had sent Ali to care for my birds. He was in the bird shelter, looking after them. . . . With a sudden vehemence, I found myself cursing my collection of hill minas. These boisterous birds—(all other birds seem quiet by comparison)—were probably chattering away at such a rate that it was impossible for Ali to hear my cries.

. I felt the power going out of my fingers and in desperation I strove to tighten my hold on the crazed creature's ears. And, with one of those unnatural bursts of strength that come when destruction is staring one out of countenance, I stiffened my knee against the tapir's chin. With renewed fury he started dragging me all around the lot, adding new lacerations to my sore and battered body.

"Ali! Ali! Ali!" I put everything I had into this final cry.

I was beginning to wonder how long I could hang on. My back was aching as it had never ached in all my days, and my chest was sore from the pounding of those hoofs. I would have to scramble to my feet somehow and get over that fence. Having survived encounters with tigers and leopards I had no intention of being wiped out by a damned tapir, an animal that had always seemed to me a sort of giant cockroach, with as much spirit and personality, under normal circumstances, as that loathsome bug.

My weakening fingers clutched the tapir's ears in a final frenzy of self-preservation and my knee, doing its best to seem a firm and determined knee, managed to maintain its wobbly intercession between me and the teeth of the four-legged lunatic that was trying to destroy me as Ali at last came running up, excitedly shouting, *"Apa ini, tuan? Apa ini?"* [What is this, master?]

It wasn't necessary for me to answer Ali's question. Screaming for the other boy to come over and help him, he grabbed a board,—one of the pieces of lumber left over after the pen had been built—and started beating the animal over the head with it. The other boy who was at the far end of the compound finally heard his screams and came tearing over.

With even more presence of mind than Ali,—(a real surprise to me, for over a period of years Ali had displayed more resourcefulness in emergencies than any native I had ever employed anywhere in Asia)—the newcomer grabbed a two-by-four scantling and shoved it into the open mouth of the would-be killer, the animal biting down on it. The surest way of saving my features was to put something besides my wornout knee between me and those vicious teeth, and the scantling did the trick.

The animal, one piece of lumber between his teeth and another being brought down on his head, backed away a few paces. As he did, Ali reached through the fence and grabbed my arm, pulling me further away from the maddened creature. At this point the other boy jumped over the fence, and, while Ali beat the animal off with his board, lifted me to my feet. Almost falling against it in my weakened condition, I grabbed the top of the fence, putting one foot in an open space between the boards about a foot from the ground. Then this boy who served as Ali's assistant—(although in this stirring operation *he* was really the leader and Ali the assistant)—gave me a great boost, which, combined with my own efforts, sent me toppling over the fence onto the ground on the other side where I landed in a limp heap. A mass of bruises, I lay there for half an hour before I could summon the strength to move.

When I stood up at last it was with the aid of Ali and the other Malay, who hustled me off to bed. The battering I had received left me black and blue from head to foot and it was three days before I could get up.

The day after I was laid up for repairs, Ali, who was looking after me, sat beside the open window of my room chewing betel nut and using for his cuspidor that portion of Katong which lay beneath my window. Ali was hardly ever without a good gob of this Eastern equivalent for chewing tobacco and he spat frequently. It seemed to help his thinking.

Ali was puzzled about that tapir. To him, as to me, the tapir was a perfect exemplification of the peaceful attitude toward life. The normal rôle of the animal was running away from fights instead of getting into them.

Ali had more to say about tapirs that day than he usually has to say about everything in the course of a whole week. Under normal circumstances he did most of his talking through the medium of gestures,—a shrug of the shoulders, a movement of the hand, a toss of the head. A few facial expressions rounded out his vocabulary.

Although he didn't bother selecting the right words, he spoke English understandably. But most of the time he was able to express himself without words.

Today, however, he needed words to unburden himself,— words supplemented by a wrinkling up of his nose, his favorite method of expressing displeasure. Normally if I asked him what he thought, let us say, of some animal that I was thinking of taking off a trader's hands, he would wrinkle up his nose if he thought the creature a poor specimen. If he thought it a good buy, he would beam all over. No words.

That nose of his was as wrinkled as an octogenarian prune as he started discussing that tapir. The animal had the devil in him, a whole tribe of devils. He spat vehemently to emphasize his point.

Ali seemed more picturesque to me than ever as he sat by that window speculating on how all those devils had got inside that tapir. He was dressed in an outfit that was standard for him unless he was at work on a dirty job. It consisted of an immaculate white starched *baja,* which is a shirt much like the top of a pajama jacket and worn over the *sarong* or skirt, which today was a red and blue affair, cut very full. On his head he wore a black velvet Mohammedan cap.

Ali wasn't in the habit of getting particularly excited about anything. His philosophy was the philosophy of *"Tidak apa?"* (Which in Malay means, "What does it matter?")

The soul of conscientiousness, he yet reserved the right to a resigned outlook. Things happened. That was life. Why examine anything too closely?

In considering the tapir that had tried to annihilate me, he made an exception to his *"Tidak apa?"* rule. It did matter. Tapirs had no business acting that way. One had enough problems in life with animals and people that were frankly one's enemies without having to face sudden attacks from what one had a right to regard as peaceful sources.

Over and over we discussed the whole race of tapirs, making many points, relevant and irrelevant.

The reader may be acquainted with the fact that tigers, leopards and other carnivora regard the tapir as a very choice dish. The tapir, needless to say, is familiar with his popularity in these quarters as a table delicacy; and he uses every resource at his command to keep out of the way of his enemies. Nature has come to his assistance in making it possible for him to stay under water for several minutes at a stretch. Consequently his normal habitat is near a river. When pursued by some killer ambitious to dine off his chops, he calmly steps into his convenient river, walking along its bottom and passing the time in the gentle pursuit of pulling up the roots of water lilies and other aquatic plants. He is as fond of these morsels as the tiger is of tapir meat.

After nibbling away for a few minutes, he comes to the surface, swimming off to some other point where there are more tasty roots to eat.

But when the jungle fruits are ripe, the tapir, unable to resist these dainties, forsakes his river. He makes for the higher ground where rambutan, checo, jack fruit and other jungle palate-ticklers fall to the ground.

Here in territory where he is easy prey for carnivora on the prowl, he vies with other herbivorous animals for his favorite delicacies. Cautiously emerging from the brush, he comes out into the more open spaces of the jungle where the fruit-bearing trees are found. In his movements is the accumulated timidity of thousands of generations of tapirs, all of them hunted animals.

Fear of attack is always uppermost in his mind. He isn't even free from it when he is near the water. More than one Dyak savage has made a meal off the remains of a tapir he has found buried in the mud along the margin of a river or swamp, the victim of an assault by a giant bull crocodile that seized its prey in the water, held it under until it was drowned and then tore it to pieces.

Practically everything Ali and I said on the subject—and our experience with tapirs had been wide—contributed to the point that it was unusual for a tapir, one of the least courageous of the perpetually hunted animals, to make an attack such as the one to which I had been subjected.

This being so, didn't the *tuan* believe that the animal was full of devils? How could a tapir act that way otherwise?

I tried to tell Ali, in simple language, that the animal's conduct represented the aggressiveness born of perpetual fear. The creature had got it into his head that I was trying to destroy him; so he tried to destroy me. If there had been a river to run to, the tapir would have headed for that instead of me. It was as simple as all that.

Ali wrinkled up his nose. He was displeased.

He kept after me until, to end the discussion, I told him that he was probably right. The creature must be full of devils.

Ali beamed. He knew all along that I would see his point. Of course the animal was full of devils!

But he wasn't finished yet.

Did the *tuan* think it wise to ship to America an animal so full of devils? Would it not make trouble for me?

This was carrying a joke too far. I finally convinced Ali that an animal so full of devils should be shipped out of Asia, which was already over-stocked with devils, with all possible haste.

For the good of my soul and that tapir's back, I was determined to resume my operations with the zinc ointment. This I did, but I confess that I ministered to his skinned back from the outside of the pen. I wrapped some rags around the end of a long stick and tied them securely in place. Then I put some ointment on the rags and with this home-made apparatus succeeded in giving him a thorough smearing. A series of these treatments proved effective and before long the tapir's back was healed. A few months later I delivered him to the Kansas City dealer who had ordered him for a small mid-western zoo. There he proved as easy to handle as a kitten.

Giant Jungle Man

I HAD just returned to Singapore after a long and arduous collecting trip that took me to the wildest of the Borneo wilds. I was resting in my room in the Raffles Hotel when I heard a pounding on my door.

"*Tuan! tuan!*" The voice was Ali's.

"What do you want, Ali?"

"Open, *tuan!* Quick! Big news have happened."

I let the boy in.

"What's it all about, Ali?" I asked. "Out with it!"

Then the boy informed me that "the grandfather of all orangs" had arrived in Singapore, the biggest animal of its kind he had ever heard of. If the reports were correct—and he had every reason to believe they were—we were on the trail of a gigantic "man of the forest" ("orang" being "man" in Malay and "utan" being "forest").

That was enough for me. If there was a record-breaking orang available, I wanted it. I hurriedly got into my clothes while Ali supplied further details.

A small boat had just arrived in the outer harbor from Jesselton on the north coast of Borneo with a party of Malays who had come to market a solitary possession that they owned jointly, an orang-utan.

Someone on board had a gift for publicity for, according to Ali, within an hour of the time the boat arrived, he had heard from several people in the market-place that the world's biggest orang-utan was in town, for sale to the highest bidder.

At first Ali was inclined to pooh-pooh the story, but when he heard it from Chop Joo Soon, the Chinese bird-dealer—an old friend of mine—he decided I ought to have the information. He reminded me that when I had told him that my next shipment

for the United States was complete, I had added that if he heard
of anything unusual he was to notify me.

I'm afraid I can't take my animals or leave 'em. I've always
got to have one more before I go home.

Ali, as I finished dressing, told me he would never forgive himself if it developed that these Malays had nothing unusual to
offer. He knew the *tuan* was tired and needed rest. He had
no desire to be disturbful. But neither had he any desire to
see those Japanese, in town collecting animals for the Tokio Zoo,
get anything that I wanted. He reminded me that the Japanese
were a very schemeable people,—(Ali's command of English was
growing by leaps and bounds, his mastery resulting in the addition of words not only to his vocabulary but to the language
itself)—and he thought I'd prefer having my rest divided (he
meant "interrupted") to taking the risk of losing an important
specimen to the collectors from Tokio. (Ali wrinkled up his
nose so feelingly every time he mentioned the Japs that I began
to feel that perhaps he didn't like them.)

The boy had two rickshaws waiting in front of the hotel.
"Lekas!" [Hurry!]" It didn't take us long to get to the Tangon
Pagar district, that part of Singapore where the docks and wharves
are located. There we engaged a Malay dug-out with three
sturdy brown paddlers and we were quickly rowed out to the
outer harbor where the boat from Borneo lay at anchor.

It didn't take us long to discover that the Malays had something
really wonderful to sell. Ali's informants had not exaggerated.
It was an amazing animal, by far the biggest orang-utan I had
ever seen. It was also bigger than any member of the species
that Ali had ever encountered, and there probably wasn't a man
in all of Asia who had had as broad an experience with these
creatures as he.

The beast weighed well over two hundred and fifty pounds
(a tremendous weight for an orang-utan). It measured eight
and a half feet from finger tip to finger tip. It was thirteen
inches across the face. The bulging cheek growths, common to
adult male orangs, the long shaggy hair about the face and chin
and the great wide mouth with the long, deadly canine teeth

combined to give this ape as terrifying an appearance as I've ever seen in an animal.

The Malays had him imprisoned in a heavy cage made of a hard jungle wood and lashed together with rattan and other jungle fibres. It was one of those ingenious pieces of carpentry that one so frequently encounters in the East.

The animal was not enjoying his confinement. His cage was too small for him and he expressed his opinion of his cramped quarters by alternately grunting and sucking in wind in the fashion characteristic of the species when angry. As I surveyed that tremendous chest and those prodigious arms with their bulging muscles and re-considered those murderous teeth I had a feeling that in a rough-and-tumble fight this shaggy importation from Jesselton could have accounted for at least a dozen men, killing as many of them as he pleased. The orang's favorite method of doing damage in a fight is to pull the foe to him with his mighty arms and rip his victim to pieces with his teeth.

There were five Malays in the group that had come over from Jesselton with the giant jungle-man. The fun began when I asked the headman how much he wanted for his hairy captive.

He and his associates put their heads together and went into conference. Then the headman, instead of naming a price, made a strange request. Would I mind dismissing my boy? They hoped I would not misunderstand. The *tuan* must not regard this request as a reflection on the boy. It simply meant that he (the headman) preferred doing business with me alone.

The headman, or *dato*, added that his English, while far from what he would have liked it to be, had proven adequate in transactions with *tuans* in the past, and that I would not need my interpreter. Time and again when Ali accompanied me to places where Malay was the language spoken, he would be regarded at once as an interpreter.

It soon became obvious that the reason why the *dato* requested Ali's dismissal was that he wanted to be able to talk freely with his comrades. Apparently it had not occurred to the spokesman that I might understand Malay. While I speak the language with difficulty, I have a sufficient knowledge of it to be able to understand the average conversation. I might miss the meaning of an occasional word but I knew enough of the lingo to be able to comprehend, without much of a struggle, what most Malays were telling one another. I saw no reason why this group should be an exception. The confidential five would spill all their secrets in my presence, including the particular technique they employed in trying to put one over on a *tuan*. Unless all signs failed, I was due to have a thoroughly enjoyable time.

In the manner of one who is making a great concession, I agreed to dismiss my "interpreter," insisting, however, that he be permitted to stay within calling distance so that in case we had any trouble understanding each other his services would be available. My purpose in doing this, of course, was to lead the group further astray in their belief that I did not understand their tongue.

"That is well," said the headman, designating a place on the deck where Ali was to wait. "But we shall be possible to do business without him. My English language is not too big but you will be able to understand what I mean to do." I understood fully what he meant to do. He meant to gyp me. His English, while not without its flaws, was easy to comprehend, as was also his manner, which eloquently proclaimed his intention to stick me if possible.

"Let's get down to business," I said. "How much money do you want?"

"You realize, of course," he replied, "what it is, this that we make offering to sell?"

"Yes, an orang-utan. How much?"

"Never before does the world see so big orang-utan."

"Perhaps. How much?"

"In many years I have seen hundreds orang-utans since I was *anak* [child] I have not looked upon one so big as this we now offer to sell."

"I'm sure of that. You're not the kind that would fool me."

"I know you realize I am not like the *orang Chino* [Chinaman]. No, I am honest fellow."

"I knew that the minute I saw you. . . . How much?"

(Time out for the *dato* to address his comrades. He is telling them that all is well. "This *tuan* will not be hard to handle.")

"*Tuan*, I have been told by 'Merican gentlemen that in your country—you 'Merican, no?—[I nodded]—will be much excitement when news have arrived that big orang-utan comes. Many will be happy to spend plenty money, he have told me, to see this orang-utan *besar*." (The last word meaning "enormous.")

He was certainly building up a case for himself. His technique amused me, but after about two dozen of these digressions, all designed to impress me with the rareness of the animal he had for sale, I decided that I had had enough.

So I said: "I understand perfectly. This is a very unusual animal. [He nodded.] It's worth more than the average orang-utan. [Another nod, accompanied by a beam of pleasure.] But it's not made of gold and it isn't studded with rubies. [The *dato* stopped smiling.] So don't ask for a million dollars. Tell me what you want and be quick about it. I've got to get out of here."

Even this didn't accomplish the desired result. The *dato* launched another speech, similarly calculated to make me feel what a great favor he was doing me in permitting me to negotiate for his epoch-making catch, the most beautiful (it was wonderful but hardly beautiful) "piece of orang-utan" that he had ever "experienced," that his family had ever "experienced," that his friends had ever "experienced," that the world had ever "experienced." At the height of this burst of oratory I found myself losing patience.

I turned heckler. Raising one hand, I fairly shouted, "I have a question to ask the speaker. How much does he want for his damned orang-utan? Or doesn't he want to sell it?" I consulted my watch by way of emphasizing that if time wasn't a factor with the speaker, it was with his audience.

After three or four more assaults on the *dato's* eloquence I managed to convince him that I wanted to hear his price,—and nothing else.

He cleared his throat in preparation for the delivery of his answer. Finally it came. If it was anyone else he was dealing with (he had never seen me until I stepped aboard that little vessel) the price would be three thousand Straits dollars. Since it was I, however, the price would be only two thousand Straits dollars, little enough, he assured me, for the Rajah of all orangs.

"You're crazy," I said. "I wouldn't pay that for a *gajah* [elephant]."

As I said this, the *dato* spoke hastily to one of his comrades in Malay. Without any difficulty, although I missed a few words, I understood this foolish headman to instruct his associate to go with all possible haste to see if he could find those representatives of the Tokio Zoo, whose presence in Singapore he had heard about. The old rogue was trying to introduce a little competitive bidding.

The headman's plan was to keep stalling me off until the Japanese arrived—I didn't have to guess this, I heard him say so with a chuckle—and then he would start a sort of auction sale, with Japan and America bidding against each other until he had sent his price sky-high.

I didn't want to lose this specimen. It was an amazing one. But neither did I want to pay a ridiculous price for it. Small monkeys are easy to handle and do not involve much of a risk but these great apes are a pure gamble. Not nearly so hardy in captivity as their smaller relatives, they present many real problems. For one thing, it is very difficult to transfer them from the food to which they are accustomed in their wild state to the substitutes which are available when they live in captivity. Sometimes one gets away with it without a hitch. The animal thrives and is healthy and happy once he's given sufficiently roomy quarters to exercise and amuse himself. But there are those trying exceptions when these big apes, unable to get used to the new diet, or suddenly stricken with lung trouble, die before anything can be done to save them.

I was in a ticklish position. If the Japanese arrived I would have to pay through the nose to get my orang. Obviously I would have to close the deal before they appeared on the scene. I made an offer of eight hundred Straits dollars, a good price. The *dato* pooh-poohed it. Turning to one of his comrades, he said in Malay, "This foolish *tuan* thinks he is going to get the better of me. But I will make him pay two thousand dollars. He cannot have the animal for less."

"Suppose the Japanese are not willing to pay that much?" (One of his comrades speaking.)

"Leave it to me. Two thousand dollars is our price."

An hour had elapsed since the time the *dato* had sent one of his cronies to find the Japanese. I was willing to raise my bid to a thousand Straits dollars ($570 in gold), but I saw no point in doing it yet. The rascally headman would not close for less than his original figure until he had heard from the Japs. That was obvious. My one hope, it seemed, was that the gentlemen from Tokio would not be willing to bid as high as the *dato* expected. After all, gold does not grow on trees in Japan any more than it does in America. Nevertheless, the prospect of competitive bidding did not appeal to me.

A half hour later the Malay who had been sent for the Japs returned—alone. He had been unable to find the Japanese. The clerk at the Nikko hotel in North Beach road did not know where they were.

He had hardly finished his story, the whole meaning of which was perfectly plain to me, when the lying *dato* turned to me, and, without batting an eyelash, calmly announced that his comrade had just brought word that some Japanese animal buyers would be over in a little while. However, he was anxious to close the deal and get back to Jesselton and if I would pay him two thousand dollars, he would let me have the animal. He would rather deal with me, he said, confidentially adding that those Japanese are sometimes a tricky lot. However, their money was as good as mine and if I would not meet his terms—

After more strenuous bargaining I landed the great orang for the thousand Straits dollars which I had fixed as my maximum. This was a fortune to the five Malays, a bigger price than I had any right to pay. But I was delighted with my purchase just the same.

It was a specimen that would surely add to my reputation in

the United States and one which could be sold at a good profit if I could get it across the Pacific in good condition.

Before leaving with my purchase, I wanted to hear the story of that animal's capture. The cleverest natives would have found it well-nigh impossible under normal circumstances to capture an orang of such prodigious proportions. These great apes do not go into traps like tigers, leopards and other jungle animals. There are very few natives that would have risked a battle with so appalling an adversary and it seemed a foregone conclusion that something must have happened to handicap the beast.

For this reason I wanted to hear the facts of the capture, curious to know in just what way the fates had set the odds against this tremendous orang-utan that was capable of routing a couple of dozen natives and killing several in the process.

The *dato* told me the story, and since he had no money to gain by lying, I daresay he told the truth. At any rate it tallied with the story Ali heard in the Singapore market-place shortly before he dashed off to drag me out of bed that I might become the owner of this orang of orangs.

Here is the *dato's* story (with much deletion of his own words, however, as his Malayan English resulted in a rambling narrative that took almost an hour to tell).

Well, *tuan*, we played a mean trick on that orang. (Laughing.) If we hadn't, you wouldn't be his owner. He'd still be roaming the jungle.

Abdul here (pointing to one of his men) found the brute's house in a big tree. (High up in some big tree the orang-utan builds a platform of branches over and around which he weaves more branches until he has a sort of nest or shelter of limbs and leaves.)

Abdul discovered the big fellow's tree-house in the jungle *tiga maken sari* from our *kompong*. (Those three Malay words mean "three chews of betel nut." The Malay frequently figures time in such picturesque terms. It takes him about twenty-five

minutes to polish off a mouthful of *sari*, or betel nut, so three
chews would be about an hour and a quarter's walk, during
which he would cover about three and one-half miles.)

It was the dry season of the year in our section. That big
orang had to go a long way for water or go thirsty, which he
did for days at a time to save himself the long journey through
the tree-tops.

It was easy to watch his movements, a task to which Abdul
was assigned. We knew the value of such an animal and we
made up our minds to capture him if we possibly could. Naturally we were in great fear of such a giant, having witnessed the
terrible results when smaller specimens went on a rampage.

It struck me that the thing to do first was to conduct an experiment at a safe distance. We filled a small tub with water,
placed it near his tree and retired to await developments.

From a clump of bushes a fair distance off we watched the
big fellow's movements. For quite a while nothing happened.
We were beginning to wonder how long we would have to wait
before our friend (though he was hardly that, eh, *tuan?*) would
decide to leave his house in the tree to see what was doing in
the world below.

He came down at length. For several minutes he devoted
himself to studying the tub and its contents. He was obviously
suspicious about something, though what actually went on in
his head no one will ever know. He got close enough to the
tub to take a drink and started bending over as if he were going
to do so. Then, very suddenly, he righted himself. He had
changed his mind. He took another hard look at the tub, his
expression plainly indicating that he wasn't at all sure that he
liked what he saw. By the time an orang gets to be as old as
this one (my captive was probably twenty or twenty-five years
old, and he might well have been more) he has had many tricks
played on him and he is nothing if not cautious.

"He's not going to drink," I said to one of my comrades. "Not
this time anyhow." I had hardly uttered these words when the
animal knocked over the tub and scrambled up his tree again.

The next day we re-filled the tub and again awaited developments. One has to have patience in dealing with these wild creatures. One would never capture them otherwise.

After a few hours the big fellow came down again, practically repeating his performance of the day before, the only difference being that this time, as he tipped the tub over with his foot, he jumped back as the contents splashed on the ground, as if expecting something to happen to him. Perhaps the fact that nothing did happen encouraged him to view the tub and its contents in a friendlier light. The third day he did not tip it over so vehemently and the fourth day he drank—first a sample swallow, then another and another, finally drinking his fill.

Each day we filled the tub, getting him used to the idea that he could depend upon this as a steady source. There were rambutans, banyan berries and other fruits not far distant, so the big fellow need make only short trips out for food early mornings and late evenings, knowing that his water was near at hand. It made things quite convenient for this lazy giant.

Then we started adding to the water a small amount of *arric*, our native gin. (Probably there is no drink in the world quite so powerful as the *arric* distilled by the Malays and the Dyaks, an innocent-looking fluid that, like other gins, looks exactly like water. It was unnecessary for the *dato* to tell me about Bornean *arric*. I sampled it once, and though it went down smoothly enough, not long afterwards I thought I was on fire. Once a Malay, in describing the concoction, said to me, "Why, *tuan*, three drops of this would make a rabbit walk right up and spit in a tiger's eye.")

Evidently the orang did not notice the taste of *arric* in the water, or did not mind it. After all, he had drunk plenty of water in his time that tasted worse than this. A thirsty animal in the jungle has learned not to be too particular, there being times when he is grateful for anything he can get, even muddy water seeming a luxury.

However, the quantity of *arric* that we used at the start was so small that the water could not have tasted much differently. Each day we increased the dose and the animal continued to drink. The *arric* taste did not seem to bother him at all. For

all we knew, he might have developed a liking for it and the
faint glow he must have experienced afterwards. The quantity
we were giving him, *tuan*, was still not large and was so well
diluted that it couldn't have had more than a mild effect on him.

When we felt that this "man of the forest" was ready for it,
we filled the tub with straight *arric*. As soon as he was thirsty
he slid down his tree for a drink, as was now his custom, the
tub having become a regular part of his life. He took a mouthful, wasn't quite sure that this was the kind of water he wanted,
retained it in his mouth for half a minute and then spat it out.
He regarded the tub thoughtfully for a time, then decided to
re-consider. He began to drink slowly and continued until he
had drained the last drop.

Then he sat down beside the tub, evidently feeling he needed
a rest. After sitting there for about five minutes he started
swaying to the right and then to the left like a mother rocking
a baby to sleep by hand. Then he got up uncertainly and
started to walk across the clearing, stumbling over something in
the process and almost falling over. In the typical manner of
a drunk who has stubbed his toe, he looked down angrily at
the enemy that was trying to throw him, some matted underbrush, and decided to deal it a kick. In doing this he lost his
balance and landed foolishly on his back-side.

He got up unsteadily, evidently concluding that something
was wrong, in which event he had better go home to his tree-top
hut. He turned around and looked doubtfully for his tree.
Finally locating the tree with his eye, he made for it, in anything but a straight line.

He managed to get part of the way up the trunk, but *arric* is
arric and when it starts asserting itself it's a serious handicap
to man or beast in a tree-climbing mood. Down slid the bewildered animal, landing with a thud on its now battered bottom.

He would teach this drunken tree a lesson! Picking up a log,
he wrathfully swung it against the trunk, the log snapping in
half and its wielder, leaning over so far in dealing the blow that
he became top-heavy, landing in a heap where he sat blinking
in silly fashion at the part of the club that remained in his

grasp. Again he rose uncertainly and started shakily across the clearing. Coming to a fallen tree, he put his hands on it to support himself, raised one leg to step over and fell down dead drunk.

When he came to, some hours later, he found himself neatly crated at Jesselton awaiting shipment to Singapore.

Shortly after the *dato* had finished his story, Ali and I, with the aid of some boatmen, loaded the king of orangs onto a lighter, and we headed for Johnson's pier. There Ali got some coolies to help us lift our cage onto a bullock cart which was sent on its way to my compound at Katong. A few days later I had the job of transferring my big "man of the forest" from his cramped box, which I considered bad for his health and his disposition, to a fine new roomy one that Hin Mong, my Chinese carpenter, had built for the newcomer.

I've had much easier tasks in my time than the one of getting this savage beast out of his old box into the new. The two boxes were nailed and lashed together, with the openings (bars removed) facing each other. Some bananas were placed in the new box as an inducement to the beast to enter his new home. The stubborn cuss refused to be tempted, for quite a while devoting himself to grunting and sucking in wind, his favorite method of expressing rage. When we pounded on his old cage in an effort to drive him into the new, he pounded back with powerful blows. If those cages had not been securely fastened together, we would have had to reckon with a terrible foeman.

After much effort, we got this great ape to go for the bananas, dropping the iron bars as soon as he entered. These bars, by the way, were spaced so close together that it was impossible for the animal to reach through. An orang as powerful as this one could have pulled a person to him, had he been able to reach his arms through the bars, and killed him in a jiffy.

Although this giant jungle-man's new cage was much more comfortable than the old one, giving him plenty of room, he showed no signs of taming down. He was in a rage most of the time. Every morning, when the boy came to clean his cage, running an iron scraper through an opening at the bottom, the animal would take the implement in his powerful grip. The boy's efforts to wrench it loose couldn't have been any less futile if he had been trying to yank a tree out by the roots. He would have to let go and wait until the animal tired of hanging on.

My orang was in fine condition when I got him ready for shipment to Hong Kong, along with hundreds of other specimens, aboard the *West Sequana* on the first leg of my journey to America. He was still a perfect example of sustained wrath but he was eating regularly. His new diet consisted of carrots, sweet potatoes, bananas, sugar cane, boiled rice, raw eggs and bread, and he was thriving on it.

At Hong Kong I transferred to the *President Cleveland*. We stopped at Kobe where I cabled my agent in San Francisco that I had a record-breaking full-grown male orang—(I included the creature's astonishing measurements in my message)—which I would sell for $5,000, a price I considered small enough for the biggest representative of this species in captivity.

A reply was waiting for me at Yokohama. It was to the effect that the Ringling Brothers circus was willing to pay $4,000 and accept delivery on the dock, which, of course, would relieve me of the risk involved in getting the animal to its ultimate destination in the United States. I accepted. This didn't allow me much profit if I added to the original cost of the animal the various incidental expenses involved, plus a decent charge for my time, but I had sense enough to know that with the Ringling Brothers circus, the finest in the world, the animal would receive excellent care and would be constantly in the limelight, which wouldn't do my reputation as a collector any harm.

So far so good. The rest was not so good. About five days out of San Francisco my prize orang developed a bad case of dysentery, which is always serious in anthropoid apes. He had suddenly achieved one of those sunken stomachs that invariably spell disaster in his species. The ship's doctor had a serum that he thought would help if he could manage to inject it. Patiently we strove to make a quick injection but we had no luck, two or three needles breaking off in the animal's fingers.

That night the Rajah of All Orangs, as the *dato* had called him, died. I tossed him over the side, cage and all. Hin Mong would have had a fit if he had seen his fine orang box go overboard. He mightn't have regarded the loss of the animal as a tragedy—he could be quite matter-of-fact about animals—but he would never have understood my throwing away a well-made crate, contaminated or not.

My experience with this orang will give an idea of the risks involved in the business of collecting wild animals. If enough specimens die en route the collector finds himself "in the red." I ought to know. It's happened to me.

Tiger Revenge

ENVIRONMENT has been blamed for many things. Maybe it's partly responsible for the wildness of wild animals.

Certainly there's nothing tame about some of their "human" neighbors. For downright cruelty, for instance, the most ferocious beast of the jungle cannot match the efforts of many a Hindu of the royal line. Anglo-Saxon villains are mere comic-strip Desperate Desmonds in comparison with a Hindu prince who has made up his mind to set new records for malevolence.

Perhaps the most expert practitioner of the art of plain and fancy cruelty that I ever observed at close range was a Maharajah who ruled one of the native states of India. He was a man with a jaded palate. His normal mood was one of sullen boredom. He had made an extensive tour of Europe in search of new thrills and when these excitements ceased to excite he returned home to see what novelties in the way of mischief he could cook up there.

Jim Wendell, an Australian friend of mine who now lives in Calcutta, was in charge of the Maharajah's racing-stable. Many of the Hindu princes are fond of horse-racing and as the horses most available for this purpose are Australian griffons, these royal gentlemen of India usually import Australian horsemen as supervisors.

Wendell, hearing I was in the district on a collecting trip, invited me to attend a "show" that the Maharajah was giving the following day. As we sat and sipped our drinks at the local club,—(wherever five or more white men gather in any corner of the globe some Englishman starts a club)—my friend urged me not to miss the royal entertainment.

His Highness's "show" proved to be a battle between a tiger and a water buffalo (a powerful bull). Bored with the tameness of palace routine, the prince sought a thrill in a combat between two animals that had no good reason for fighting each other.

Nothing was overlooked to insure a bloody battle. By royal command, the tiger had been given practically no food for two or three days,—just enough to stave off weakness. By way of getting the buffalo good and mad he was made to go without water for some time. If there are any water buffaloes that have ever done anything to you and you want to annoy them, just see that they don't get any water. You'll get quick results.

As an added guarantee of perfect buffalo fury, some small spikes had been driven into the animal's shoulders. Now, if there's anything a buffalo doesn't like, it's a spike in his shoulder, —or even an ordinary nail, or a mere thumb-screw, for that matter. The idea just doesn't appeal to him.

If you want to stage a murderous tussle, you can't do much better than bring together in a walled enclosure a ravenous tiger and a parched water buffalo that has suffered the added insult of spiked shoulders.

The combatants were turned loose from cages. They didn't lose much time making it plain how they felt about each other. The tiger opened with a leap designed to land him on the buffalo's shoulders. The buffalo shook him off, lowered his head and charged. The tiger eluded him and once again sprang for the enemy's shoulders. He landed but couldn't keep his footing. Again he was shaken off but this time he drew blood, his front claws digging into the back of his adversary's neck.

This didn't do much physical damage but it did plenty by way of multiplying the fury of the buffalo. Again he charged and this time his aim was better. He caught the circling tiger amidships and sent him spinning on his back. The charge of a full-grown bull buffalo has spelled many an animal's doom. It is a charge that carries all before it. If the enraged bovine, one of the most terrible of fighters when aroused, had been quick enough he could have ended the fight then and there with his horns. But he was too slow in his frantic attempt to pin the tiger down and gore him. More than one tiger has met his death in a fight with a buffalo that managed to sink in his terrible horns before the enemy had recovered from one of those awful charges.

The tiger, partly pinned down, wriggled loose and poised himself. He leaped. In a fraction of a second he was hanging from the buffalo's left forequarter, his hind claws unshakeably imbedded in the animal's withers, his forepaws cruelly sunk into the shoulders, while with his murderous teeth he dug deep into the back of the neck. With an agonized bellow that was more of a sustained groan, the great jungle bull sank to his knees. Reaching out with his left forepaw, the great cat brought his claws around to a position in front of the buffalo's head. With a powerful thrust he cut down into the features which became a sickeningly gory mass. As he dug deeper and deeper with those hideous claws he pulled the probing paw downward as though he were manipulating a giant glass-cutter, and then when a final dig into the blood-spattered head gave him a grip that could not be broken, he braced himself with the other forepaw and gave a great yank toward himself that snapped the buffalo's neck.

The battle was over. The great horned fighter, in fitful gasps, was breathing his last.

The tiger continued to slash away at his fallen foe. He had conquered and was now ready to enjoy the fruits of victory. His sides were sore from the roughing the great bull had given him and one paw was out of commission—(the left hind leg which had somehow snapped in the tussle and now hung loosely) —but the main consideration was that here was a feast after a long fast and a hard fight.

You will have to pardon my reference to the tiger's victory. I assumed, of course, that he had scored one. It seems that I was mistaken. As the hungry cat started the first course of his banquet a shot rang out, the first of a series.

These little leaden tributes, all aimed at the tiger's head, found vulnerable resting places there and soon the tiger was no more. One of the Maharajah's guards, who had been standing by during the fray, served as executioner.

It seems that the Maharajah, no longer amused, found the limping tiger an eye-sore. An incapacitated tiger approximated his idea of a nuisance, and this one, having fulfilled his destiny by relieving a few minutes of the royal tedium, was ordered shot.

I caught a glimpse of the prince as he descended from the platform just outside the walled enclosure from which he had watched the spectacle. The puffiness of his features suggested a head made of putty and stained dark to give the proper Hindu look. In each of the sacs that depended from the lower eyelids you could have stuffed a hen's egg. The unpleasant curl of the doughy lips that contributed further to the general swollenness indicated that his princely highness was displeased.

The fight hadn't lasted long enough to suit him, I afterwards learned. After elaborate preparations, all he got for his trouble was a brief skirmish. It was galling. No wonder he had the tiger shot, poor man. Hadn't the silly beast wound up the fight in a hurry instead of dragging it out endlessly and showing his bored chieftain a good time? A tiger as lacking in consideration as that deserved what he got.

I looked around for Lal Bahudar, my native boy-of-all-jobs, and prepared to leave. Lal, more conservative than the rest of us who had watched the battle from the wall of the enclosure, had perched himself among the beautiful red blossoms of a near-by plane tree. Lal scrambled to the ground and ran toward me excitedly, emitting as whole-souled a *"Soure Cabatcha!"* as ever greeted my ears. (This is the Hindu equivalent of a familiar four-syllable Anglo-Saxon oath that casts aspersions on a man's maternity.)

In this quaint and playful manner, Lal was merely expressing his opinion of the execution he had just witnessed. In his brain there lingered an echo of something he had once heard his wicked master say (yes, I have much to answer for!) for he added, by way of making his meaning doubly clear, "He'sagodamshame!"

Lal spoke broken English, in a typical native sing-song. He had a habit of running his words together, into a jumble of syllables, sometimes unrecognizable.

Just as I was about to credit Lal with humanitarian instincts, he unleashed a hodge-podge of words that made it clear what was bothering him. What he regarded as a "godamshame" was not the killing of the tiger but the fact that the beast had not been permitted to eat a square meal before he was sent to his doom.

Lal was tantalized by the idea of man or beast needlessly dying with an empty stomach. We discussed the subject at great length.

I tried to make Lal see that the question involved was not whether the tiger should have been permitted to have a final meal but whether it was sporting to make an animal fight for his life in combat with a dangerous opponent and then, when he had won, shoot him down in cold blood merely for the fun of seeing him expire.

I simply could not get my idea through Lal's head. He was a comparatively kind-hearted Hindu, which means that, while not nearly so bloodthirsty as native royalty, he was not exactly merciful in his attitude toward wild animals, regardless of the circumstances. Had he understood what I meant by the sporting attitude he would have dismissed it as foolish sentimentality. Why should anyone want to let a tiger, world-old enemy of man, live? But it would have been so easy to let him have a last meal of buffalo meat before bumping him off. Over and over again he made his point, underscoring it each time with an eloquent *"Soure Cabatcha!"* He kept it up until he had made the prince a direct descendant of all the stray she-dogs since the year one and therefore not a prince at all but a rank mongrel.

A year later I had occasion to return to the scene of the tiger-buffalo fight. I had some good orders for black buck antelope and this section of northern India was the ideal place to get them.

As a matter of course, I looked up my friend Jim Wendell, who supervised the Maharajah's racing-stables. Over a whisky and soda I kidded him about working for a cruel rascal.

He took it good-naturedly. "After all," he said, "a man's got to live."

"Why don't you turn horse-thief?" I asked. "I hear that's a good graft and you can be in business for yourself instead of working for a royal louse who'd throw his own mother into a ring with a cobra if he thought a good fight would result."

"I cheerfully admit," said my Australian friend, "that I have no love for the Maharajah. Hardly a day passes without my imagining myself in the act of embroidering my initials on his posterior with a red-hot poker."

"Why don't you do it?" I asked. "It's a great idea."

"I couldn't very well do it alone," he replied as he downed another whisky. "I'd have to have help. Someone's got to hold him down while I work the poker."

"What's the matter with me?" I said.

We had another drink and then we shook hands and vowed not only to carve my friend's initials on the Maharajah's buttocks but to add my own. I had never before seen F. H. B. in a burnt-leather effect on a Maharajah and I thought it would be quite a novelty.

Another drink and we revised the whole plan. The new scheme was to burn our full names in spencerian script on the royal rear, appending the date, or at least the year, in Roman numerals. We agreed that this would add a desirable touch of classicism.

We shook hands again, had a final drink, vowed that we should be friends unto death, bid each other a touching farewell and parted for the night.

The following day found my friend in an entirely different mood. You will be quick to realize this when I tell you that he greeted me in this fashion. "Frank, I've been thinking things over and I think you're a damned hypocrite."

This was a bit sudden, to say the least.

"What do you mean?" I said.

"All your righteous indignation about the Maharajah's cruelty gives me a pain. You think you're a saint because you don't kill animals."

"Hold your horses," I replied. "I hate princes who have animals killed to gratify their sadistic impulses and I despise the tea-party jungeleers who make their kills for the rotogravure sections of the Sunday papers. The next time I see a picture of a hunter standing with one foot on the head of a lion or tiger that he has just killed, I'm going to commit murder. I have nothing but respect for real hunters. The greatest of them all is the Sultan of Jahore. He is not one of your platform huntsmen. He meets his wild game on an even footing, out in the open, without a regiment of natives stacking the cards against the animal he is after. He has taken his life in his hands hundreds of times. An account of his exploits would make the greatest of all chronicles of big-game hunting. Beside his feats, those of most so-called big-game hunters pale into silly insignificance."

At this point Wendell grew sympathetic. "You're all out of breath," he said.

"Shut up," I said, "and let me finish. You just said I think I'm a saint because I don't kill animals. You're talking through your hat. After all, my business is to collect wild animals and bring 'em back alive for the zoos and circuses. How the hell could I bring 'em back alive if I killed 'em?"

"I'd never thought of that," said my Australian crony. "Beg pardon. I take it all back. How about a little drink?"

Again my friend had a complete change of heart. In India this is not to be taken as an indication of a mercurial nature; it should be taken, until real signs of instability present themselves, merely as a reminder that the man one is dealing with is an inhabitant of the tropics, which do strange things to the most constant of natures.

"I got annoyed with you," he said, "because there was another 'show' of the Maharajah's I wanted to invite you to, and I expected you to turn me down after hearing you talk about his cruelty. A cruel bastard if there ever was one—but why remind me? After all, I'm in his employ and when you tell me what a rat he is, you make me feel like one myself. Here I am, an Australian in India, working for a Hindu prince. I'm not quite sure how it all happened. But, here I am. God knows I'd like to be somewhere else.

"But that's all beside the point. The Maharajah's having another 'show' the day after tomorrow. That's what I started out to tell you. I think you ought to see it because you'll probably never again in all your life see anything like it. Don't ask me if it's another exhibition of cruelty. Of course it is. What the hell do you expect of my prince by this time—tender-heartedness, or what?

"Although I must say that the skunk has one soft spot in his make-up. He's crazy about that little boy of his. I didn't think the dirty savage had it in him to feel kindly about anyone.

"But to get back to the show. The prince is really outdoing himself this time. You told me that you've been thinking about writing the story of your experiences. If you have anything like that in mind you can't afford to miss this exhibition."

My friend rattled on in this fashion for a full fifteen minutes. You'd have thought from his passionate sales-talk that he had something to gain by my presence. The truth of the matter was that he didn't want me to miss what he considered an extraordinary spectacle.

He was very secretive as to what was going to take place. My questions netted me no information as to the nature of the proceedings. "If you're interested," he concluded, "turn up at the stables shortly after noon the day after tomorrow."

I appeared at the specified time. Lal Bahudar accompanied me.

In an open space between two of the structures that housed the prince's race horses we came upon a cage inside of which I saw one of the most magnificent specimens of the Royal Bengal tiger I have ever beheld.

Three or four *syce* (native stable-boys) were at work on the cage which was of the compressible type, similar in principle to the kind used in modern zoological gardens for surgical operations on savage animals. For instance, if the supervisor of a zoo has a dangerous beast that has to have a tooth extracted, the patient is transferred to a compressible cage, one side of which is pushed in on slides until the animal is wedged in and held tightly in place as though he were gripped in a vise.

The *syce* slid the adjustable side of the cage over till the tiger, which snarled its disapproval, was squeezed into a space so narrow that it was impossible for the animal to budge. Head and body were held absolutely rigid. Then the clamps were applied to the narrowed cage and the tiger was an utterly helpless prisoner.

I noticed that he was able to move his paws a few inches, though he was unable to strike out with them. As I stood there quietly speculating on the exact amount of play those paws had, the *syce*, who were evidently giving some thought to the same subject, started lashing each paw to the nearest bar of the cage with rope.

Lal Bahudar was enjoying himself thoroughly. On the whole, he was a rather decent barbarian,—honest and dependable. A less enthusiastic enjoyment of the tiger's discomfiture would have been too much to expect from him.

Evidently he knew what the next move was going to be, for when another groom, a very stocky chap, appeared bearing a pair of heavy iron snippers, Lal emitted a shriek of sheer delight. These snippers were similar to the big powerful kind that blacksmiths employ in removing old horse-shoes.

In businesslike fashion the newly arrived *syce* approached the cage, and, without any loss of time, gripped one of the tiger's claws with the snippers and gave a great yank. The enraged animal strained at the bars and emitted an ear-splitting cry of anguish. It was one of the strangest tiger cries I have ever heard. It started as one of those fearsome throaty snarls, grew in volume to a weird agonized howl, and then died down again to a guttural growl that somehow seemed more ferocious than the louder cry and plainly bespoke, in combination with the horrible expression in the eyes, the most awful, and the most justifiable, lust to kill that I have ever seen in an animal anywhere.

The jerk of the snippers had loosened the claw from the bed

of flesh and gristle where it had its roots and the stable-hand snipped it off while the blood spurted out. Again the infuriated animal emitted a howl of pain and strained at the bars till they sank into his sides.

If you can imagine anyone pulling your finger-nails out by the roots you have a pretty good idea of what that tiger suffered as the *syce* with the snippers cold-bloodedly made the rounds of the cage and yanked those claws out one by one.

I watched the performance with a feeling of hatred for the royal swine that was responsible for it and disgust with myself for having remained a spectator so long. I lay claim to no high moral principles and I have an instinctive distrust of those who shout their virtues in the market-place; but I afterwards had a real feeling of shame for having watched that outrageous spectacle as long as I did.

The *syce* with the snippers had just finished pulling the last claw, gristle and all, to the surface. With sinister calm he snipped it off, examined it meaninglessly, and let it drop to the ground. With his toe he turned it over, as if fascinated by his handiwork, and then he prepared himself for the second phase of his task.

The beast was now moaning, but what my ears still heard was that final agonized shriek, a cry that epitomized the physical suffering, the melancholy, the venomous hate, the murderous longings, that consumed him.

I stood there staring at the ground for what seemed half an hour but was probably three or four minutes. Someone banged me on the back. I looked up. It was Wendell.

"I think you need a drink," he said.

I didn't feel much like conversation. I felt another whack on the shoulder and again I heard, "I think you need a drink."

"I think you're right," I replied. As I spoke I found myself staring straight ahead to where the imperturbable *syce* of the snippers was performing another job on the tiger. This time he employed a large needle very much like those used by veterinarians in stitching up wounds in horses. I easily recognized the material in the needle as surgical catgut. It wasn't very difficult to recognize the place that was being stitched. Even a man in a fog—and I was in the midst of a very thick one—could recognize it as the mouth. The nerveless *syce* was coolly sewing the tiger's lips together, through the bars of the cage.

Perhaps I lay too much emphasis on the *syce's* nervelessness and coolness. After all, it didn't take much of either of these qualities to perform the task in hand. The tiger's head was so tightly wedged in that it was impossible for him to do anything with his teeth. In case there *was* any possibility, this was removed the minute some careful soul conceived the rope-work that fastened the jaws together.

In view of which, perhaps I should revert to my original estimate and refer to the *syce's* cold-bloodedness rather than his coolness. I knew very little of the gentleman but I know a great deal about Hindus and it is safe to say that if there was any danger involved, this seemingly courageous stable-hand would have fled with a speed that would have shamed the records of our greatest sprinters.

While the *syce* finished his job Wendell took me over to his quarters for a drink.

"I need one as badly as you do," he said.

We walked along in silence for a few minutes.

I broke the silence. "Now that they've yanked out that tiger's claws and sewed his lips together, what are they going to do with the poor devil?"

"Oh, you'll see."

"I will like hell."

"Oh, come on."

"I've seen all of that rotten mess I intend to."

"Get a good skinful and you won't mind it, Frank. There isn't much I can't stand with a bellyful of Scotch."

"You haven't answered my question. What are they going to do with the tiger?"

"Throw him to the dogs. An old pastime of the prince's. Renders a tiger helpless and tosses him to a lot of big dogs. Gets a kick out of seeing how soon they can tear the tiger to pieces. Today's show ought to be the best he's ever pulled, or the worst, whichever way you look at it. You ought to see the brutes of dogs he's got. Six of 'em. That's one more than he's ever used before."

"You aren't going to attend, are you?"

"I've got to . . . Christ! Don't remind me what a stinking job I've got."

"Beg pardon, Jim."

"I don't blame you for staying away. This isn't going to be a fair fight. Just a bloody massacre."

We were now in Wendell's quarters. He produced a bottle of Scotch and we had a drink that wasn't productive of much conversation. I recall mumbling a few words in praise of the whisky. It was all I could think of to say. I felt all washed out.

We had a second drink. I started feeling better but still I could think of nothing to say. I sat there staring at the bottle and wondering how soon I could ask for another drink without seeming a hog.

It occurred to me that I was staring at the bottle too pointedly; so I looked at Wendell for a change. Suddenly it struck me that he had a very fine face. This had never occurred to me before. I had always liked him tremendously but it had never entered my head until now that he was sensitively put together and that he probably suffered a great deal in his queer job. I had always thought of him as a rough-and-ready colonial who couldn't be fazed by anything.

His plight disturbed me but I was secretly glad to know that Asia could unsettle a stout-hearted chap like Wendell. It was reassuring; for Asia has unsettled me on many an occasion. In my many years of work as a collector of zoological specimens, this strangest of continents has produced some wobbly moments in me; and these moments have filled me with doubts and misgivings.

My silence began to get under Wendell's skin. Suddenly he broke out into a great jumble of unrelated sentences. . . . "Crazy game, isn't it? Crazy country, crazy people. What the hell does it all mean? But what does anything mean? Suppose the prince didn't throw a helpless tiger to a pack of dogs? It would still be a lousy world, wouldn't it? Let him have his fun. What the hell do I care? It's none of my damned business and it's none of yours. . . . Inherited brutality, that's the answer. The prince's father was even worse. Yes, worse; ask anyone that knew him. We're unreasonable, that's what we are, Frank. Unfair. Even a little intolerant. . . . Yes, I know all about it. The prince is a cruel scoundrel. But he learned it from his father. What do you expect? There's the prince's little boy. When *he* grows up he'll be cruel too. He'll see so much cruelty all around him that he'll regard it as the accepted thing, as part of the business of preparing to be a prince. And, anyhow, who cares? Let 'em all kill one another off, human beings and animals. It's getting damned hard to tell which is which. Have a cigarette. India can stand a few casualties. She's horribly overcrowded. It's too bad they're usually the wrong ones. Don't stare me out of countenance. Look at the bottle for a change. Have a drink. Don't have a drink. Do anything you damned please. See the Maharajah's show. Don't see his show. Who cares? Please yourself. Blow your brains out if that'll make you happy. There's a gun over there in the top drawer of my desk. Christ! It's getting late. I've got to have a look at those dogs. I'm supposed to keep 'em mad at the world in general and tigers, in particular. Got any ideas? Think I'll try putting on a striped suit and spitting in their eyes. Let's get out of here. The prince'll raise the devil if I'm late. He's a stinker that way."

Wendell was himself again. His long soliloquy, instead of wearing him out, seemed to pep him up. On the way back to the stables he was his old genial self again; as we strode along he seemed positively happy. One comes to regard such changes of mood as a commonplace in India. The thing's in the air.

I did not attend the "fight" between the tiger and the dogs. Pardon the quotation marks. Pull a tiger's claws and sew his lips together and you can't expect much of a fight.

But there was plenty of drama. The cruel exhibition, as planned, should have resulted in the loss of only one life, the tiger's. In addition, one human being and one dog perished. That was where the unexpected entered.

Wendell and Lal Bahudar (who watched the proceedings, or most of them, from his old perch among the flaming red blossoms of an adjacent plane tree) supplied me with the details of what took place.

The helpless tiger and the six dogs were turned loose in the walled enclosure. The dogs were of tremendous size and great ferocity. They were a cross between a mastiff and an Irish wolf-hound. Almost invariably the result of this combination is a huge vicious animal. I have seen quite a few of these dogs in India. They are used for boar-hunting and sometimes are known as "boar-hounds." The colorings are brown and white, black and white, plain black and plain brown.

The tiger, the ends of his paws gruesomely blood-stained and his mouth distorted into a grotesque expression as a result of the catgut that sealed his lips, was a ghastly sight to behold. Half-bewildered, he hobbled about in circles on his bloody stumps, probably trying to figure out why this new torture was being visited upon him. He had a right to expect a rest for the day after the earlier horror that had been his portion.

The dogs did not spring at the enemy on sight. Dogs have too much native caution for that. After all, a tiger is a tiger.

Discreetly they edged closer and closer to the hobbling foe, backing him against the wall. For a full minute, according to Wendell, they stood this way. The inaction of the big cat emboldened one of the dogs to come close and snap at the hind quarters, hastily withdrawing. All the tiger did by way of reply was to lift one of his aching paws. That was all. The dog that had snapped at him, repeated the performance and the others, encouraged by the tiger's inactivity, joined him. In a second they were all snapping away at the impotent enemy, barking furiously as they attacked.

To save himself the tiger started rolling over on his side toward the middle of the enclosure. By sheer dint of his weight he succeeded in scattering the dogs and gaining a respite. His sides were bleeding but no serious wounds had been inflicted. The dogs had not managed to sink in their teeth. The wounds were all on the surface.

Again the dogs cornered the foe, all of them piling on after one of them had sampled a mouthful of the loose skin around the flanks. This time the tiger was painfully mauled and chewed up. But nothing approaching a serious blow had yet been struck.

The tiger was in a blind fury. With claws in his toes and no catgut binding his lips, he could have routed a dozen such dogs and left half of them stretched out on their backs with their entrails hanging out. One of the dogs leaped at him and he knocked him over with a great slap of one of those toothless paws. Pain was written all over the tiger's face as he struck the blow with that bloody limb. It was agony to defend himself and it was agony to be roughed and bitten by these miserable canines.

The dog he bowled over with a thrust of that bloody paw leaped at him with murder in his heart. Teeth bared, the savage cross-breed struck at the tiger's mouth. He bit deep into the lips on the right side, breaking the catgut and enabling the tiger to get one of his big teeth free. Lunging madly, the infuriated cat knocked the dog over, trampled on him and dug into his belly with that one great tooth that was free, working it like a can-opener and ripping open the canine's guts.

The other dogs scattered in terror. The plight of their fallen comrade shattered their morale.

And then the outstanding thrill of the day set the spectators —(the prince and his party on the platform and the native palace attendants on the wall)—on their collective ear. Gathering all his strength, the tiger made a great leap to scale the wall. It was a terrific assignment for one so maimed. By one of those miracles of determination he just made it, his belly scraping the top of the wall as he fell rather than jumped over the barrier. As he scrambled over the top, a shot rang out and a bullet from the rifle of a royal guard buried itself somewhere in his bottom. The bullet, instead of slowing up the beast, seemed to have the effect of spurring him on. With all the speed he could muster he raced onward on those gory stumps. By now he was calloused to the pain. He had no destination. All he wanted to do was to put some distance between himself and his torturers.

Already the palace guards were in hot pursuit. Shots rang out but they missed their mark. The tiger, as wounded as he was, was lengthening the distance between him and his pursuers.

Straight ahead was the *midan,* or parkway of the palace. On, on, he raced.

A few dozen yards ahead three native women could be seen, the royal governesses. They had the Maharajah's son in tow, the future prince.

The royal ladies, in accordance with strictly normal conduct, scattered and fled in terror.

On, on, ploughed the crazed jungle cat. Right in his path was the deserted heir to the throne. All he saw was a human being of very small size,—one ideally suited to a murder-bent tiger whose prowess had been sadly reduced by the drawing-out of claws, the sewing-together of lips, the bites of vicious dogs, and a bullet wound for good measure.

With a slap of one of the clawless paws he sent the Maharajah's four-year-old boy spinning. Then, while shots rang out all around him, he dug his one free tooth into the heart, into the neck, into the eyes.

The future occupant of the throne, the rightful heir of the prince, vested with privileges to torture whomsoever and what-soever he pleased, died like a dog at the hands,—or rather, the bloody paws—of another member of royalty: the Royal Bengal tiger.

Then, just to show that he was not above dying himself, the worn-out tiger, now half-dead anyhow, took all that the rifles of the oncoming guardsmen had to give, and expired.

It was all pretty rough on the Maharajah's little boy; but who says there is no justice . . . now and then?

Wanted: Two Rhinos

I was in the office of Dr. William T. Hornaday, then Director of the New York Zoological Park. This was back in 1922.

After discussing some lesser assignments, Dr. Hornaday reopened a subject that had been close to his heart for some time. "Isn't there some way we can secure an Indian rhinoceros?" he asked. "You know I've always wanted one."

I appreciated the confidence that this eminent zoologist displayed in me in discussing the possibility of securing one of these rare animals, the great single-horned, armor-plated rhinoceros of India which is now practically extinct in that country.

Dr. Hornaday, with the zeal of the honest-to-goodness zoologist who will not take no for an answer, pressed his point. I did not feel very optimistic about the prospects but I found myself weakening. Dr. Hornaday's faith in me made me feel that I ought to make a strenuous effort to secure for him the prize he sought.

The Indian rhino, as far as India itself is concerned, is virtually a non-existent animal. In former years it ranged all over northern India away up into the United Provinces and as far south as southern Bengal, and it was, in those palmy days, the greatest of all big game known to man. It is the largest, the most awe-inspiring of all rhinos, an Indian bull rhinoceros being much greater in size than the common African variety.

In the little state of Nepal, which in size is the Asiatic equivalent for a country like Montenegro in Europe, the Indian rhino has always been regarded as royal game, no one except the Maharajah and those friends and associates to whom he gave special permission being allowed to hunt it. For this reason the species has survived in Nepal and quite a number of them are to be found in the southeastern part of the country, which comprises the foothills of the Himalayas.

The more I thought of the project the more it fascinated me, —and the more I was stumped by the problem of Nepal's iron-clad governmental regulations which not only forbade strangers to hunt the Indian rhino but actually did not permit foreigners to enter the country! These were the difficulties that had floored me in the past on those occasions when my ambitions as a collector had betrayed me into visualizing myself as the proud possessor of one of these rare animals that very few hunters, including the greatest, have even seen, much less shot or captured.

It was a diplomatic mission as well as a collecting trip. It involved getting in right with someone close to the ruler of this powerful little kingdom that brooks no interference in its affairs and lets the whole world go hang as it goes about its business, demanding nothing of other countries except that they do the same thing.

Even England, with the tremendous power she exercises in Asiatic affairs, has only the faintest kind of look-in in Nepal. By a special arrangement whose negotiations taxed the diplomatic talents of the Foreign Office,—(for the Nepalese are a stubborn people to deal with)—a lone British attaché hangs his hat, and does little else, in Khatmandu, the capital. His rôle is that of "adviser" to the Maharajah, having utterly no connection with or control over any of Nepal's official business or its law-making. This unofficial representative contents himself with keeping a watchful eye on the Russian bear and doesn't challenge the wisdom of letting the Nepalese severely alone.

The only other white man permitted in Nepal is an electrical engineer who supervises the Maharajah's power-house in Khatmandu. Sometimes His Highness craves for his primitive country some of the benefits of modern civilization, like electrically lighted streets, which are to be found in the capital. But as soon as the white men who crossed the border by special permission to make the installation had completed their task, they were hustled out of the country. Only one was allowed to remain, the engineer in charge of the plant, and he is as carefully watched as if he were constantly plotting to run away with his royal master's favorite wife or to carry off on his back the wall of Himalayas which give Nepal the greatest natural fortifications in the world.

As I sat in Dr. Hornaday's office that day there flashed through my mind the many obstacles that had to be surmounted before I could hope to bring any Indian rhinos out of Nepal. I like tough jobs, as evidenced by the stubbornness with which I pursued my quest for some of the "firsts" that I have brought back to America. (By "firsts" I mean specimens never before seen in America alive, among my contributions being the anoa, or pigmy water buffalo of Celebes; the babirussa, rarest and least known of the wild swine; the proboscis monkey, the long-nosed monkey of Borneo; the siamang gibbon, largest of the gibbon apes, and others.)

But the search for Indian rhinos was so much tougher an assignment than any I had ever had before that I had a momentary feeling of blueness over the possibility of disappointing Dr. Hornaday, who had succeeded in interesting another well-known zoologist in his Indian rhino project, Dr. Charles Penrose, President of the Philadelphia Zoological Society, and a brother of the late Boise Penrose. They had decided between them that if I would undertake an expedition with the object of securing two rhinos, one for each of the zoos, their institutions would assist in financing the project. These two men knew as well as I did that the expense of such an expedition would be too great to render it practicable from a profitable standpoint, so that the only way I could possibly have accepted the proposition was for them to share in the expense in case of failure and to pay me liberally for the animals if I delivered them.

They adopted so sporting an attitude toward the venture that I found myself taking a more optimistic view; and when, in addition, Dr. Hornaday said, "You have never failed me and I'm sure you won't fail me now," I made up my mind that I was going to make a success of the enterprise if I had to tunnel my way into Nepal and drag a couple of Indian rhinos out of the country on my back.

After all, Dr. Hornaday had never expressed a wish for any specimen that I had not been able to bring to him sooner or later. The anoas mentioned above were a striking example. Three years before I had been in this same office and the director had expressed a desire for specimens of these pigmy water buffalo for the New York Zoo. Like the Indian rhino, there were none in the whole length and breadth of America. I had gone all the way into the interior of Celebes after an almost two years' search and brought out a pair of these rare little bovines, which are still on view in the Bronx Park Zoo.

On May 20th of that year I sailed for Hong Kong, on the first leg of one of the most important collecting trips I have ever undertaken. While the Nepal expedition for the Indian rhinos was my big objective, I also had other important orders. The St. Louis Zoo had commissioned me to secure for them a collection of Indian waders (cranes, storks, flamingoes), also some gibbons and antelope. Then there was an order for a whole zoo which I had contracted for with the city of Dallas. I had spent three days in Texas, not long before I sailed, consulting with the Dallas authorities. I outlined plans for a moderate-sized zoo, naming a complete list of animals and birds with which to stock it and making suggestions as to the cages, pens and paddocks. I left the city with a contract to deliver within one year's time about five hundred specimens of birds, mammals and reptiles.

I also had an order from Al G. Barnes, the circus man, for three elephants, two tigers, two tapirs and two orang-utans.

The New York Zoo, in addition to the Indian rhino, had commissioned me to get a pair of snow leopards, a pair of markhor goats and a few smaller animals. Philadelphia, too, did not confine its order to the rhino, my supplementary commission from Dr. Penrose being for a pair of anoas, a pair of snow leopards, one orang-utan and a pair of binturongs.

I also had a few smaller orders. I merely mention these additional orders to give you an idea of the extent to which my business had developed and the scale on which I was operating.

In this chapter I shall confine myself to the expedition into Nepal for the rhinos.

My diary reveals that I arrived in Singapore on the 28th of June. There I made preliminary arrangements for the trapping, and, in some cases, the purchase of the specimens I was after. Then I sailed for Calcutta.

At Calcutta I had a stroke of good luck. One of the many inquiries designed to help me discover someone who could be helpful in getting me on the right side of the Maharajah of Nepal resulted in the information that General Kaiser Shum Shere, a nephew of the Maharajah, was in town. He had come down from Khatmandu in his official capacity and had established a sort of Nepalese headquarters in Middleton Row, in the European section of Calcutta, where he had taken a large house for the season.

I had to get an introduction to this Nepalese prince; that was obvious. Various schemes popped into my head. I finally hit upon a very simple plan that involved an old friend of mine, a lady of considerable social standing who lived in Calcutta. I was fairly sure that if I asked her to invite General Shum Shere for tea and include me among those invited, she would do so.

She cheerfully fell in with my plans and the tea was arranged. Shum Shere proved to be a dapper little man of about thirty-five, with a dapper little beard. He was neatly attired in white flannel trousers and a tweed coat. When one remembers how many native princes of all sorts and varieties in that part of the world never miss an opportunity to deck themselves out like musical comedy field marshals in the grand finale when the king enters, you will realize how agreeably surprised I was on finding General Shum Shere to be an unpretentious, businesslike sort.

Rather casually—for I did not want to press my business too hard—I mentioned the fact that I was after a pair of Indian rhinos. All I wanted to find out for the moment was whether I was right in my belief that there were some left in Nepal. To my delight I learned that the Nepalese borders sheltered what were practically the last survivors of the species. As I thought, they were royal game, controlled by the Maharajah. The prince evinced interest in my expedition, did not encourage or discourage me, and wound up by inviting me to call on him at his house in Middleton Row. This was real progress.

In the Park Street section of Calcutta which takes in Middleton Row, most of the houses and grounds are enclosed within a high wall, with great iron gates at the entrances. On arriving at the gate of Shum Shere's house a few days later—(I didn't waste much time in taking him at his word)—I found ferocious-looking Gurkha troops on sentinel duty. In his scabbard each of the fierce-visaged devils had three ominous knives. As I eyed the barbaric roughnecks I decided on a polite approach.

But my honeyed tones availed me nothing. They didn't understand what I was saying. I had made the mistake of calling without an interpreter. I tried sign language. This was also a dismal failure. Then one of the Gurkha lads made a gesture of his own. He used one of his knives for the purpose. With it he pointed to the street. A second Gurkha removed a knife from his scabbard and pointed streetward. Obviously the boys were inviting me to take the air. I decided to leave.

The next day I returned, accompanied by Lal Bahudar, my No. 1 Indian boy, a native of the Nepalese border country, who spoke the language as fluently as he did Hindustani. He shouldered his way right past those fierce-looking Gurkha sentinels, shouting to them in a queer dialect as he ploughed ahead. I learned later that he told them I had come all the way from America at the General's special request and that if they interfered they'd get into trouble.

I was soon ushered into a rather sumptuous apartment. General Shum Shere, dressed in the height of Nepalese fashion, greeted me effusively. The transition from the white flannels and tweeds to the Asiatic habiliments in which he now appeared —trousers of a pinkish silk, very baggy down to the knees where they became tight-fitting, and a sleeveless jacket of green velvet over a white silk shirt—was a bit sudden.

If he had been of a heavier build, and a noisy bombastic type, the General might have succeeded in looking pretty silly in his pink pants and bright green coat. As it was he looked merely colorful, and as neat as he did in his flannels and tweeds. Perhaps the fact that this Nepalese outfit was carefully tailored and a perfect fit also had something to do with the General's being so pleasant a departure from some of the foolish-looking Asiatic aristocrats I had met before.

Be that as it may, the General was a modest and unpretentious little chap, with none of the pompousness one expects to find in an Asiatic prince.

In physique he did not live up to one's conception of the celebrated adventurer, yet he is a great *shikari*, or "mighty hunter," one of the greatest in all of Asia. It was Shum Shere who in 1921 arranged and carried out the much exploited tiger and rhinoceros hunt for the Prince of Wales during his visit to Asia, when he bagged a number of the big striped cats and a record rhino.

Shum Shere managed to be cordial without resorting to the effusiveness that is so common in the East. There is a high percentage of extremists among Asiatic hosts. Either they won't let you past the front door or, once inside, they make such a fuss over you that you find yourself growing uncomfortable.

I was motioned to a chair while the General sat on a richly upholstered divan. A servant brought cigarettes and whiskies and soda so that soon we were settled down to a friendly chat. Shum Shere was educated in England and speaks the King's English with a studied correctness, only his slightly sing-song delivery reminding one of his Eastern origin.

After exchanging pleasantries for ten or fifteen minutes we got down to business. Yes, there were Indian rhinos in Nepal. He had told me that before at the tea given by my friend, but it was heartening to hear him repeat it. No, under no circumstances could I hope that the Maharajah would make an exception to the rule declaring the rhino to be royal game. There was as much chance of that happening, he assured me, as there was of the Prince abdicating and asking me to be his successor.

Did he hold out any hope for me? Was there any chance of my securing the rhinos?

Yes. (This was cheering.)

How?

Well, it was like this. The Maharajah regarded everything in Nepal as part of the natural resources of the country. He doubtless viewed the rhinos in this light. The Maharajah was a practical-minded business man, frankly interested in converting any of the country's natural resources into cash. How could he otherwise hope to maintain the splendid government he gave his five million subjects with a modern capital at Khatmandu devoted to the betterment of the people? Yes, the Maharajah would probably be willing to talk business.

But naturally enough he, Shum Shere, a mere general, did not attempt to speak for His Highness. He would telegraph the Maharajah and find out whether the nation could spare two rhinos, and, if so, how much they would cost.

Four days later I heard from Shum Shere. Could I come right over?

This I did, jauntily. The General sounded like business.

This time the Gurkhas made no attempt to stop me. The one that seemed to be the leader of the squad, a sort of top sergeant, eyed me in rather friendly fashion, for a Gurkha. By this I mean that he did not look as if he wanted to run one of his swords through me.

Shum Shere did not waste any time in getting to the point. I could have two Indian rhinos for 35,000 rupees.

This is about $12,600. It's a lot of money to invest in a couple of animals that have to travel 16,000 miles before you can hope to get your money back. Animals sometimes have a habit of dying on your hands before you can cash in.

And, as in the matter of owning an automobile, it isn't the initial cost alone that turns one's hair gray; the upkeep does its bit toward that end.

It takes considerable money to keep two rhino bellies packed with food over a 16,000 mile journey, and the transportation charges in getting 'em back to civilization constitute another item that becomes rather sizeable. Unless you can afford luxuries

I wouldn't advise you to import any Indian rhinos, even if you can get the Maharajah of Nepal to O.K. your project.

I told Shum Shere that 35,000 rupees was a lot of money. I didn't see how I could pay that much.

Would the General be willing to telegraph His Highness at my expense and see if the country couldn't part with that portion of its natural resources represented by two rhinos at a lower figure?

Of course! At once!

Shum Shere was nothing if not businesslike. He lost no time in getting off the message I suggested.

Late the same week I again heard from the General. He was sorry. Extremely sorry. But 35,000 rupees was the lowest figure His Highness could possibly consider. He, Shum Shere, had just received a message to that effect. The expedition to secure the rhinos would necessitate the use of many soldiers and elephants, and much equipment. As the gentleman from America realized, it was a tremendous undertaking to set out to secure two Indian rhinos alive. In Nepal there were hunters that knew how to shoot rhinos and bring them in dead, but capturing them alive was a new business. It was a hazardous, expensive enterprise.

I got the impression that even if I were the Maharajah's brother he couldn't afford to let me have two live rhinos for less than the price named. In fact, I was given to understand that even though I was buying only two specimens, I was getting the benefit of the wholesale price.

Not wishing to reduce the Nepalese nation to a state of poverty by making serious inroads into its natural resources at a starvation figure like 30,000 rupees, the maximum I felt I could afford to pay, and being exceedingly anxious to bring back two Indian rhinos on the hoof, I agreed to the price of 35,000 stipulated by His Highness.

I regarded it as a losing deal from the financial standpoint but felt that if I could bring the rhinos back it would be a fine thing for my reputation.

We closed the transaction and I was delighted when Shum

Shere told me that he would personally head the expedition for the animals I sought. This meant that the job would be intelligently organized and prosecuted, for the General is a truly great *shikari*, a man who has won the respect of the greatest hunters in Asia.

The deal for the rhinos settled, I decided on a collecting trip that took me through Burmah and down the Malay Peninsula to Singapore where I wound up with a great many specimens, including elephants, tigers, smaller animals and birds.

It was arranged that I was to keep in touch with a representative in Calcutta who was to be notified by Shum Shere as soon as the latter had captured the two rhinos. Then I was to proceed to Nepal for the animals.

Some weeks later I returned to Calcutta with a number of specimens that I had collected on the way up from Singapore. Some messages from Shum Shere had been relayed to me to the effect that he was making good progress in his rhino hunt and expected to have news of the capture before long.

I then went up into the United Provinces for additional specimens and had not been back in Calcutta many days when the good news finally arrived. Shum Shere notified me that he had captured two fine Indian rhino calves—(my order was for calves)—one weighing a ton, the other about a ton and a quarter. I was very happy over these tidings and delighted beyond words with the additional information that Shum Shere was on his way to Calcutta on official business and would meet me and give me full details as to how I was to secure delivery of the animals at the camp that had been established between Khatmandu and Bilgange. This involved special permission to enter the country, which would be granted because I was a friendly soul helping the Nepalese nation to market her "natural resources."

Before leaving for the rhino camp in Nepal on what proved to be the strangest journey of its kind I have ever undertaken, I asked Shum Shere for first-hand details of his expedition and how he had captured the calves. Having given him some pointers during our early interviews on how I thought he ought to go about it I was anxious now to know if he had followed my sug-

gestions. Besides, it's always interesting to learn how the other
fellow operates.

My order for rhinos came at a good time, Shum Shere told
me. Rice-growers had been complaining to the government at
Khatmandu for some time that rhinos had been stamping down
their crops, making "wallows" of the fields (flooded for irriga-
tion at this season) and in general making nuisances of themselves. These complaints were coming in with such frequency
that His Highness predicted an unnatural end for these "natural
resources" unless they started behaving themselves.

So that when the Maharajah received Shum Shere's message
to the effect that he had a customer for a pair of rhinos I'm sure
His Highness must have forgotten the dignity of his office and
turned a few Asiatic handsprings. His business sense, however,
did not leave him in his enthusiasm; for he remembered to say
that he couldn't possibly let me have two rhinos for less than
35,000 rupees.

In fairness to the old boy let me add that capturing rhinos
alive is a pretty costly business and he must have been put to
considerable expense. In fact, I doubt if more than 20,000
rupees of the total I paid him were profit. After all, the only
inexpensive way of getting rhinos was to shoot them; and I'm
sure if I had asked for a pair of dead ones the charge would
have been much less.

The Terai, which stretches for a thousand miles through Asia,
is the most wonderful stretch of forest known to man, harboring
more game and wild life than any other wild lands in the world,
including those of Africa, which do not compare with it. The
great Nepalese Terai is richer in game than any other part of
this tremendous forest. One factor that keeps it so is the stern
decree of the government forbidding foreigners to enter the
country.

Into that part of the Terai that finds itself in the south central
part of Nepal, General Kaiser Shum Shere led his expedition
for the Indian rhinos.

Shum Shere had *carte blanche* to kill as many rhinos as he
pleased in the course of the expedition on account of the damage

they were doing in their migrations to the rice-fields, these pil-
grimages invariably resulting in the utter ruin of acres and acres
of the crop on which so big a percentage of the populace depended for subsistence.

As he was on the look-out for calves, he devoted himself to
looking for nursing mothers. It was hard work to track these
down and capture them. He could have shot down plenty of
them in the rice-fields but to try to capture them there alive
would have meant a skirmish that might have resulted in the
destruction of whole crops belonging to needy planters.

So he sought them out in wilder territory.

After days of reconnoitering, the General, who was working
with a force of thirty elephants and well over a hundred Gurkhas,
surrounded a female rhinoceros with a good-sized calf. He shot
down the mother, knowing that the rest was easy. By this I
mean that it is well known to those who are familiar with the
habits of the rhinoceros family that a rhino calf will stand beside
the dead body of its mother until decomposition starts to set in.

As the old cow dropped in her tracks, rope fencing, about four
feet high and interminably long, was quickly brought up and
thrown around the calf, making an enclosure of probably an acre
in extent. A small army of Gurkhas managed the rope fencing,
and they gradually closed in on the young rhinoceros until it
was hemmed within an enclosure of only twenty-five or thirty feet
in diameter.

The animal put up a game fight, the General said, it being
necessary to use his entire force of men to keep the fencing
taut and prevent the baby rhino—(a mere infant weighing about
a ton)—from dashing through. The flexibility of the rope enclosure, even when tautly held, prevented the calf from injuring itself in its frantic efforts to break loose.

At this point in the proceedings, logs and poles were cut from
the forest and brought up to the rope corral. These were driven
in the ground close together and banked high with earth on the
outside. The rhino was left this way for several days with the
rope fencing stretched taut inside of the log corral, so that the

animal could not butt its head against the logs in any further frenzied attempts to escape.

Milch goats were brought from a distant settlement and a gruel of boiled rice, goat's milk and sugar was fed to the animal, in addition to jungle leaves which were cut daily by the attendants.

When the little prisoner—(if it's all right to describe one-ton of rhino calf in that fashion)—had become sufficiently tractable and its restlessness subsided enough so that there was no longer any danger of its injuring itself, the rope fencing was removed and the animal was left in the log enclosure.

A second calf was captured in the same manner.

Later on both animals were transferred to cages, and after a long and wearisome trip on buffalo carts through the rugged, hilly country of southern Nepal, they arrived at the camp north of Bilgange where they were being held for me.

Shum Shere made the rice-growers happy and the rhino world sad by bringing down with his own rifle twenty-one of the mammoth beasts during the hunt, including the two cows that were with the calves he captured. He told me that he had never before realized how easy killing animals was in comparison with the job of capturing them alive; and he ventured the further opinion that capturing the rhinos was a cinch compared to my job of getting them back to the United States alive.

I recall showing Dr. Hornaday photographs of some of the rhinos that Shum Shere had shot down as vermin. These pictures of the dead pillagers of the rice-fields had been given me by the General. I'll never forget Hornaday's horror over the fact that these rare and almost extinct patricians of the animal kingdom, these survivors of the great race of Indian rhinos that had practically ceased to exist except in books telling of their mighty feats, should have suffered the ironic fate of being shot down as public nuisances.

So far so good. There were two rhinos waiting for me in Nepal. But my work had only started.

What follows will give the reader some idea of why the life of a wild animal collector is not exactly a picnic.

Delivered: Two Rhinos

BEFORE leaving for Nepal to get the rhinos I wanted to deposit the purchase price, 35,000 rupees, in a Calcutta bank, the money to be paid to Shum Shere as soon as the animals were delivered to me in satisfactory condition at a point where I could load them on a freight car. My plan was to release the money by telegraphing to the bank from Raxaul as soon as the Maharajah's representatives had gone through with their side of the deal.

Shum Shere, to my surprise, refused to have anything to do with the financial arrangements. He leaned backwards in his honesty, insisting that if he handled the money at any point people might think he was making money out of the transaction whereas he was merely helping his uncle the Maharajah dispose of some of Nepal's resources. He was glad to do a little thing like that for his uncle and his country without pay and he simply couldn't consider appearing in the financial arrangements for fear that his participation might be an indication to the un-enlightened that his interest in the whole business was a selfish one.

No, no, no. A thousand times no. The American gentleman was wasting his time.

Not only did he, Shum Shere, have no desire to take part in the financial arrangements for the personal reasons already mentioned but he doubted that he had the authority to do so. When you bought something from the Nepalese government you took cash with you, and made payment on the spot, and got out. It was a rule.

The more he thought of it the surer he became that he would be acting in violation of one of the royal regulations involving payments due the Nepalese government.

But wasn't this a special case? After all, wasn't the General a high prince of Nepal and wasn't it perfectly proper for him to act as his government's financial representative?

No, no, no. Ten thousand times no. Would the American gentleman be so kind as to consider the matter closed?

The prospect of carrying on my person all the way to Nepal 35,000 rupees in cash to pay for the rhinos, plus the sizeable sum I needed to cover the cost of transporting them to Calcutta, did not appeal to me at all.

A letter of credit would have been utterly useless as there are no banks in the isolated part of the world for which I was heading. Nor are there any hotels or other institutions to facilitate the safe handling of money.

I estimated that I should have to carry approximately 50,000 rupees (which was then about $16,000 in our money) on my person. The more I thought about it the less I liked the idea. Carrying this much money on one's person is risky business anywhere in India, and particularly up in the border countries where more than one man's throat has been cut for less than a hundred rupees. In fact, in many of these out-of-the-way districts they cheerfully cut your throat for nothing. There are Hindu knifesters who seem to be striving to preserve their amateur standing, fellows who require no financial inducements, not even expense money, to slit a man open from ear to ear. All the inspiration they need is a dislike for you and a lonely road. Of course, if an investigation reveals that you have some money on your person, they unofficially turn professional, like some of our amateur athletes.

Despite the precautions I planned to take, as I hastily reviewed the whole situation in my mind, I feared that somehow it would leak out that I had a fortune in rupees on me and that somewhere on the way to Nepal I would be singled out for the attentions of some flirtatious bandit who did his courting with a knife.

Shum Shere was sympathetic. He was adamant in his refusal to accept payment for the rhinos through a bank in India but he kindly offered to furnish a bodyguard of three Gurkha soldiers to accompany me. He made no effort to conceal his belief that I would need them.

Without further ado he called in one of his officers and gave him an order in Nepalese. The officer went out and soon reappeared with three of the examples of Gurkha ferocity that guarded Shum Shere's house. I recognized one of them as the Nepalese numbskull who made menacing noises with his throat, dilated his nostrils as if he were smelling me preparatory to eating me, and stamped his foot when I insisted on sending in my card on my first visit to the General's place. As he eyed me uneasily I saw in his look a combination of sulky embarrassment and ill-concealed displeasure that I did not like and I quickly decided that I had no desire to put myself in this malodorous— (I forgot to mention that he smelled to deep Hades)—villain's hands. His comrades weren't much better to look at or to smell.

None of these soldiers around Shum Shere's place seemed to have any distinctive uniform. They were clothed in the ordinary tight-fitting trousers and sash-like belt of the North country and either the short Nepalese jackets or ill-fitting coats fashioned after European style. Different types and colors of material were represented in their garb. The only uniform thing about them was their aroma.

No, I'll have to amend that. There was also a definite uniformity about the big Gurkha knives they carried, each of the weapons (a cross between a good-sized butcher knife and a broad-sword) as capable of cutting my throat as anyone's else, I couldn't help thinking.

The three Gurkhas now before me looked more like brigands than soldiers. Shum Shere designated them as my bodyguard and I stood scrutinizing them for a few seconds, wondering whether I should prefer to take my chances with them or with some of the savage hill tribes and bandits along the border.

Shum Shere must have read my thoughts for he immediately started reassuring me. After placing my safety in the hands of these men, he declared, they would die fighting for me. When a representative of the Maharajah of his (Shum Shere's) stand-

ing gave these men a trust, it was a matter of life and death
with them and they would sooner die at their own hands than
have anything happen to me.

The doubtful aroma they exuded suggested that perhaps they
were already dying, or, in point of fact, were quite dead on their
feet,—(the East is a great place for miracles)—but it would
have been indelicate for me to point this out. After all, the
securing of my Indian rhinos was as much a diplomatic mission
as anything else, and I discreetly refrained from unnecessary
flippancies.

In fact, I was all seriousness. Some of it seems amusing in
retrospect but I don't mind saying that at the time of my interview with Shum Shere I was plenty worried over the necessity
of carrying a large sum of money on my person from Calcutta
to the wilderness that is Nepal.

The General was trying to help me. There was no question
about it. I didn't see how I could gracefully turn down his
escort, as little as I thought of the wild-eyed Gurkhas who comprised it. I accepted with thanks and arranged to start north
by the train leaving Calcutta the following evening at eight
o'clock.

Most of the next day was spent in buying supplies and in
making other preparations. This included a visit to the bank
where I displayed my letter of credit and asked for fifty thousand
rupees. On account of the size of the sum—(in India that is a
fortune, comparable in the eyes of a native to a sum like a
million dollars in the United States)—the manager asked me
to step into his private office. Such transactions are never made
across the regular paying teller's window.

I've handled venomous snakes with fewer misgivings than I
experienced in handling that money. In fact, if instead of the
rupees, I had just dropped a curled-up cobra in my pocket, I
couldn't have felt more nervous. And I'm hardly what you
would call the nervous type.

I've had some hair-raising experiences in handling animals
but I've seen so many more deaths in Asia result from money
matters than from contacts with animals, that I've never had

any fun out of being a walking treasury. I prefer to take my chances with tigers and leopards.

That night, a quarter of an hour before the train's leaving-time, I arrived at Hourah station with Lal and a body servant named Johereim, and a dozen coolies carrying canned goods, a cooking outfit, bedding, etc. I had fifty thousand rupees in gold and in one-thousand rupee notes, principally the latter, tied up in a piece of silk cloth and fastened around my waist under-neath my clothing. The promised bodyguard, the nondescript trio who were going to die for me if necessary, were nowhere to be seen. Lal and I searched the station as diligently as if we actually liked the rascals but nothing smelling like them could be found. I waited at the entrance gate until a few minutes be-fore train time, when I concluded that the three trusted Gurkhas were not going to make an appearance. I decided not to bother with them but to take my chances without the aid of their carving-knives and fierce looks. I swung aboard the waiting train, with almost a feeling of relief that they had failed to show up.

Lal opened his remarks on the subject with as sincere and ringing a *"Soure Cabatcha!"* as I had ever heard him utter. He did not take as cheerful a view of the situation as I did. In the failure of the Three Reliables, my protectors unto death, to show up he saw a dark plot to accomplish my undoing. They would spread the news all over Calcutta that the *sahib* was on his way to Nepal with much money and on my arrival there I would be stabbed in a thousand places by an army of bloodthirsty brigands.

My theory was that the three bad boys from Nepal had started to celebrate their vacation from guard duty and the impending trip to the *vaterland*, had consumed more than was wise, and were now lying somewhere, drunk.

Lal didn't think much of my theory. He shook his head gloomily and predicted dire happenings.

The following day, about twenty hours after we had left Cal-cutta, we pulled into Mokamaghat. There we were to cross the Ganges River to Athmal Gola, proceeding next to Raxaul where the railway terminates and also where India ends and Nepal begins.

The idea uppermost in my mind was to get to the rhino camp as fast as possible, secure my rhinos, get them to the Raxaul freight yards with the aid of the Maharajah's representatives, pay for them and be rid of that troublesome money—and be off for Calcutta. I had quite a collection of animals and birds waiting for me there and I wanted to get back, assemble the whole lot and return to America with them. I have my own ideas about how animals and birds should be cared for and I was a little uneasy as I remembered the slipshod methods of even the best care-takers one can find in Calcutta.

So you can realize how I felt when on pulling into Mokamaghat I learned from the excited station agent that the Ganges River was in the throes of one of the worst floods it had ever known. I judged from the terrific downpour toward the tail-end of our trip to Mokamaghat that the monsoons had probably set in but I had no idea that we were running into a storm that was flooding that whole section of India.

The Most Holy of Rivers was swollen so far beyond its banks that railway communication with the northern country had been completely cut off. Lal and I momentarily forgot that the Ganges was a sacred river; we had some unholy things to say about it. But Lal did more than swear. Again he saw a dark plot to undo me, this time the Ganges River joining the conspiracy. He shook his head mournfully and declared that while he hoped for the best, if he were in the *sahib's* boots he would prepare for the worst. His superstitions, all rushing to the surface at once, pretty nearly floored him, poor devil.

Almost all the bridges north of the Ganges were out of commission, railroad tracks were washed out, and everything was in a hell of a mess.

I was told by officials that it might be well over a month before we should be able to proceed to the border. Again I found myself thinking of my big collection of animals in Calcutta, including four recently acquired Assam elephants; and of the stock at Singapore that was awaiting shipment to America. Feed bills were running up heavily and there was considerable risk of losing the animals by leaving them too long in the hands of those unreliable natives. But the rhinos, which could do more for my reputation as a zoological collector than all the other specimens put together, were across the border.

I had a tough decision to make. Having got as far as Mokamaghat, I hated to turn back; and I also hated the idea of leaving all my birds and animals indefinitely in Singapore and Calcutta.

Neither prospect was particularly pleasing. Mokamaghat was full of a queer assortment of stranded nondescripts and I didn't see much fun in living with this gang for perhaps five or six weeks, with nothing to do but guard that infernal money which was beginning to get on my nerves.

After thinking the whole matter over, I decided it would be impractical to wait for the monsoons to subside. Through the combination of runners and that part of the telegraphic service that was not out of commission I succeeded in getting a message to the authorities in Nepal. I told them that it would be impossible for me to get to the rhino camp for several weeks and that I would have to return to America with a big shipment of animals. This I did not want to do until I had assurances that they would hold the rhinos for me. About eight or nine days after I sent my message I got one back saying that the Maharajah understood my plight, and that the rhinos, which were in excellent condition, would be held for me until my return from America.

This was cheering news. With the knowledge that those two rare zoological prizes were still mine, and that I could gather them into the fold at a later date, I left for Calcutta in good spirits for a man whose plans had been messed up by a flood. What a relief it was to get rid of my cash at the bank!

Two weeks after my return to Calcutta I steamed down the Hooghly River on the S.S. *Kum Sang* with my four elephants 'tween decks and practically the entire deck space of the small coastwise vessel loaded with crates and cages of birds and animals.

I could ship on the *Kum Sang* only as far as Singapore, where we unloaded our collection and took them out to the compound to await an American boat due to sail for Los Angeles and San Francisco nine days later.

The day we arrived in Singapore was a regular circus day for the residents there. Fourteen large bullock carts and two motor-lorries transported my cages and animals from the dock out to the compound, followed by the four elephants.

Thousands of natives and not a few whites followed us through the streets. A few times, when we had to stop for traffic, the curious crowded around us in such mobs that we could hardly move.

With the vast Singapore collection augmented by this big shipment from Calcutta, I now had the biggest collection of live animals and birds ever assembled in one place with the possible exceptions of the big zoos in New York, Philadelphia, London and Hamburg.

This is not the place for details of my return to America with this record-breaking shipment. This, after all, is the story of those two Indian rhinos.

On my return to America I disposed of my great collection. With the various animals and birds on the way to their proper destinations, I breathed easily again and decided to visit Dr. Hornaday in New York before returning to Nepal.

I called on him and made a full report. He was delighted to learn that I had located an Indian rhino for him and one for Dr. Penrose. He was the soul of patience; his sympathy with my problems was complete. And I recall how he marvelled over my casualness in discussing a second long journey to far-away Nepal after the disappointments of the interrupted trip from which I had just returned.

Several weeks later I again found myself in India, on the way to Nepal via Mokamaghat, with Lal assisting me in the matter of guarding my fortune in rupees at night (for I was again forced to carry cash), and with Johereim attending my wants during the day. The damage done by the monsoons and the great flood had been repaired and travel was again normal.

At last, after many months, I found myself in Raxaul! I looked around for a *dak* bungalow (government rest house). I had been told that I should find one here. I learned that my information was incorrect and that there was no such accommodation.

A small railroad bungalow not far from the station and just outside the limits of the native town was the only possible habitation where a *sahib* might put up. In these frontier towns the Indian railroads maintain what are known as "railroad bungalows" so that when their division superintendents or other British railroad officials find it necessary to remain overnight in the out-of-the-way places, where suitable homes or hotel accommodations are not to be found, the bungalow is at their disposal. A native servant is in charge, keeping the place in order and ready for occupancy whenever these officials arrive.

While I checked and sorted my luggage which had been set out on a platform at the railroad station, I sent Lal to interview the servant in charge of the railroad bungalow to ask permission for me to put up there. The servant sent back word that one of the railroad *sahibs* would be arriving in an hour or two from Bhikna Thore and that I should have to get his permission. However, he suggested that the luggage be brought over to the bungalow veranda as it was beginning to get dark. While the coolies were carrying my boxes and bags across from the station, I inspected the bungalow. It was quite a comfortable house of plastered adobe walls and high roof of thatched rice straw, built on a cement platform wider than the bungalow itself so as to constitute both a floor for the bungalow and a veranda. There was a large center room and two smaller ones on either side. The large room was furnished with a hand-made wooden dining table, three plain chairs and a wicker couch. One of the smaller rooms was comfortably furnished for a sleeping room. There was a connecting alcove which contained a galvanized bath tub (wherever there's an Englishman you'll find a bath tub of some kind) and a big stone jar of water with a dipper. The other room was unfurnished.

I sent Johereim to the near-by bazaars to buy a chicken. He

returned with a likely looking one and with this and some of the stuff from my provision boxes he and the bungalow servant started preparing dinner for me. The idea uppermost in my mind was to take a bath. I was grimy after the trip and the galvanized tub looked pretty good to me.

I entered the little alcove and started undressing. I suppose I should have waited for the Englishman's permission before taking a bath but it didn't seem important enough.

I draped my clothes over a stool near the tub, placing a gun on top of the heap. I had removed the small percentage of gold contained in the silken sash in which I carried my money around my waist. The gold I had placed in my trousers pockets and the sash containing the thousand rupee notes I now wrapped around my neck. After tying it securely so that it clung to my neck like a great plaster, I proceeded to wash myself. Two or three times I reached over to see if I could grab my gun quickly if I needed it, and, finding it within easy reach, I went on scrubbing myself.

I had done a good job, except on the neck, which on account of the peculiar circumstances that prevailed, I was unable to scrub. I was about to start drying myself when I heard someone enter the bungalow and start raising hell with the servant in charge.

The newcomer was the English railroad official. What he didn't tell that poor bungalow servant wasn't worth telling. How dared he permit strangers to usurp his quarters? Who was this American who had the gall to walk in with his servant and promptly make himself at home? Where was the fellow anyhow? He had a few things to say to this brazen intruder.

I could hear the servant, who seemed to be sobbing as he spoke, say that I was taking a bath.

"Taking a bath!" roared the Englishman. "Who told him he could take a bath?"

Then I could hear my genial host stomp over to the alcove where I stood stark naked, with nothing on but a neck-band stuffed with money.

"I say!" He started as he eyed me in bewilderment and rage. "What does this mean?" For a second his eye rested on my revolver, then he looked up at the peculiar arrangement around my neck.

I saw nothing to worry me in this irate Englishman, who looked as if he might be a decent sort when he wasn't blowing off steam, so I picked up a towel and started drying myself.

"You'll excuse me, I hope, for not having some clothes on," I addressed him. "I wasn't expecting you quite so soon."

"I wasn't expecting *you* at all," he retorted. I thought that was pretty fair sarcasm and decided at once that this growling bear wasn't half bad.

Then I explained what I was doing there. I had expected to find a government *dak* bungalow, and, failing to find one, had temporarily located here. I hoped I hadn't put him out in any way. The Englishman grunted a few times as I told my story but he seemed to be calming down. He stared hard at the decoration round my neck, so I decided to make an explanation. "Sore throat," I said. "Damned nuisance."

And it was too,—the money, not my throat, which was a good throat and quite a help in breathing and swallowing.

Perhaps this affliction of mine softened my involuntary host. After telling me, with a kind of sternness that didn't sound very convincing, that he wasn't used to having strangers walk in on him in this fashion, he relented and told me I could use the unfurnished part of the bungalow.

I invited the Englishman to share the dinner which had been prepared for me but he declined my offer. "I've got my own food," he said. "My mistake," I replied. That's all the conversation that took place during the meal.

I believe he would have appreciated some of the delicious hot food which Johereim served me but he was suffering from a familiar ailment, British standoffishness, and this prevented familiarity on so short an acquaintance; so he sat opposite me at the table moodily mincing at his cold cuts while I enjoyed a first-class meal.

After dinner the Englishman thawed out. With pipes lighted and a whisky peg before us, we talked well into the night. He seemed interested in my experiences with animals and I got a great kick out of his stories of railroading in this strange and wild country. He was in charge of that division of the Bengal and Northwestern Railway which runs along the border of Nepal from Raxaul to Bhikna Thore and a hundred miles or so further on.

As we prepared to go to bed, he said to me out of a clear sky, "Be careful with your money."

"What money?" I asked, with a start.

"The money you had round your neck in the tub. You remember,—your sore throat." He smiled as he said this. So did I, foolishly. I was amazed. How in blazes did he know I had money in that sash? I didn't ask him, and he didn't tell me. To this day I haven't the faintest idea how he found out.

He broke into a laugh, a pleasant laugh. "I'm careless with my money too," he said. This was as ironic as it was amusing. I thought I had been so careful!

"If you've got much of it on you," he added, "keep it out of sight. The blighters here are very fond of money." With this he was off to bed.

The next morning I saw my English friend off. He was on his way up the line to a point between Raxaul and Bhikna Thore. His method of travel was nothing if not picturesque. His conveyance was a railroad hand car. A heavy armchair was placed on the car and he seated himself in this. Two natives seated themselves on the floor of the car. Two other natives got behind to push. The Englishman explained as he opened a parasol that this was his favorite method of getting around. When the two pushers grew weary, the boys on the car relieved them. They would alternate until they reached his destination. He had travelled thousands of miles in this fashion, he explained as he was off with a wave of the arm,—the boys sending the car down the tracks at a merry clip.

I had kept the Nepalese authorities posted on my movements by telegraph. They knew I was at Raxaul, stopping at the railroad bungalow, and they were to send representatives to meet me.

Not long after the Englishman's departure these representatives arrived,—two Nepalese who had come down from Bilgange, in accordance with arrangements made by General Shum Shere, to escort me across the border and on to Bilgange, whence a trail led up into the foot-hill country where the rhino camp was located.

My escorts were mounted on small horses or mountain ponies. They had brought an extra one for me. These ponies, bred in the Nepalese hills, are diminutive in size but hard as nails.

Elephants awaited us at Bilgange for the trip from here to the rhino camp. For a hardened collector I found myself getting pretty excited as we neared the camp.

My delight on finally reaching the animals, after months and months of anticipation, may well be imagined. I fairly slid off the big elephant on which I was riding before it had a chance to kneel.

Lal was so tickled he did the Asiatic equivalent of a handspring, a cross between a somersault and a cartwheel, if you can imagine anything as crazy as that. He accompanied his acrobatics with the most joyous cackling I'd ever heard from him.

The rhinos were wonderful calves, in splendid condition. I was happier than I had been in as long as I could remember.

The animals were in big heavy crates made of logs and big limbs cut and put together in the jungle. These cages were built in a most ingenious fashion, no nails being used, the rough-hewn timbers so dove-tailed and doweled together as to be thoroughly solid. It was almost incredible that these firm, well-made cages had been constructed with only the use of an adze, mallet and a crude hand-wrought native chisel.

And then the fun began.

The man in charge of the rhino camp was a Nepalese official, a pompous person who acted as if he was in the habit of giving orders to the Maharajah.

He had joined us at Bilgange where I was amused by the Napoleonic attitudes he struck as he barked out trivial commands to the half-scared Gurkha escort that accompanied him.

I was so occupied with thoughts of the closeness of my rhinos that I paid no attention to the fool. I thought his greeting needlessly gruff and I didn't see any occasion for his scowl but he seemed so unimportant a detail that I dismissed him from my mind.

He didn't lose much time asserting himself when we arrived at the rhino camp. His English was poor but he didn't have any trouble telling me, as I stood before the cages admiring my prizes, that he had taken care of the animals long enough; and that he would now turn them over to me and take payment for them. The animals were about as much use to me away up here in the jungle in these great heavy crates as they would have been in their original wild state.

It didn't take much imagination to see what would happen if I did this officious bonehead's bidding. He would break all speed records in vacating the camp; and with only Lal and Joherem to help me get two or three tons of rhino to the railroad yards in distant Raxaul, I would certainly be up against it.

I flatly refused to make payment at the camp.

The American did not realize what he was saying. Would he be good enough to pay the money at once and not waste any more of the time of one of Nepal's busiest officials? As he said this he struck a military pose, doing his best to look like a field marshal.

My fingers itched. I never felt more like clouting a man on the nose. But that wouldn't have accomplished much. There were at least thirty Ghurkas in and around the camp and I had no desire to have their carving-knives wind up in my innards. Some of them started crowding round as I snapped out my reply. I would pay for the rhinos when they were loaded onto the cars at Raxaul, and not a minute sooner.

This declaration was in reality merely a more emphatic version of what I had already told him. Nevertheless it had a strange effect on him. First he spat on the ground. Then he raised both arms in the air and waved them around frantically, to the tune of a series of shrieked exclamations which Lal afterwards told me were simply excellent cussing in the Nepalese dialect. Then he returned to his garbled English, capping his outburst by calling me a pig.

I said nothing. Again my fingers itched. But that was not my only emotion. I also wanted to laugh. In all my experience

I had never encountered a more ludicrous ass. I stood there alternating between a desire to break his neck and laugh in his face. I wound up by doing the latter. What else could I do when this funny Nepalese, arms akimbo, poked his face into mine, and with what he doubtless considered a fierce look but which was merely a stupid glare, announced that he would give me five minutes in which to make payment? It was the best joke I'd heard in a long time.

My laughter was interrupted by a command to the Ghurkas from this comic-opera official who, I afterwards learned, was a major in the Nepalese army. He barked out something in Nepalese and the Gurkhas lined up in a ragged row behind him. They had an expectant look, like chorus boys waiting for their music cue.

The major, who had dropped back a few paces, beckoned to me to join him. I refused. Whereupon he pompously strode over to where I stood, the Gurkhas advancing a similar distance behind him.

Then the major, shaking a finger in my face, told me that I was a fool; that he was aware I had been instructed to bring cash with me; that he knew full well that I had this money on me; and that if I didn't pay for the rhinos at once he would be forced to take the money away from me.

This was going too far. A joke is a joke. Musical comedy soldiers have no right getting that fresh. I removed my revolver from its holster, turning it over in my palm for effect. Then I significantly stuck it in the front part of my belt where I could grab it quickly. I had no desire to fight the Gurkha army but I was perfectly willing to plug a few of these boys if they forced a scrap.

Needless to say, I did not want a knife and gun party if it could be avoided. I was in Nepal to get those rhinos and I knew enough about this country, which had no use for white men and excluded them, to know that a skirmish with the authorities would probably result in the confiscation of the animals. And, what with all those knives, there was a possibility of my losing more than the rhinos,—perhaps an ear or an eye.

I meant to shoot only to defend myself. I stepped back a few yards, removed the pistol from my belt, fingered it again for effect, and put it back in place. Then, by way of emphasizing that I was ready for anything, I took some cartridges out of my pocket, ran them from one hand to the other a few times, and put them back in my pocket.

All the time I was trying to figure out a strategic move calculated to impress the major with my importance.

I started by telling him that General Shum Shere was one of my oldest friends. In Calcutta he and I were inseparable. I practically lived at his house there.

The major's widening eyes showed that I was making progress. I went on. And on.

How could I have secured special permission to enter Nepal if I hadn't been an old comrade of the General's? The General, in securing the rhinos for me, was merely doing me a friendly service. True, I was to pay for them; but little did he, the major, know how I had to plead with the General in Calcutta to get him to consider taking my money. Shum Shere had told me a hundred times that it was a small enough service to a friend to secure a pair of rhinos for him as a present. After all, Nepal was full of rhinos, and they were trampling the rice-fields. They would all be shot as pests anyhow, so why not give an old friend a pair?

If he (the major) thought this was merely a business deal, he was sadly mistaken. My friend Shum Shere would hear of my abominable treatment. He would hear how the major had threatened to take my money from me by force. He would hear how—

But that was as far as the major would let me go. He was melting by the second. His manner plainly indicated that I had scored. If I had told him that I was in the habit of putting Shum Shere on my knee and playing with his whiskers, the major would have believed me. Raising one of his arms, he pleaded with me not to say anything to General Shum Shere. It was all a mistake. He (the major) understood he was to take payment here at the camp but if the American gentleman said no, no it was. I had him on the run. I saw no point in abandoning my hard-boiled tactics too soon. I would think it over. Perhaps I wouldn't say anything to Shum Shere.

He wanted a promise, a definite promise.

So I made one. I would not tell the General how badly I had been treated if the major would immediately start making arrangements to help me get the rhinos to Raxaul. There he would have to load them onto the cars. Then I would pay him, and only then. And I would not tell the General that there was a major in the Nepalese army who deserved to be shot.

The major agreed with alacrity. He would help General Shum Shere's good friend get the rhinos to Raxaul.

I never appreciated the truth of Kipling's poem about the man who tried to hurry the East so much as I did during the days that followed. Most of my time during the day was spent with the rhinos, and some of the nights too. I made three or four trips back and forth between Raxaul and the rhino camp, traveling by elephant as far as Bilgange and from there either by mountain pony or in one of the rickety horse-drawn *gharries*. While waiting for the major to complete his arrangements (there were many delays on account of the red tape involved in securing permission for a troop of Gurkha soldiers to make the trip to Raxaul with the rhinos), I devoted myself to negotiating at Raxaul with the railway officials for the flat cars I needed for shipping the animals, and to a number of other important details involved in getting my valuable freight back to Calcutta.

By this time plenty of Nepalese must have known that I had considerable cash on me and I did not relish those trips at all. I now kept my revolver handy at all times, being called upon twice to scatter, with shots in the air, suspicious-looking natives in the underbrush along the road. But perhaps I misjudged them. Maybe they were only playing hide-and-seek.

More than once I thought the major was walking out on me. Every time there was a fresh delay I decided he must have discovered that General Shum Shere and I were not such great cronies after all.

But this was not the case. He was actually making haste, for a Nepalese. Finally he completed his arrangements and the rhinos started on the first stage of their sixteen thousand mile journey.

It was a great sight to see our odd caravan coming down through the jungle. The two huge crates were loaded on big bullock carts drawn by four water buffaloes each. Alongside marched forty or fifty Gurkha soldiers to steady the load and help push the carts out of mud holes, ruts, etc., while directly back of the carts came three elephants, each carrying a huge load of fodder for the animals. This consisted of green leaves of the jack fruit tree which were cut before we left the rhino camp and piled about eight feet high on top of each elephant. Following the elephants were a couple of bullock carts carrying our supplies, and one of the little Nepalese *gharries* in which Lal and Johereim were riding. The major and I were mounted on ponies and we acted as grand marshals for the parade, riding up and down the line, keeping everything in order.

By now the major was pretty friendly. I told him he looked every inch a general on his pony. God help any of Nepal's enemies that dared tamper with so fine a figure of a man, I added. The major loved it. In point of fact he had less figure than the rhinos we were transporting; but flattery was his weakness and I played to it. It was all in the game.

After three days of hard going we reached Bilgange and a temporary camp was made. I went on into Raxaul with Lal, had a good rest at the railroad bungalow and was back shortly after daylight the second morning, when the caravan again got under way. Owing to the almost impassable roads, it was a two-day trip to Raxaul. On arriving here I expected to get the animals immediately loaded onto cars so that we could take them out on the late evening train, but when we pulled up before the railway station, the station-master informed us that the two flat cars which he had ordered sent up from Muzufferpur, the next divisional point, had not yet arrived. We therefore had to make camp here and wait until the next afternoon.

The major was beginning to grow impatient. In my anxiety over my precious cargo,—those three or more tons of rhino that had made so much trouble for me,—I had forgotten for almost a whole day to compliment the biggest ass in Nepal and he was becoming low in spirits.

I cheered him up considerably when I told him that next to General Shum Shere he was the finest man I had met in Asia, but even then he wasn't any too cheerful. He hinted that he was growing tired and would like to be on his way home.

Before he had a chance to ask me for the money again, I told him I would write Shum Shere and tell how nobly the major had seen his task through to the end,—how uncomplainingly he had aided me until the rhinos were on the cars and on their way to Calcutta. He grinned foolishly and accepted the situation.

The following afternoon the cars arrived from Muzufferpur. It is needless for me to say how tickled I was. The Gurkha soldiers were again called into service (the major barking out far more commands than were necessary and with a vehemence that the situation didn't call for), and the two rhinos, none the worse for their rough trip on the bullock carts, were set onto the cars.

This done, the major and I (with the decrepit old *babu* who acted as station-master and Lal as witnesses) entered the railway office where I opened my clothing, got out the silken sash that served as my wallet and counted out the 35,000 rupees I owed the Maharajah,—tossing in an extra hundred rupees for the major to buy himself a sword against that day when he should become Field Marshal of Nepal.

The old *babu's* eyes almost popped out of his head as I counted out the money,—more rupees than he had ever seen in all his life. The major wasn't any too calm either. His hand trembled with excitement as he signed the receipt.

And soon we were off. Lal and I rigged up shelters of boughs and leaves over the crates to keep out the burning rays of the sun, and the balance of the fodder which had been brought down by the elephants was loaded on the flat cars with the animals. These frontier trains are made up of both passenger and freight cars, so a first-class compartment was available for me. One of the Nepalese boys who had been attending the rhinos ever since their capture agreed to accompany me to Calcutta to assist Lal in watching and caring for the animals en route, so when we left Raxaul I placed him on one of the cars and Lal on the other to guard the rhinos, Johereim tending my needs in my compartment.

I had got my prizes to the rail head. It might have seemed that the worst of my troubles was over. But that would have been reckoning without a new danger that promptly developed,—the Eastern lust for an aphrodisiac that was reputed to be borne on the heads of my rhinos.

To all Asiatics the horn of the rhinoceros has great restorative powers, especially in matters sexual. A book could be written around the superstitions and myths that abound in Asia about the miraculous rejuvenating properties of this substance.

To many Asiatics, the worst of all ailments is sexual impotence, and when this is coming on there is only one remedy: rhino horn. The Chinese will cross the Himalayas to the Nepalese border for rhino horn, paying thousands of rupees for a small bag of the cure-all. In China this is disposed of at fancy prices to the wealthy. I know of an instance where a sixty-year-old Chinese aristocrat, with over twenty concubines, regularly sent emissaries over the back-breaking Himalayas for rhino horn. The complaints of his favorite concubine had induced him to import quantities of the infallible remedy at fancy prices. I understand that he did not always get rhino horn. It seems there are bootleggers in every field, everywhere. He got a percentage of rhino horn, with other kinds of horn tossed in.

One of the bloodiest murders that ever took place in China had for its motive a shipment of rhino horn, among the biggest ever gathered together. The shipment changed hands three times, two dealers perishing in the struggle for possession. The rich Chinaman who financed the original expedition to the edge of Nepal for this big consignment of the wonder-working restorative eventually received the goods that, theoretically, made him the richest man sexually in China; but he was made to pay through the nose by the bandits that eventually made delivery,—the price that he paid amounting to a small fortune in the Orient.

The Chinese method of using rhino horn is to dry it thoroughly and grind it into a powder, which is then mixed with a liquid and taken internally.

The Malays look upon rhino horn more as a charm than as a medicine and no Malay will ever overlook an opportunity to rub his hands over a rhino horn, and if he is so fortunate as to have a small piece to carry in his pocket, the god of luck will never forsake him.

The Hindu view is much like the Chinese; to him rhino horn is the horn of sexual plenty. Only in the method of using it does he differ. Instead of powdering and drinking it, the Hindu sucks on a small piece of the magic restorative.

More than one aging and fatigued Hindu has vowed by all that was good and holy that if he could only get hold of a good bit of rhino horn, of the right size and shape to keep comfortably under his tongue, there wasn't a virgin in all the land that was safe in his presence. In India this is one of the oldest cries of the played-out *roué*.

The horns of my young rhinos were just beginning to grow out and it behooved me to keep a close watch on them, especially when our train stopped at stations along the way; so it was with some reluctance and much cautioning that I left Lal and the Nepalese boy in charge of the two cars and went to my compartment to wash and rest.

I got out at almost every station along the way and assisted the two boys, standing guard over the animals with a good heavy walking stick, which I found it necessary to use on several occasions. Wherever there is a railroad station in India there are many native idlers and loiterers,—shiftless Hindus whose chief emotion seems to be curiosity about the next train. These idlers would crowd around at every stop we made, some of the bolder ones making daring efforts to snip off pieces of the soft horn of my calves. I wielded my cane, bringing a lump to more than one thieving Hindu head, and Lal and the Nepalese boy whaled away with long sticks, yet we had our hands full; and in spite of all our precautions, on the second morning out of Raxaul we found a hole at least an inch square and almost two inches deep gouged out of the tender young horn of one of the rhinos. Some Hindu, avid for rejuvenation, had carved himself a piece of horn big enough to make a few dozen of the little buttons, which, if diligently sucked, make sexual menaces of the feeble and doddering, and which would add thousands of "YOUNG NATIVE GIRL ATTACKED" headlines to the front pages of the land—if anything like that could possibly be news in India.

The incident seems unimportant at this writing but I don't mind saying that I was furious when I discovered what had happened to the horn of one of my rhinos. I immediately questioned Lal and the Nepalese boy but my investigation yielded nothing. Some Hindu had been too quick for them.

At Athmal Gola on the north bank of the Ganges River, the Bengal and Northwestern Railway terminates. On arriving here I had to charter a boat. I sent Lal and Johereim scouting about for coolies while I entered into negotiations with several Hindu owners of the big clumsy sail boats that ply about this busy section of the Ganges. I succeeded in getting these piratical navigators wrought up against one another to such an extent in their competitive bidding for my cargo that I managed to get the rhinos carried to Mokamaghat at a reasonable figure.

I had telegraphed from Muzufferpur to the station-master at Mokamaghat, requesting that two cars be ready on my arrival there, but we had been so long in arranging for the boat and getting across the Ganges that the cars which had been held for me were used for some other purpose and it was late that night before I was able to get the animals loaded again and headed for Calcutta.

I needn't tell you how happy I was when we finally arrived in Calcutta. I tried to store the animals in a friend's garage in Ballygunge, a suburb of Calcutta, but the building proved too small. He then suggested that I deposit the cages on his front lawn, which I did. The comparative seclusion of the place minimized the problem of driving off natives who were on the lookout for the shining road to those mythical sexual excitements that all Hindus seemed to be seeking. Only a few of the bolder

natives invaded the privacy of that lawn and they were easily
chased away.

An amusing record of my rhinos' visit to my friend's place in
Ballygunge is to be found in the March 29, 1923, issue of *The
Englishman,* a paper published in Calcutta. The story is written
in that drowsy, good-natured style that characterizes so much of
English colonial journalism. Here it is:

"RHINOS" ON A BALLYGUNGE LAWN

Difficulties of Accommodation

A rhinoceros is all very well in a zoo, but he makes a strange
house guest. And when there are two of him, he is even stranger.
At least this is the opinion of a certain Calcutta gentleman—his
name shall remain a secret lest crowds of his friends should trample
down his flower garden in an effort to see his impromptu menagerie—who is entertaining a pair of the horned pachyderms pending
their departure by steamer for America.

The rhinoceros are the property of Mr. Frank Buck, the well-
known naturalist and wild-animal collector. Mr. Buck secured
the animals in Nepal, and took them by bullock cart to Raxaul,
and brought them to Calcutta by railway on Monday. As it was
impossible to get them shipped for several days, one of Mr. Buck's
friends offered to house the "rhinos" in his garage until the time
for their departure. The pair was consequently taken to Ballygunge, but the promised garage proved too small to take both.
Today, the animals stand on the front lawn of a little white
bungalow in Ballygunge, looking out at the world through the bars
of their crude wooden Nepalese cages.

One of the animals is a small one, weighing scarcely two tons,
but the other is quite well developed. They appeared to be in good
health when an *Englishman* reporter called to look at them, although a bit cramped for space. Their appetites are not impaired
by the fact that they get no exercise. There are no immediate
prospects of their getting any exercise, either, for no one will
volunteer to take them for a walk on leash.

Note the discreet use of quotation marks around the word
rhinos.

Note also that *The Englishman* gives me credit for heavier
calves than I actually had. "One of the animals," they generously said, "is a small one *scarcely weighing two tons,* but the
other is quite well developed." The one to which *The English-*

man kindly attributed two tons weighed in reality one ton, while the one they thought "well developed" weighed between one and a quarter and one and a half tons,—good weights for youngsters. (Note—Full-grown Indian rhinos have been known to attain a weight of six tons, which is well in excess of what the average elephant weighs.)

An American ship, the S.S. *Lake Gitano,* bound for Hong Kong, was in port when we reached Calcutta. She was due to sail in a week, which was good news. I arranged for passage for Lal and myself and the rhinos and the many other specimens I was bringing back. I had two fine shipping crates made of heavy teak planks for the rhinos, got my other specimens properly caged and crated for the trip and we sailed from Calcutta on the 30th day of March, 1923, with the rhinos and other specimens as deck cargo.

Heavy seas were encountered in the Bay of Bengal and several times we had to call out the crew during the night to move or lash down the big rhino crates (the new hard-wood cages with their occupants weighed more than three tons together), and also to move and tie up the two full-grown elephants which were carried on one of the aft hatches. The *Gitano* was a small boat, loaded so she was uncomfortably low in the water, and with the sea running heavy we had to be continually on guard. With the ship's decks barely five feet above the water there was constant danger of the decks being awash.

The *Gitano* called in at Penang on the Malay Peninsula and from there I took a train down to Singapore, leaving Lal in charge of the animals. I beat the *Gitano* into Singapore by a full day and on her arrival there had the specimens at the compound moved down to the dock and ready to be loaded, for the ship was to remain at Singapore only a few hours. The trip from here up to Hong Kong was without incident. I had made telegraphic arrangements from Calcutta for shipping out of Hong Kong on the S.S. *President Wilson* and fortunately our boat and the *Wilson* pulled into Hong Kong at the same time.

The two ships made fast on either side of the dock and the

transshipment of my animals was made. As fast as the crates and cages were lowered onto the pier from the *Gitano* they were heaved aboard the *Wilson*.

I had calculated on stowing my cargo on the aft decks of the *President Wilson* but, owing to the fact that this portion of the ship had recently been reconstructed and the aft decks turned into third-class quarters for the carrying of Filipino steerage passengers, the only available space for my cargo was on the forward deck. These big Pacific liners are sufficiently high out of the water so that in ordinary weather this is a safe enough place to carry the stock. While I should have liked a more sheltered section for my specimens, I took without complaint the only space that was available for me. I did manage to find a shelter away up on the hurricane deck for most of my birds, but the elephants were placed on top of number one hatch and the rhinos were set down between the first and second hatches, while the smaller crates containing my anoas, orang-utans and various other animals were stacked up against the forward bulkhead.

By this time I had a right to expect some peace of mind. I had sweated buckets of blood in getting my rhinos to the point where at last they were on the way to America.

I discovered that I weighed twenty pounds less than when I originally set out for Nepal. I was pretty well worn with the task of getting those troublesome Indian rhinos headed for the States, and I felt like easing up a bit.

I didn't get the rest I was looking for. The reason: a typhoon.

All hands were called out. My cages and crates were made fast with canvas coverings. The seas, lashed by murderous winds, mounted higher and higher and finally broke in torrents over the bow.

The captain—that grand old seaman Henry Nelson—issued orders that no one was to go forward. I stood on the bridge and watched mountains of water break over the forward decks. I knew the elephants were safe enough as they had the advantage of the hatch's elevation. The force of the waves, in other words, was broken by the base of the hatch. The smaller stock was covered with canvas and well lashed against the bulkhead; so I felt reasonably sure that they would stand the storm too.

But I was much concerned about the two huge rhino crates. Though they were well lashed when we first hit the storm, they were taking a terrific pounding, the kind that loosens deck cargo. Once heavy crates of this kind get loose, the tremendous force of the waves may at any moment send them spinning across the deck; and when this sort of cargo does shift it takes everything on the deck with it.

As daylight broke next morning, I was on the bridge scanning the forward deck to see what harm the terrific seas of the night had wrought among my animals. The elephants were trumpeting loudly as they faced the howling wind and the tons of sea water that came rushing over the ship. As a great wave would burst over them, they would brace themselves, leaning forward and taking the full force of the wave on their big, broad foreheads.

At intervals between the huge waves that enveloped the whole forward deck and the salt spray that splashed through the rigging, I could barely see the two rhino crates and it looked from the bridge as though one of them had started to shift. Soon there was a clear moment or two between waves and I could plainly see that part of the lashings on one of the rhino crates had given way and that the crate was shifting a few inches with each lurch of the ship.

The storm had now been in progress for about thirty hours. Captain Nelson was on the bridge where he had remained all night, and where I had joined him. I yelled to him about the shifting of the rhino cages. He couldn't hear a word I was saying. The shriek of the wind and the roar of the giant waves drowned my voice.

Finally, by the process of bellowing in his ear I managed to make myself understood.

"No news to me," he said. "I'm afraid they're gone."

"Gone?" I echoed, stunned. It would be awful to lose those rhinos after the struggle I'd made to get them this far.

"I'm afraid so," the captain replied, roaring in my ear to make himself heard above the terrific din of the wind and sea. "The next big one that comes over will either smash that crate up against the main mast and break the damned box into a thousand pieces, or crash it against the other crate, loosening that too, and sending them both overboard. What the hell do you care? There's lots more rhinos where those came from, ain't there?"

I liked the captain. He was a great scout and a fine mariner. But his last remark was a heart-breaker. I would have preferred being washed overboard myself to seeing anything like that happen to the animals I had fought so hard to bring back to the United States.

I asked the captain to let me have a sailor to go forward with me and help me re-lash the crate.

"You're crazy," he said. "Do you think I'd order a man out at a time like this?"

Well and good. I'd go anyhow and see what I could accomplish unaided. I had no intention of losing those rhinos without putting up a battle.

I started below. The captain yelled a warning to me: "Don't you go up forward, young feller! The first real wave that hits you will carry you over the side."

But I did go forward. Everything was battened down so I couldn't get onto the forward deck from below, but I went out on the main deck, watched my chances between waves, and climbed hand-over-hand along a wire cable to reach the deck below. By dodging behind ventilators and masts as great masses of water came over the deck with a rush and a bang, I finally reached the rhino cages. They had survived a few more of the punishing waves than the captain thought they could stand but they were wobbling all over the place and in a few more minutes anything might happen.

What an assignment I had given myself! The cage that had started slipping had to be tightened immediately. If it was not made fast it would carry the other cage with it. I would just about get a line made fast around it when a huge wave would strike the ship with a tremendous blow and I would crouch down behind the mast, letting it break the force of the blow, to keep from being washed overboard. In this manner for nearly an hour

I worked in the midst of those towering waves that kept pounding over the deck.

When the cage was at last made fast I was so worn out that I didn't know how I was ever going to scamper back to safety. I managed to drag myself along, however, my joy over the knowledge that my rhinos were safe giving me strength. Watching my chances to get from one shelter to another, exposing myself along the open deck only during the lulls between waves and climbing back hand-over-hand to the main deck and up to the bridge, I found myself once more where my friend the captain stood.

"Good work, Buck," he said. "But I'm damned if I understand it. Risking your neck for a couple of lousy rhinos!"

I was too worn and bedraggled and drenched to make an explanation.

"I'm glad you made it, Buck," he said as he warmly shook my hand. And just as I was about to be overcome by emotion over his delight with the success of my exploit, he added with a grin, "No skipper likes to return to his home port with his log recording a passenger washed overboard. It doesn't look good."

Then he broke into a laugh and banged me on the back. "And now go and get some dry clothes," was his parting shot. "I don't like pneumonia cases either. They're a nuisance."

A few hours later the storm started to die down. Our five or six hours of actual typhoon and over twenty-four of terrific old-fashioned wind-storm had given everyone on board some pretty anxious moments and no one objected in the least when the sea started behaving itself. We didn't have much peace, however, for we ran into two more raging wind-storms, not much less violent than the first, before we finally arrived in San Francisco. All in all, it was one of the toughest voyages I ever made, more than once my resourcefulness being taxed in my efforts to provide adequate protection for my floating zoo.

I cleared my animals through the customs at San Francisco and then shipped them to their various destinations.

Through the good offices of Dr. Hornaday I was able to get special accommodations for the rhinos that brought them east in very fast time.

I'll never forget the joy Dr. Penrose expressed over the success of the expedition.

Nor am I ever likely to forget the events of May 22, 1923. On this day, exactly a year and three weeks after Dr. Hornaday had said to me, "Buck, I'm still hopeful of getting an Indian rhino some day," Dr. Hornaday, Raymond L. Ditmars and I stood by while zoo attendants opened up the front of a huge teak-wood crate and a splendid young rhinoceros walked out of its traveling quarters into its permanent home at the Bronx Zoo in New York. I've often wondered if the visitors to this famous park who stand daily before the rhinoceros paddock realize what it meant in work, risk, worry and expense to place that animal there.

Dr. Penrose and Dr. Hornaday each generously paid me a bonus of $1,000 in addition to the tentative price of $7,000 per rhino which we had fixed. This gave me a total of $16,000 and it wouldn't take much bookkeeping to show that I didn't make any money on the deal. As near as I can figure, I broke even. But I had had a valuable new experience in my chosen field and my prestige as a zoological collector had been greatly increased. I had the two most valuable specimens in the country to my credit, the only Indian rhinos in the whole of America.

Both of these rare animals are in excellent condition today. The New York specimen now weighs about two and a half tons, the one in Philadelphia about two and a quarter tons. They will put on considerable more weight before they attain their full growth.

The New York specimen, the bigger of America's two living examples of Nepal's "natural resources," still bears the mark of the sex-crazy Hindu who gouged out a piece of the horn. As a result of this native's vandalistic bid for rejuvenation (or perhaps he was a dealer who sold little buttons of rhino horn to his virility-seeking brothers), the horn of the New York rhino separated as it grew up and this animal today appears to have a double horn.

Whenever I am in New York and I am lonesome for memories

of one of the most strenuous expeditions of my life (and it's funny how in my field a fellow sometimes longs for living reminders of the hardest of his hard knocks) I go up to the Bronx Zoo and look at the Indian rhino and mentally say something like this, "Hello, you damned nuisance. I love you for all the trouble you caused me."

Jungle Laundress

OF the thousands of monkeys and apes I've brought to America from Asia perhaps the most interesting was a female orang-utan I picked up in Pontianak, Borneo. She was sold to me along with four other members of her species by a Malay trader who'd been up bartering among the Dyaks.

I did not know at the time that I'd bought anything as unusual as Gladys proved to be. (That's the name my favorite ape later achieved, though I couldn't possibly tell you how or why.)

Of the five orang-utans I took off the trader's hands, two were little babies in baskets, two were about half-grown and the other —Gladys—was almost full grown. She was about two or three years removed from the age of eleven to twelve when members of her sex and species, dismissing the follies of youth, take upon themselves the cares of motherhood. A care-free young lady, with a genius for sociability, she devoted herself to the business of making friends and keeping them amused.

When I pick up a group of orang-utans in this fashion I don't know whether they're fresh from the jungle and wild or whether they are animals that were raised as pets from infancy. The natives of British North Borneo and Dutch Borneo will never pass up an opportunity to raise a baby orang-utan and hold it till some trader appears to acquire it for a few guilders or an axe, tobacco, salt, cotton cloth for *sarongs*, or any of the other staple articles used in bartering for local goods. Such animals come to the collector tame and are easy to handle.

It is useless to ask the trader who in turn sells to the collector whether he is offering tame or wild monkeys for sale. Half the time he doesn't know; and, when he does know, he won't tell for fear he'll give the wrong answer and spoil a sale. The collector who knows his business can generally answer for himself the

more important question: are these sound and healthy specimens?
Once he is reasonably sure of himself on this score (it is impossible of course to be absolutely sure) he takes his chances on all
other points.

After a man has spent as many years in the trade as I have, he
forgets to worry about whether an animal is wild or not. In the
course of handling hundreds of the jungle's most ferocious inhabitants, animal savagery becomes a commonplace. There's a
way of handling the worst of them.

But it's convenient, in handling animals you haven't trapped
yourself or bought under circumstances that give you some idea
of their characteristics, to know something about them. This is
particularly true in the case of orang-utans. One that has been
raised as a pet, for instance, will have a much better chance of
thriving in the collector's compound if it is given the liberties
one can safely give a domesticated ape of this variety.

The only safe course until you've had a good chance to observe
your orangs and classify them, if they are anywhere near full
grown, is to treat them all as rascals, which is what most of
them are. Put your hand too close to the bars of one of these
tree-dwellers that resents his captivity and there's a good chance
that you'll get only part of it back; or, if you get it all back, it
won't be in working order.

Along with many other animals, these five orang-utans found
their way before long to my compound in Katong. As I supervised the job of installing them in the shed one of the five reached
out through the wooden bars of its cage and gently touched my
arm. The approach of a tame orang is unmistakable. There is
no grabbing, no frantic reaching, none of the quick stealthiness
that one finds in members of this simian family that have evil
intentions.

I stopped to observe the movements of the animal that had
touched me in this friendly fashion. I was getting my first real
impression of Gladys. Moving a little closer,—but ready to
withdraw in an instant in case I was mistaken—I encouraged the
lady to show how sociable she could be. Again she reached out
and stroked my arm.

Continuing the experiment further, I took an axe and smashed a few of the wooden rungs, much like heavy broomsticks, that are used to bar up the boxes used in caging orang-utans. She poked her head, or part of it, through the opening and nuzzled against me as I moved closer. Not once was there a display of teeth. The animal was as tame as they come.

In a few minutes I had Gladys out of her cage. Never have I seen such ecstasy in an ape—and I've seen some happy ones. She gently put her arms around me and held me for a minute, rubbing her face against my hand when that was over. Then she stroked me again with her hands, completing her display of joy by dancing up and down in front of me and eagerly looking up as if to say, "Where do we go from here?"

Soon I had Gladys installed under the house, which stood three feet off the ground. She was almost four feet high when she stood upright, but that did not matter, for I put a collar around her neck and gave her ten feet of chain and she used the space under the house merely for sleeping quarters.

While Gladys had no desire to escape, she frequently pined for more liberty than her chain afforded and usually she knew what to do about it. In fact, she managed to free herself from every collar I put on her until I resorted to one that was fastened on with a padlock.

I would have cheerfully given her her liberty but she worried the servants and the two friends that shared the house with me. In fact, Andy Mack told me that if Gladys didn't stop entering his room and throwing his things around he'd have her arrested for disturbing the peace. He didn't mind what she did to the things a fellow couldn't trip over, like socks and ties, but when she started scattering his shoes all over the floor, complicating his 3 A.M. tipsy entrances, that was serious and he wouldn't stand for it.

Gladys also had a playful habit of climbing all over the house, the roofs of the sheds in the compound, and occasionally a neighbor's dwelling. In fact, once she almost scared the wits out of the young man next door who worked in a bank in Singapore. She peered in at him one morning while he was bathing,—unladylike conduct, I was forced to admit—though I had to correct the lad when he insisted that it was a gorilla he saw at his window and that "he" (the gorilla) had "his" teeth bared and was about to break through the window when he scared the monster off by pounding. I will not here correct all the inaccuracies in this statement. I will say, however, that I emphatically pointed out that Gladys always let closed windows alone. She never hesitated to climb through an open window to say hello but forcing her way into a place was out of her line. Those who didn't think enough of her to provide access to their quarters simply had to do without her society. She had her pride, did Gladys.

Then there was the complaint from our *caboon*. He once caught Gladys rubbing her face against the brown cheeks of his little baby. Gladys, her maternal instincts asserting themselves, had developed quite a fondness for the child and would mother it whenever she got a chance. She enjoyed swinging the child's hammock back and forth and so did the child for that matter, but the *caboon* objected, and as I didn't want to lose our gardener I was forced to curb these attentions of my affectionate orang-utan.

One of Gladys' favorite pastimes was looking for me around the compound. Once she decided she wanted to put her arms around me, she would hunt all over the place and when she failed to find me around the compound she would try the house. This always annoyed the servants who thought that the place for an orang, tame or otherwise, was in the jungle.

Gladys, however, was a determined girl and once she made up her mind she wanted to see me she would continue her search until she found me. These searches were sometimes complicated by the fact that I was in Singapore while Gladys was trying to find me in Katong. Once I found her waiting for me at the road. She had got used to seeing me drive home in my car; and failing to find me on the premises, she waited (for how many hours I'll never know) till I drove up, joyously scrambling over the door and taking a seat beside me.

Although Gladys was as harmless as a kitten, I eventually found it necessary to secure the padlock mentioned above and

restrict her to such territory as her original ten feet of chain permitted her to roam. She was probably greatly puzzled by the
curtailment of her liberty for only the day before she had performed an act of real usefulness. Ali had opened the door of one
of the big bird cages too wide and one of the minas flew out.
Filling the air with triumphant chatter (it will be recalled that the
mina is a chattering bird that can outtalk a parrot when in a
garrulous mood), she flew all over the grounds with Ali in frantic
pursuit. After a half hour's chase, the boy and the bird were
all fagged out and when Ali made a final weary dash, driving the
worn-out bird in Gladys' direction, it was a simple matter for the
orang-utan to grab the squawking mina, which she did very gently,
holding it so carefully that not a feather was rumpled.

As the boy came running up, Gladys handed him the fugitive,
stroking it tenderly by way of farewell, the noisy bird replying
unfeelingly by pecking at the hand that was petting it.

Gladys was philosophic about her confinement. After all, it
was better than life in a cage. She was able to exercise and get
the sun and probably that is why, after a few days, she seemed to
forget that she had a padlocked collar, and she was again her
exuberant self. I've never seen an animal with a similar capacity
for enjoying life. Everything that went on around her interested
her. Keen, alert, responsive, she was closer to the human species
than any other ape I've ever handled.

Gladys, among other things, was an excellent chambermaid.
She got the maximum results out of the bundle of straw and the
blanket I gave her for her bed. In fact, she made a ceremony
lasting about a half hour out of the nightly business of making
her bed. She would spread out the straw, step back a few feet
and survey her work, re-arrange the straw, step back again for
another look and repeat the performance over and over again
till she decided that all was well. Then she would lay out the
blanket on top of the straw and lie down, rolling over until she
was completely wrapped up. Sometimes the end of the blanket
would not wind up at a point that enabled her to tuck herself in
securely, and when this happened she would unroll herself and
go through the performance again and again until she was so

rolled up that there was no chance of the blanket coming loose while she slept.

Whenever I would see Gladys go through a performance of this kind I would find myself growing curious about her past. These amusing little customs and habits were, of course, traceable to her early life in captivity. What was that life? I would never know exactly but this did not prevent me from speculating on it and trying to piece Gladys' story together.

Needless to say, I am not an animal trainer. Many animals that I have sold to circuses have been converted into fine performers but I have no interest myself in teaching animals tricks or stunts. It is out of my line entirely.

This is not by way of saying that I am not interested in trained animals. I am; but I must add that I find it much more absorbing to watch an animal like Gladys go through some routine that she has picked up herself than to watch the antics of animals trained to do certain tricks after rigorous discipline.

One day I was passing Gladys' place under the edge of the house on my way to the compound. In my hand I carried a tin wash-pan of water in which was soaking a big square piece of ordinary cotton cloth that I was about to use in washing a minor wound on the leg of a small animal. As I went by, my favorite orang-utan reached up and stopped me. Curious to see what she wanted, I stood by and did nothing. She was obviously interested in what I was carrying. (It was the customary thing for her to examine anything I had in my hand. I never discouraged the practice as I was on the lookout for reactions that would throw some light on the past life of this animal that interested me so.)

With both hands Gladys reached up for the wash-pan. I let her take it. She carried it two or three feet and then sat down on the ground with the pan in front of her, between her legs. She removed the rag from the water and began to scrub it with her fists like a laundress. Then she doused it in the water again, swished it around, removed it, put it between her fists again and rubbed away vigorously as before. There was about five minutes of this, winding up in a final dousing of the rag. After first soaking it thoroughly, she picked it up with both hands and proceeded to wring it out, like an experienced washerwoman. Then she carefully unfolded it and shook it out. Then, putting one corner between her teeth she stretched it out flat with her hands. This done, she ran her eyes over it carefully to see if it was clean all over. Satisfied that it was, she walked over a few feet out of the shadow of the house to where there was some sun and spread the rag out neatly on the grass.

Gladys had gone through all the motions of an Asiatic woman washing clothes, winding up with the method of drying that they use. Partly, at least, I could now piece together Gladys' story. She had been raised in a native village, right in the bosom of the family. How she got there has to remain a matter for speculation; although a reasonable enough supposition is that when a baby she accompanied her mother in a raid on a durian tree on the outskirts of the village. (The durian is a jungle fruit about as big as a medium-sized cantaloupe, the favorite fruit of both apes and natives; it has a hard prickly rind, containing a soft, cream-colored pulp, of a most delicious flavor, though somewhat offensive odor.) The natives, as frequently happens, might have speared the mother to get the suckling babe.

More than once in a Borneo village have I see a woman nursing a baby on one breast and an infant orang on the other. Always there is that hope that a trader will come along and buy the ape.

Gladys probably grew up with the children of the family, playing with them and accompanying their mother to the river bank on wash day. There it is customary for the children to help and Gladys, not to be outdone, doubtless decided she would do her bit too. It was probably somewhat in this fashion that she learned the gentle art of laundering.

Gladys got to be so much fun that frequently I took her to Singapore with me where she became a familiar figure. She enjoyed nothing more than an automobile ride and when I would unleash her and let her climb into my car for one of those trips to Singapore she would embrace me so completely that I would have to disengage myself before I could drive. Then she would sit back in the seat like a lady out for an airing, confining her displays of affection to an occasional pat with her hand or a rub of her cheek against my arm.

My business over, Gladys would sit down with me in the bar of the Raffles Hotel while I had a gin sling. Occasionally I would let her have a small glass of beer. Once, to see what she would do, I removed all chairs but one, in which I sat down, pretending to be unaware of Gladys' existence. Undaunted, she slid a chair over to the table and seated herself, reaching for my glass by way of announcing that she was ready for her beer.

On the way back to America Gladys was the pet of the *President Cleveland* (captained by my old friend George Yardley, one of the greatest of skippers, with whom I've made eleven of my forty crossings of the Pacific). I had her installed on the boat deck where her chain gave her plenty of room for exercise.

As soon as the women on board heard of Gladys' accomplishments as a laundress they made regular trips to the boat deck with water-soaked handkerchiefs which Gladys would rub with her fists, wring out and spread out on the deck in the sunshine.

The news also spread that my amusing orang-utan was fond of tea and at tea-time more than one lady would have her afternoon cup with Gladys. As much as Gladys liked beer, it was as nothing compared with her fondness for tea.

Once a lady on board accused Gladys of snubbing her offer of tea-time refreshments. The orang drained the proffered cup of tea but refused the sandwiches and cakes that accompanied the offer. It was necessary to explain that Gladys had got into the habit of eating out of a plate. I had taught her this at Katong and, unless very hungry, she would ignore food that was placed on the bare deck. After all, that's no way to treat a lady. The food was placed on a plate and Gladys ate it.

The wireless operator of the *President Cleveland* developed quite a fondness for Gladys. In fact, some of his frivolous associates referred to her as his "girl." He would pet the orang and feed her apples and bananas, and she in return would rub her head against him, and, in her more affectionate moments, embrace him.

One day Gladys, who still knew how, resorted to her old trick of unfastening her collar, which I had forgotten to padlock. A few minutes later she was in the wireless operator's quarters, looking for her friend. Failing to find him, she looked around to see what mischief she could do; and, evidently deciding that the bed was not properly made, pulled it apart. She was making a neat pile of the bedding in the middle of the bunk in an effort to arrange it like her own straw bed when the operator entered.

He let out a yelp of dismay, for overhead was a high voltage wire that ran through his quarters into the wireless room, and if this animal that was in the habit of climbing all over everything, decided to investigate that wire she'd be a dead orang-utan not long after she touched it.

The operator sent a boy to get me and I came running in and claimed the exploring Gladys. The operator afterwards told me that he sweated blood in the few minutes that intervened between the time he sent for me and my arrival. He stood there, he told me, ready to stun his favorite monkey with a water pitcher if she made a move in the direction of the wire.

The operator was kidded for the rest of the trip by the officers of the ship who accused him of secret tête-à-têtes in his cabin with Gladys. "He tried to steal Buck's monkey," was the way one of them put it. "Buck had to break down the door to get her out."

Before the trip was over Gladys also made a reputation as a book-worm. A lady visitor brought a book with her and sat beside the orang and read. When the woman put the book down, Gladys picked it up, and, opening it up, held it for a full minute in the manner of a person reading. The fact that she held it upside down did not seem to affect her interest in what she found on the pages.

My parting with Gladys was the saddest animal farewell I've ever known. I hated to part with her. As she required the kind of attention she could only get in a good zoo, circus or similar place, I had to let her go. Besides I needed the $750 that she would bring. I sold her for that price to the Municipal Zoo in Madison, Wisconsin. I could probably have secured a much better price if I had offered her to the movie people. One of the big companies, it developed, was looking for an ape such as Gladys, that could be taught to act.

But I had no regrets on that score. Perhaps Gladys had no ambitions to become a movie queen. In Madison I knew that she would have a good home and that her affectionate nature and interesting character would make her many friends.

Holter's Traps

IF ASIA had an official census-taker and one of his jobs was to list the soldiers of fortune, that task alone would keep him busy for a long, long time. From everywhere they come, these picturesque legions who obey the silent but overpowering commands of General Boredom. On, on, they march in all directions, swarming all over the continent and waging grim and determined warfare against the dread scourge of ennui.

Some years ago—I believe it was in 1918 or 1919—I was in Medan, which is the biggest city in Sumatra. I was sitting on the veranda of the DeBour Hotel sipping a gin pite, a drink that suits the climate perfectly and which consequently is very popular there. A good percentage of the business transacted in Medan is done over a tray of gin pites, and before anyone accuses me of trying to mystify the reader let me point out that this drink is none other than the familiar gin and bitters. But in Medan they'd be puzzled if you asked for it by that name. You must ask for a gin pite, or, if you want to go completely native, a Bols *mera*. In either case you'll get a gin and bitters, and you won't be sorry either for somehow no other drink seems to sit as well in Sumatra.

I was on the Island rounding up some animals and birds, and my work done, I was taking my ease. I was to return to America soon, after picking up some other specimens that I had gathered together at two or three other points, and I was enjoying one of those few periods of relaxation that a collector of animals manages to squeeze into his strenuous program.

As I slipped back in my chair revelling in the fact that I had no immediate task to perform, a servant touched me on the shoulder. Would I be good enough to step to the telephone?

I got up, hoping this wasn't going to be another call from

some animal trader who had something to offer for sale. I had collected all the specimens I needed to fill the orders I had from zoos, circuses and dealers back home and I did not feel like listening to any more Medan sales talk.

I was delighted when I found that the call was from an old acquaintance, Albert Holter, an interesting soldier of fortune. The last time I had seen Holter he was running a tea estate in Ceylon and I was agreeably surprised to find him in Sumatra. He had heard from a trader that I was in Medan at the DeBour Hotel and had rushed to the nearest telephone to call me. I invited Holter to join me for a gin pite and dinner. He was a colorful chap and the prospect of a few hours with him appealed to me. I also welcomed the opportunity to reciprocate in a small way the hospitality he had shown me when I was a guest for a week on the tea plantation he managed in Ceylon. He explained hastily that new interests had recently taken over the tea estate and that in the reorganization that took place he had lost his job and he was now in Sumatra to— But he would tell me all about that as soon as he reached the hotel.

Holter had dedicated his life as a very young man to the goddess of adventure and he was still at it. Before he took up his work in Ceylon he had been a trader in pearls in the Persian Gulf and a minor executive in a tin mine in the Malay country. Then there was a whole string of other interesting assignments he had had. All in all he was as striking a trooper as I had met in all my experience with Asia's great army of soldiers of fortune.

Holter was half English and half Dutch. At the time of the visit to Sumatra to which I make reference here, he was about thirty-six or seven. As I sat waiting for him I kept wondering how badly the loss of his tea estate job, the best he'd ever held, had affected his morale. I recalled that he had met with a long series of reverses and when finally he had landed this post in Ceylon he had acted very much like a more than usually tired soldier of fortune, footsore and weary from the march, and grateful for a billet that promised a comfortable living without a struggle. The work was light,—and there was good food, good lodging, a pretty fair salary, and wine and women in abundance. After all, as he pointed out, these were inducements not to be lightly dismissed. Even a restless soul such as he, a chap with something stewing in his guts that gave him that urge to roam from place to place, could see the practical advantages of a berth such as the one he had in Ceylon. And if I thought the work was dull I was mistaken. Not by a damsite, Buck! If you think that running a tea estate hasn't its interesting side, listen to this, old man . . . and then he would go into a lengthy recital of his duties, each point that he made designed to show that everything connected with his work contributed to the annihilation of boredom. What a relief from the monotony of the days when he traded in pearls in the Persian Gulf! There was dull work. It made him sick to think of it. And how much superior to that stupid job he had had a few years back in the tin mine in the Malay country. How he ever survived the dreary drabness of that berth he'd never understand. After a few months of it he was becoming as inert as a clam, and if he hadn't got out when he did God only knows what would have happened to him. . . . You know what a sluggish job does to a man, Buck. . . . I recall nodding sympathetically.

As I sat waiting for Holter to join me on the veranda I found myself framing a few sympathetic words to say to the poor devil. It was tough losing a post like that.

Not long after his telephone call, Holter turned up. He swung up the path leading to the hotel as jauntily as if he had never had a stroke of bad luck in his life. Certainly no one would have taken him for a man who had recently lost the best job he had ever held.

We shook hands warmly, Holter releasing his hand of greeting to pound me on the back. Beaming his delight, he stepped back a few yards like a man seeking to improve his perspective on a picture, and fairly shouted as he surveyed me from head to foot: "Well, if this isn't a treat! You're looking great!"

I found myself admiring the cheerful front he was putting on. Soldiers of fortune do their share of belly-aching when things go wrong and it was refreshing to meet one who knew how to take a sporting attitude toward his reverses.

That was the trend of my thoughts as I invited Holter to have a drink. He sat down beside me and we ordered gin pites. We sat and sipped our drinks, my friend entertaining me with the latest bar-room story. I could think of only one thing as he talked away with what I decided was the most unnatural exuberance I had ever observed: how tragic it was for a soldier of fortune to decide it's time to settle down and then, after landing a good job, to be fired and have to put on his marching shoes again and take to the road that leads to God knows where.

The final swallow of my gin pite found my compassion taking the form of words.

"It's too damned bad," I said.

"What's too damned bad?" Holter echoed.

"Your losing your job."

"Hell! that's nothing. Ceylon is the dullest place in the world. I'd have gone crazy if I'd have stayed on that tea estate much longer. Did I ever tell you how monotonous the work was? It was awful. Never knew such boredom in all my life. It's just as well that they fired me. I'd have had to quit sooner or later or go mad. I suffocate when I'm on a job that isn't interesting. It was different in the days when I was in the Persian Gulf. Trading in pearls kept a man interested in life. Something always happened to keep things from getting dull. Every time I thought of those days when life had a thrill and then suddenly realized that I was mired to the waist in a stupid routine job in Ceylon I felt like putting a gun to my head. Then I'd think of the great old tin-mine days in the Malay states. There was a job. Something happening all the time. No two days alike. Adventure. Excitement. Thrills. Color. Romance. 'Goddam those lousy tea people,' I kept telling myself. 'If they think they're going to stifle me they're mistaken. They can keep their stinking job. I've got to get out. I've got to get a taste of life again. A man like me can't live in a cemetery.' I started soldiering on the job. A blind man could have seen it. I didn't do a lick of work. I spent my time trying to figure out what place I wanted to head for next. When the reorganization took place, the new crowd fired me. It shows they know their business."

Such a beautiful series of contradictions! And now that it was no longer necessary to feel sorry for Holter—(he was the liveliest tragedy I had seen in some time)—I began to enjoy myself.

"To hell with the tea business," he went on. "Too tame. I'm going into a man's game. Of course you've heard of the bounty on tigers that Sumatra's big rubber and tobacco interests recently established? Fifty guilders for every tiger you kill. Christ! I can live on a hundred guilders for a month here if I have to. And think of the excitement. You don't know what it means not to have to talk to the tea people any more, to have the kind of work I like again. I can't stand bores, Buck; the tea people are all like that. Think of it! Two tigers a month—just two—support me. And I'll get ten a month or know the reason why."

I asked Holter if he had ever hunted tigers before.

"No. Why hunt 'em? That's too much like work. I'm going to trap 'em. Lots of 'em."

And he went on to tell me that he had located just the right trap for his purpose,—an importation from America with great jagged interlocking teeth. It was tremendously powerful, reminding him of a giant bear-trap. He had located a half dozen of the devices in Medan after a search that took three days and he was ready to start out for the interior after his tigers.

When he got through there wouldn't be a tiger left in Sumatra to kill off the bullocks and water buffaloes (that served as work animals) and the goats (that were widely used on the plantations for meat). The big cats would stop terrorizing the plantation workers. Life would again be normal in Sumatra.

Holter, to a greater extent than any other man I've ever known, had the capacity for being carried away by his own words. It wouldn't have surprised me a bit if he had suddenly jumped up from his chair on the veranda, shouted, "I can't wait any longer!" and gone off after his tigers.

In the midst of one of his most impassioned outbursts, Dahlam

Ali walked in to report that all was well with my birds and animals.

"That's a great boy you've got there, Buck!" exclaimed Holter when Ali had left. (Ali, though past fifty, was still a "boy," as all native workers are.)

I cheerfully agreed. Ali, I told him, was probably better posted on Asiatic animals than any man in the world, brown or white.

"Is that a fact?"

"So far as I know it is."

"Come on, Buck. Do you mean to say he's better posted than you?"

"Yes, in the matter of wild life in its original state. A good deal better. I know more about handling animals once they're caught. That's my job, knowing how to feed and take care of 'em, how to make 'em behave when they get too fresh, how to make 'em survive a strenuous voyage across the Pacific, and things like that. Bringing 'em back alive,—that's *my* specialty."

I was trying to change the subject. Holter's enthusiasm over his tiger project seemed a little pathetic.

But he was soon at it again. Without knowing it at the moment, I was providing him with more ammunition.

"You're leaving for America soon, aren't you, Buck?"

I nodded.

"What will you do with that boy of yours?"

"Send him back to Singapore. On my return I'll pick him up there."

My Hindu boy, Lal, usually returned to America with me but never Ali. Several years before, Ali was brought to America by the Hagenbeck-Wallace Circus. He was a picturesque figure in his *baja* and *sarong,* and added a nice touch of color to the circus's many parades. He also served as an animal care-taker. But Ali never liked America. He thought the people were a little crazy. Nobody seemed to know what he was doing. Having visited America, he understood why the *tuan* spent so much time in Asia. He was picked up by a circus representative in Singapore where he sold pets to sailors. With a basket of parrots and monkeys he would go out into the bay in a dinghy where foreign ships lay at anchor, and hawk his wares. After two years with the circus, he yearned for the Singapore water-front and his monkeys and parrots and a good chew of betel-nut; and he left America with a sigh of relief, vowing never to return. I picked him up some years later after he had wandered all over Asia, leaving his water-front for the wilds, and in the process acquiring an amazing knowledge of wild animal life. He had lived with the Dyaks of Borneo, the Batiks of Sumatra, the Sakais of the Malay Peninsula, and with other forest tribes; and he knew these strange Asiatics and their jungles as well as he knew Singapore Harbor. I told all these things to Holter in answer to a series of rapid-fire questions. Ali fascinated him.

"I'm going to ask you to do me a favor, Buck."

"Shoot."

"I want to borrow your boy. He'd be a great help to me in trapping my tigers. With a boy like that to give me pointers I can't go wrong. Don't turn me down, Buck. This is the greatest work I've ever undertaken. It's going to put me on the map. I can feel it in my bones."

"It's all right with me if it's all right with Ali. It may be eight or ten months, perhaps a year, before I return to Singapore. His time is his own till then. Let's ask him."

"Urge him to do it, will you, Buck? I know he'd do anything in the world for you. It means a lot to me."

After dinner we talked the matter over with Ali. He readily agreed to work for the *tuan's* friend, his compensation being fixed at $25. in Singapore money per month. As much as I liked Holter, a fascinating adventurer if I'd ever met one, I couldn't help feeling that I was dumping a rather unstable amateur on Ali's door-step. Unquestionably he was more than a little bug-house and Ali was on record as being opposed to crazy people. But perhaps he would not find in this Dutch-Englishman the kind of insanity that displeased him in Americans. Holter's insanity after all was the kind that passes for sanity in Asia. And, on second thought, why worry about Ali? He was the soul of resourcefulness and few problems having to do with the world of animals worried him.

A few days later I left Medan with my Sumatra collection. My own affairs occupied my mind so completely from then on that I didn't have much time to think of Holter and his tiger-trapping expedition. Once or twice I thought of him and wondered how much success he had had. I found myself hoping that he had bagged at least enough tigers to keep him in gin pites for a few months.

One afternoon, about a year later, I was seated at a table in the bar of the Harmony Club in Batavia, Java. I had just arrived from the Philippines where I had picked up some birds (and where I was the guest of my old friend Major Fletcher at the military post in Zamboanga).

I had not been in the room more than a few minutes when I heard a familiar voice cry out: "I'll be damned if it isn't Buck!"

Looking up I saw Holter, a few tables away, waving to me. I was delighted to see him. I was anxious to hear all about his tiger-trapping venture (and his latest Greatest Proposition in the World). I thought I should have to wait until Ali, who was to meet me in Singapore, told me of the Holter expedition to rid Sumatra of its striped cats; but the fates had decreed that I should get it first-hand from the father of the enterprise himself.

"Come on over!" Holter yelled.

This was a brand-new Holter. Usually this energetic adventurer would jump up when he spied a friend, and, fairly hurdling everything between him and the familiar face that had caught his eye, come tearing over on the run, spilling his most recent enthusiasm en route.

I got up and joined him at once, puzzled by the fact that he remained seated as we shook hands. Normally his was an acrobatic hand-shake, the palm of his right hand meeting yours with a rush as its owner leaped at you. Looking down I saw the answer. Holter was minus his left leg. An old-fashioned pegleg had supplanted it. He either lacked the funds to buy an artifi-

cial limb or such luxuries were not procurable in this part of
Asia.

"That's tough, Holter," was about all I managed to say.

"Hell! that's nothing," he replied. "Let's have a drink."

I could hardly wait to hear about his tigers but I quickly decided not to have anything to say on the subject until he brought
it up himself. The Holters of Asia develop strange reticences
about subjects that were once pet enthusiasms and I had no
desire to touch this luckless rover in a sore spot.

"I'm glad of this opportunity," he started, "to thank you personally for your boy's services."

"Forget about it. Glad to help you out."

"Forget about it? You don't realize I'd probably be dead if
it wasn't for that boy. I can't forget a thing like that."

Then he told me his story.

It was to that section of northern Sumatra which has become what is probably the world's finest rubber and tobacco
district that Holter went for his tigers. When he arrived with
Ali the Tiger Rush was in full swing. The news that fifty guilders was being offered by the wealthy planters for each animal
killed had had its effect on the natives for miles around. The
day Holter arrived the excitement was at its height for only
the day before two fine bullocks had been slain by tigers. The
hunt was on in earnest.

Holter and Ali established headquarters in a native *kampong*
in that part of the interior which lies about midway between
the cities of Belawan Deli and Singkel. They lived in one of
the typical houses made of bamboo and nipa palm and built
off the ground on stilts.

As soon as he was settled in his quarters Holter was all for
getting busy. With Ali advising him in the matter of location,
my Dutch-English friend set out his line of traps, stringing them
out over a wide expanse of jungle.

A tiger-trap of this kind is not baited. The main idea is to
place it in a game trail and conceal it under leaves and loose
earth. A tiger on the hunt is sure to seek out a jungle path

frequented by prospective victims as they move up and down the forest,—wild boars, deer, tapirs and other tasty morsels.

Ali was extremely useful in this phase of the work. He couldn't have had a surer eye for locating a game trail if he was one of the animals that regularly used these shortcuts to almost any given point in the jungle.

In fact, Ali was so useful that he (Holter) began to feel like the Malay boy's assistant. One of the first signs of the jungle amateur (though Holter was blissfully unaware of this) is sheepishness in the presence of the expert knowledge of a bright native. Holter sounded a bit silly to me as he told me how it irked him to have the boy continually be the first to think of the right thing to do. "It was damned annoying, Buck," he said, "to have to follow the boy's lead in practically everything. He's a wonder, and I respected his judgment; but I'll admit that more than once I felt like kicking him for being so damned smart. I began to feel after a while as if this was Ali's expedition, not mine. For three or four days in a row we made a round of the traps together, Ali advising and cautioning me in so many matters as we made our way from trap to trap—(it took several hours to cover them all)—that after a while I found the boy a steady source of irritation. I was aware, of course, that he knew what he was doing but his calm assurance began to tantalize me. I know damned well I had no right thinking so, but I found myself feeling that the boy was trying to show me up."

Late one afternoon Holter decided to visit one of his traps a few miles from his *kampong*. A tiger had been reported in the district and he was anxious to see if he had had any luck. So far he had not earned any of the planters' guilders and he was growing impatient. His cash reserve was rather low and this added to his anxiety.

He had cheerfully given Ali permission to attend the marriage-feast of a village headman,—(in fact, he was glad to be temporarily rid of the all-knowing Malay)—and he looked forward to tramping the jungle alone. "I decided," he told me, "that my rifle provided all the protection I needed. It was foolish, I afterwards realized, to go alone into the jungle at this hour; but it gave me a feeling of independence that I could not resist."

He set forth as jauntily as if he were going for a stroll along a boulevard. After all, only one mile of his walk was through actual jungle. He would be out of the forest before dark. The walk from the edge of the jungle to the *kampong* he didn't mind at any hour. It was a straight walk and with every indication of a repetition of the unclouded moon of the night before he saw nothing but enjoyment in the stretch from the border of the jungle to his little bamboo house on stilts.

"The story of my missing leg," said Holter, "is the story of a bad guess. I've got rotten luck that way. That goddam boy of yours—(thanks again for letting me have him)—always guesses right. In addition to knowing the jungle, he's outrageously lucky. . . . Have it your way, Buck. But I stick to my story. The boy's lucky. And I'm not. Who but a luckless devil like me would have had the accident I did? It would never happen to one of your stupid natives. The beauty of the jungle is lost on them. They walk along blindly, as unconscious of the wonders around them as if they were without eyes and ears. . . . You're wrong, Buck. They're a lot of blind swine. They don't feel the things I felt as I strolled along. All they experience is the sensation of possible danger. They're all caution. Fear, that's what consumes 'em. That's why they're so damned smart. If you spend all your life fearing death you're bound to learn something about the business of avoiding danger,—certainly more than the chap who doesn't give a damn when he croaks.

"I don't have to tell you what happened. I walked straight into my own trap. You know what those infernal things are like. Opened up, ready for a victim, they spread out in a sort of circle, over a foot in diameter. As I walked along I brought my left foot down on the trigger that sets the spring into action. The jagged jaws of the trap sprang to. The device seemed to leap up at me as if aiming for my neck. It caught me just below the knee. You'd have thought it was propelled by a million demons. The impact was terrific. The vicious teeth, digging in deep, banged against the sides of my leg as if released by a blow from a ten-ton hammer.

"As steel and bone collided I was flung to the ground. My body was whipped down against the turf as if I was a great carpet-beater being brought down by some tremendous force against the expanse of rug that was the earth.

"It was, in other words, as if some giant had picked me up by the legs, swung me over his head and slammed me down to the ground with all the strength at his command.

"The steel points imbedded themselves cruelly in the flesh of my leg, seeming to eat their way in deeper and deeper as if bent on worming their way through and snapping the limb in two.

"I pushed my free foot against the spring of the trap and struggled as effectively as I could in my weakened condition—(the blow from those jagged steel jaws had stunned me badly)—to force it open. I was wasting what strength I had left, in the frantic process ripping more flesh from my leg. My struggles couldn't have been more futile if I were pressing my shoulders against Gibraltar in an effort to send the great rock splashing into the Mediterranean. I was a prisoner, torturously held captive by the device that was supposed to catch tigers for me and earn me some badly needed guilders.

"I yelled for that damned boy of yours, forgetting in my near-delirium that I had gone off without him, glad to be rid of him. I cursed him for neglecting me. That's what happens to a man's mind when he's caught in a steel trap.

"Night was coming on. As you know, twilight in the Sumatra jungle finds millions of mosquitoes on the wing. I'd lash out with my arms and drive a swarm away and another army would take their places. They were all over me, digging into me from every angle. They even got into my ears, and on my eyelids, biting away for all they were worth. . . . How about another drink? You don't expect me to finish this story without another drink, do you? . . . I'll have the same. . . . Breathing heavily as I was after the shock of being thrown, I even succeeded in sucking up a few of those mosquitoes into my nostrils, that's how thick they were.

"And then there were the ants. I needn't tell *you* what jungle ants are. Attracted by the smell of blood, they swarmed all over my leg in countless battalions, greedily digging into the flesh. It was futile to try to fight them. You know what the little villains are like. Drive off one gang of 'em and another million appear on the scene. And what was the use? How could I wage an offensive against 'em without raising hell with my wound? They had dug down deep into the flesh and it was even more painful to try to dig 'em out than it was to let them gnaw away.

"And then my imagination started getting the better of me. I remembered all the stories I had heard of the murderous performances of ants travelling in great armies,—of formidable animals they had killed, swarming around by the billions and billions and digging away until nothing remained but the bones. I myself have seen the bleaching skeleton of a python that had been attacked and vanquished by one of these nations of tiny killers travelling in a great irresistible phalanx." (I knew how Holter felt. I've seen a movement of ants ten inches wide and a mile long,—one of the most terrible forces of destruction in the jungle once it had the inclination and the opportunity to concentrate on an enemy.)

"My desperation was growing by the minute. Fairly consumed by mosquitoes and ants, I wrestled frantically with the spring of the trap, making another vain effort to part those cruel steel jaws.

"Then I tried to do something with the heavy spike by means of which the trap, which was fastened to a heavy chain, was anchored to a tree. The spike, driven several inches into the trunk was as firmly in place as a rivet in a girder, and my efforts could not have been more ineffective if I was trying to pull some steel-work apart.

"All I succeeded in doing was to rattle the chain furiously and stir some wild life into action. Remember that I had placed the trap along a game trail and consequently there was life all around me. Almost simultaneously with the first real clanking of the chain any number of night birds started giving their calls.

Or perhaps they were making a racket right along that I was not conscious of till now. And I became acutely aware of all kinds of rustlings and stirrings in the underbrush around me, my imagination no doubt contributing its share.

"But I did not have to depend on my ears. There were things I could see,—for instance, a family of wild pigs pattering along the trail. A member of the group, the biggest boar of the lot, drawn on by the smell of blood, came running over to where I lay. Spying a human being, he fled as though chased.

"The experience with the wild pigs was unimportant in itself but it gave me some crazy thoughts. If my blood made it so easy for a stupid boar to locate me, what about a tiger or a leopard? You've told me time and again that normally a tiger, let us say, smelling a man would avoid the spot. But the smell of blood would lure him on, wouldn't it? That's the way I figured. If one of the great cats smelled my bleeding leg he'd be attracted to me, wouldn't he? That's what kept running through my mind as I lay there. And every time I'd hear a noise that suggested the stealthy approach of a large animal I'd visualize a tiger or a leopard in the act of pouncing upon me and clawing me beyond recognition.

"Again my ears got busy and picked up and interpreted every sound within range. I heard the agonized shriek of a bird. It might have been the cry of some feathered creature caught by one of the marble cats that one finds in this part of Sumatra. Then there was a series of grunts, suggesting wild pigs, or possibly bears picking up food from the ground, and following these grunts there was a sharp squeal, suggesting an assault on one of the pigs by some carnivorous beast. Then there was one of those thin shrill shrieks suggesting a rodent being seized by a snake. Animals kept calling to each other. And at regular intervals I could hear some sizeable body crashing through the heavy jungle,—perhaps one of the tigers I was after, perhaps the very one that had been reported in the district that day. It might just as easily have been something harmless like a tapir but I had set my heart on being in constant danger and you can easily picture the tortures I suffered in consequence.

Much of the jungle traffic doubtless represented the movements of the small nocturnal animals like civet cats, musangs and porcupines but after I had been in the trap long enough they all became tigers.

"Meanwhile the ants kept swarming all over my wounded leg and the mosquitoes kept pecking away at me till I was in a frenzy of torment. All the sounds around me merely served to remind me again that I was in the thick of all kinds of wild life and I succeeded in convincing myself that sooner or later I would be the victim of a deadly attack of some kind or other. The reality of these maddening ants and mosquitoes added to the things I conjured up in my fevered brain made me want to do away with myself. And you know how I love life, Buck. It was a strange rôle for me. Yes, I wanted to die. Funny, isn't it? There was my rifle just out of reach. It had been knocked out of my hand when the impact of the closing trap had thrown me. I struggled desperately to reach that gun but it was several inches beyond my most frantic stretch. No man was ever keener to blow his brains out. Then I saw a heavy stick close to me, and a perfectly insane idea popped into my head. I tried to club myself over the head with it, but it proved so badly rotted it broke in two. I cursed and wept. I was not to be delivered from my agony. My death would be slow and terrible. Hideous hours of hell on earth, each an eternity, before release. I screamed like a lunatic. Perhaps some other fool had ventured into the jungle late and would hear me. Of course I was wasting my breath.

"Overhead in the branches the monkeys awakened from their sleep mocked me with their crazy chatter, tree-frogs joining the chorus with their weird singing.

"As I lay there on my side I found myself suddenly looking straight up. So thickly were the trees interlaced in most places that one got the impression of the jungle having an inky black ceiling. Here and there faint splashes of moonlight seeped through, suggesting leaks in the jungle roof that were letting in light.

"Above the chatter of the monkeys and the singing of the

tree-frogs I would hear an occasional agonized howl, suggesting to my not too experienced ears (although that boy of yours had taught me a lot) a gibbon suddenly awakened by some beast of prey on its trail.

"Some twenty-five or thirty feet up and to the right where a sprinkling of moonlight mixed with the jungle blackness and lent shape to things, I could see a strange limp body that seemed to be slowly moving in all directions at the same time. The bad light made it impossible for me to tell what it was but it was utterly unlike anything I had ever seen in a tree in all my life. Suddenly it dropped to the ground with a strange hollow thud not more than a dozen feet from where I lay. Tell me I'm crazy, Buck, but I believe to this day that it was a giant snake of some kind that went through this performance. Whatever it was, it scurried off and was gone in a couple of seconds." (Holter had given a pretty fair description of a big python dropping out of a tree on his way to his next stop in the jungle. Too bad he couldn't have witnessed the sight under better conditions. I've always considered it one of the jungle's greatest spectacles. A python weighing as much as two or three hundred pounds has been known to drop in this fashion from a height of thirty or thirty-five feet. And the clever devils manage it without injury too.)

"I don't remember much of anything after the falling of that strange body. About all I recall is making a final feeble effort to drive off those ants and mosquitoes that were tormenting me beyond endurance.

"The rest of the story I had to get from your boy, and others. Wait till you meet him in Singapore. He'll probably tell you what a nuisance *Tuan* Holter proved to be." (Holter was right in his surmise, I afterwards discovered. Ali never discussed the Dutch-Englishman without wrinkling up his nose and that meant the worst.)

Ali, it seems, returned from the marriage-feast in the village about an hour before midnight. When he arrived at the little shack where he lived with Holter he was surprised to find the *tuan* out. A series of inquiries revealed that the white man had not been seen for hours.

Ali quickly concluded that his master had probably set forth on a tour of inspection of his traps. Holter had not been having any luck and Ali had prevented him two or three times from making anxious visits to his traps at hours that the boy considered unsafe.

Ali quickly recruited a searching party among the villagers. Bearing torches and armed with krisses and bolos they set out in search of Holter. Ali knew where all the traps were and he was therefore able to conduct a businesslike search. The *tuan*, he was sure, must be near one of those traps.

"As far as I could determine," continued Holter, "it was sometime after midnight when they found me, after first visiting two other traps. I had been a prisoner for at least six hours. How many of those hours had elapsed when I lost consciousness I'll never know.

"I was a stark raving madman when I came to. I didn't know much of anything until I found myself several days later in the hospital here. They had taken me by boat and ox-cart to Padang, where a rough job of amputation was performed on my leg. Then I was brought here to Batavia where I could get good hospital care. And I've been stuck here ever since. For months my leg was so bad I couldn't get around. I was up against it financially but I managed to borrow some money from an old friend. The past few months I've been fed up with Batavia. I've got to have action, Buck. I go to seed when I stick around in one place. I've been thinking things over the last few weeks and I've got a plan."

"That's fine."

"Yes, I know what I'm doing at last. The trouble with me in the past has been that I haven't picked the right things to do. Some of 'em gave me a little action—what are you laughing at, Buck?"

"Your casualness about your tiger expedition. If you call that *a little action*"—(already Holter had forgotten his own recital of his thrilling experiences in Sumatra).

"It was pretty exciting on the whole but it wasn't just the right thing for me. No opportunity. No scope. I've got a good idea at last. It's going to put me on the map. I can feel it in my bones, Buck."

"What are you going to do?"

"Something practical for a change. Got wind of a gold strike in Borneo. Fortunes are going to be made and I intend to get my share. I'm outfitting now and leave next week for Banjermasin."

When I joined Ali in Singapore it was hard to get him to say much about Holter's tiger expedition. He was sorry that *Tuan* Holter had had such a bad time but the man should have known enough not to enter the jungle alone at that hour. Things like that always made trouble for everybody.

I told Ali that *Tuan* Holter thought he (the boy) was very smart and knew his business, refraining from adding how piqued Holter had been over Ali's superior knowledge.

Ali was unimpressed. In fact, his reply was to the effect that he regretted he couldn't say as much for *Tuan* Holter. By way of emphasis he gave his betel-nut an extra good chew and spat hard.

A few days later, in one of his talkative moments, Ali gave me a fairly detailed picture of the tiger expedition, in which he included his principal reason for not liking Holter. The man had forgotten to thank him for saving his life.

I was unable to join Ali in regarding this as a grave oversight. You can't expect a fellow who risked his neck as regularly as Holter did to remember a little thing like that.

"And, besides, Ali, he thanked me. After all, I'm the boss."

Chips Lends a Hand

I was in Dallas, Texas, laying out plans for a zoo with Director of Parks Jacoby. The Al G. Barnes Show was in town, and, once I had concluded my arrangements with the municipal authorities—(an order involving the complete stocking of the type of zoo that I suggested)—I found myself hanging around the lot where my friend Al G. was entertaining the local citizenry with his performing animals.

Having sold Barnes the bulk of his collection, I had an interest in that show that went beyond my normal interest in animals. These were *my* animals—at least I had owned them in the days when I brought them out of Asia—and I always got a kick out of hearing how they were getting along. Had this tiger or that elephant developed into a good performer? Was that black leopard any better-natured than he was in the days when I brought him and dropped him, a snarling rascal who'd as soon claw you as look at you, on Al's doorstep? . . . And a hundred other questions that were on the tip of my tongue whenever I ran into this old friend who for years ran the best all-animal show America has ever seen.

Al G. and I had a long talk one day in which he mentioned his needs in the way of new specimens. He was particularly anxious to get a good-sized orang-utan, not necessarily full grown but big enough to make a good showing. Joe Martin, his famous orang, had "gone bad" on reaching sexual maturity, as most anthropoid apes in captivity do. He had attacked several people and Al did not want to take any more chances with him. This meant that the greatest of all performing orangs had to be kept in his cage where he was now a member of the non-performing group, a mere exhibit in a travelling menagerie. What a comedown for Joe who had once been featured in the movies and starred in the Barnes Show, one year capturing the place of honor on the billboards! No longer was it safe to lead him out into the center ring where for so long a time he had earned the plaudits of the mob. Knowing something about the problems of a sensitive animal of this kind when full sexual ripeness suddenly arrives to complicate his life, I knew what a tough time Joe Martin must have had and I sympathized with him in his uneven struggle against the demons of maturity.

The king of circus orangs dethroned, another animal had to be found to take his place. But perhaps I should alter that. Al Barnes was not hopeful of securing another Joe Martin. He told me so. "If there's ever another one like him I'll be the most surprised man in the business." (The nearest approach to him in my own experience was Gladys, the orang-utan described in these pages in the chapter "Jungle Laundress," the most loveable, intelligent member of the species I ever handled.) Barnes said he would be satisfied if I could secure for him a specimen tame enough to lead out into the ring,—or one that had been partly tamed. The animal need not be one capable of developing into a performer. The main thing was to secure an orang that knew how to behave himself, or at least had a nucleus on which to found a career featuring good behavior.

On my next trip to Asia I looked around everywhere for an animal that would meet Barnes' requirements. When I would run into an animal that was tame enough he would be too small. When I would get on the trail of one that sounded as if it was of the right age and the prescribed docility, it would turn out to be crippled or of delicate health. Always a hitch somewhere.

Chop Joo Soon, a Chinese animal trader in Singapore, with whom I had done considerable business and who knew of the type of orang I needed to fill my Barnes order, notified me one day that he had just the thing. His specimen proved to be an excellent one, although he had apparently forgotten the tameness clause. His animal was of the right age and the right size but he was about as tame and manageable as a fresh-caught panther. In fact he had just been brought in from the Borneo jungle. He was so fine an orang, however, that I decided to buy him regardless of whether or not he would do for Barnes. If I could not land a better behaved specimen, I would try to tame him down sufficiently to make him a useful member of my friend's show. If this proved impossible I would bring him back anyhow and sell him to a zoo. A good-sized orang-utan can always be sold in the United States.

The shipment of which this orang was a part was a very big one. It was one of the biggest of the many floating zoos with which I have returned to the United States. As I needed more help than Lal, my capable Hindu boy, could give me, I asked the mate of the ship on which I was crossing the Pacific to select another helper for me from among the sailors. I often do this, never having any trouble getting the assistance needed. There is always some member of the crew whose duties are light and who welcomes the opportunity to pick up a little extra change.

Having mentioned the fact that I needed a man who was husky, the mate suggested the ship's carpenter, a big powerful American. Chips—(he was known by no other name)—had more spare time than any other available member of the crew, and would be just the man, the mate said.

Chips, I afterwards learned, was the bully of the forecastle, and I suppose one of the reasons the mate suggested him as my helper was a secret hope that the extra work would keep the burly braggart so busy that he wouldn't have time to make trouble for his brother sailors, which had long been his specialty. Proud of his strength, the carpenter would perform feats that none of his comrades could match, and then proceed to call them a lot of weaklings. Many fights resulted, Chips invariably coming out on top. His specialty was beating up smaller men and boasting about it. He had lost favor with the officers and was due to be dropped as soon as a good man could be secured to take his place.

The mate was so anxious to keep the big roughneck busy that he was even willing to let him pick up a little extra change. I imagine he would also have been glad to see him pick up a few little injuries in his work with my animals.

Chips' standing with his fellow sailors, however, was no concern of mine. I had asked for a husky helper and the mate had supplied one.

The carpenter was a rare bird. Shortly after I was introduced to him he asked me to feel his muscle. This I did, withdrawing my fingers too quickly to suit him.

"You hardly felt it," he said, taking hold of my hand and placing it on the bulging biceps of his right arm. "Feel again."

I obliged. "Some muscle," I said.

"You bet it's some muscle," Chips agreed.

"How much do you suppose I can lift?" Chips asked.

"I haven't any idea," I replied.

"Well, what would you guess?"

"Oh, I guess you could do some pretty heavy lifting. Those are great muscles you've got there."

"You said it. Like iron. Feel!"

"I just did."

"I know, boss. But feel again. It's bigger now."

Again I obliged. After all, I was crossing the Pacific with this clodhopper as one of my helpers and we might as well get acquainted.

Chips was at me again, trying to make me guess the number of pounds he could lift. As I stood there trying to frame a suitable reply, one that would convey my confidence in his ability to walk off with the Pyramids on his back, I heard one of the elephants straining at his chain. This animal was tied up on the aft deck between the bulkhead and the No. 4 hatch.

As the restless pachyderm kept rattling his chain and stamping his feet, I said, "I wish that elephant would stop milling around."

"Do you want me to put a stop to it?" asked Chips who knew as much about elephants as I know about Greek dancing.

"Never mind the elephant, Chips. I've got other things for you to do."

"We ought to teach him a lesson, boss."

I had a hard job convincing him that he'd better do as I said. He was all for grabbing an elephant hook and showing the animal "a thing or two."

"Never mind the hook, Chips. Throw him some hay. That may quiet him down."

"Don't you think I'd better jab him a couple too, boss?"

"No."

Chips looked crestfallen.

"Just the hay?" he asked.

"Yes, just the hay."

A half hour later the elephant had quieted down. Triumphantly Chips came over to where I was working on some birds and announced the fact that he had made the elephant behave.

"That's fine, Chips."

"If he makes any more trouble, boss, let me handle him. I've got his number."

"Swell! . . . By the way, what did you do besides throw him some hay?"

"Well, you see— Oh, I just— Well, the first thing I did—"

"That's great," I interrupted, not wanting to embarrass him too much. "There's nothing like having a system." Then I quickly gave him another job to do to spare him—and me—the pain of further explanation.

A few days later I was forced to admit that Chips wasn't overestimating his strength. I wanted some tigers shifted around and the big carpenter, unaided, moved them about in their heavy cages as if they were so many kittens in baskets.

"That's great work, Chips." (There really had been no need for Chips to do the job alone. Lal was there to help but Chips spurned assistance. "This is man's work," was the way he put it.)

"There's no one else aboard that could 'a' done it," was how he received my compliment.

"I'm sure of that."

"Osgood thinks he's strong, boss. Have I told you about him? He's a roach, is Osgood. That's what—a roach. Thinks he's got muscle. I'll bet if he was asked he'd say he could 'a' done it. He's that lousy, is Osgood. Ask him, boss, willya? It'll be a great joke. If he says he could 'a' done it I'll clip him on the snoot. I'll point him out to you, boss, and you ask him. It'll be great sport."

I declined the invitation. This left Chips gloomy, for he was obviously aching for an excuse to "clip" Osgood. But I cheered him up when I said, "You needn't tell me you're stronger than Osgood, or anybody else. You're the strongest man I've ever seen, bar none." And it wasn't far from true. The necessity of having to keep on telling it to Chips, however, grew a bit painful after a while.

One day I said to the carpenter, "Chips, I've got a real job for you."

"I'm your man, boss."

"It's a job that takes strength and nerve, Chips. I wouldn't think of asking anyone else to do it. There's no one else on board that's got the muscle to do it. Certainly Osgood couldn't do it." I knew this would make Chips feel good.

"That roach!" was all he said.

I explained to Chips what the nature of his task was. "I'm going to take the orang out of his cage and you're going to help me do it."

I wanted to see if I couldn't tame down this little demon before reaching San Francisco. After all, Barnes wanted a manageable specimen, and, if possible, I didn't want to disappoint him. If I could get a collar around the animal's neck and take him out of his cage daily, in the process getting him used to the idea that I was a friend, not an enemy, some progress would be made toward taking the fight out of him. Once he got it through his head that he was safe in my company, and saw how much fun it would be to be let out of his cage for exercise in the warm sun, he'd be a different animal. One can't ever be sure about these things but that was my guess about this particular orang.

"We're gonna take Shrimpo out of his cage?" asked Chips. This was the name he had given the ape.

"Yes."

The carpenter's disappointment was obvious. "Hell! I thought you had a real job." Chips had never taken the orang seriously on account of its shortness of stature. It was less than four and a half feet in height, which was no reason to assume, as Chips had done, that this was not a formidable creature. An orang can't be judged by its height. The short back legs give an impression of squatness that has more than once resulted in an underrating of the fighting powers of these dangerous apes.

Chips had evidently not taken the trouble to notice that Shrimpo's arms, for instance, were all out of proportion to his height. They were enormous, with great bulging muscles. I thought I had a pretty sizeable pair of biceps—(I weighed about 200 pounds at the time, most of it bone and muscle, thanks to years of strenuous work that was death on fat)—but Shrimpo's were much bigger around than mine. Chips had also failed to notice the animal's big mouth and wicked teeth,—or, if he had noticed them, he had lacked the perception to see that this ape was not to be taken lightly. As a matter of fact, Shrimpo was a good match for the average two or three men.

"This is a real job, Chips," I said. "You'll find that out when we get started."

"Quit your kidding, boss," said Chips, as he disdainfully eyed Shrimpo, in front of whose cage we were standing. "If that little feller got fresh I'd put him on my knee and spank him."

"Don't be so sure of that, Chips. But we'll go into that later. I want to explain how you and I are going to get the ape out of his cage and hold him while Lal puts on the collar."

"What!" exclaimed Chips. "Three people to put a collar on that little runt! Gimme the collar. I'll do it myself."

Lal started grinning.

"What the hell's he laughin' at?" roared Chips. "I suppose he thinks I can't do it alone. He thought I couldn't move those tiger cages alone either."

"Calm down, Chips. This is different from moving tiger cages."

"You ain't tellin' me that monks is worse than tigers, boss, are you?"

"When they're loose and the tigers are boxed, yes." Chips didn't seem capable of getting anything through that thick skull of his. "We're going to get started now, Chips," I said. "Here's the dope. First we'll knock the front of the cage out. I'll make a quick reach for him and grab a wrist. Then—"

"Let me do that part, boss. I'll show the little shrimp."

"Don't interrupt. I'll grab him first. I've done it before. Looks easy but it isn't. It takes experience. I'll drag him out of his cage with a swift yank. Your job is to grab the other wrist quickly. We'll stretch his arms out straight, like this. (I stretched out my arms till they were parallel with the floor of the deck.) Then, while we're holding the little devil, Lal will snap a collar, with chain attached, around his neck from behind. Then we'll all let go together, jump back and run the end of the chain around a stanchion."

"There's nothing to that," said Chips.

"Let me finish. It'll take every bit of strength we've got to keep that animal's arms stretched out. Don't fool yourself about that. He's a powerful little cuss. If I should let go he'd make a quick lunge for you, to break *your* hold. He could snap your wrist with one bite. But I'm not going to let go. How about you? If you let go, *I'd* be in the same danger."

"Say, boss, you don't think that little roach is going to bother *me*, do you? I've handled bigger roaches than him. Take Osgood. One day—"

"Never mind about Osgood. We've got to get busy. Do you understand what you're to do?"

"Hell! there's nothing to understand. It's as easy as—"

"Remember what I said before. If one of us lets go the other will probably get hurt. Maybe badly hurt."

"There's a swell chance of me letting go, boss! If I couldn't hold a little flea like that I'd—"

"Let's go!" I said.

I proceeded to pry off the iron bars of the cage with a crowbar. The occupant didn't wait to be yanked out. The idea of getting out of his cage appealed to him. With an angry grunt, which was his way of saying, "Get out of my way!" he stepped forth. As he did I grabbed one wrist, Chips grabbing the other. We pulled his arms out straight, firmly holding him as we had planned. The carpenter had followed instructions and seemed to have a very good grip on the wrist he was holding.

The orang, boiling over with rage, was making frenzied efforts to reach us with his teeth, violently twisting and bobbing his head.

His struggles to get at us were nothing to worry about, for we were holding him securely; but that head was moving in all directions in a perfect riot of twists and squirms, making it impossible for Lal to get the collar on. The only sounds that came from the animal were the alternate grunts and sucking-in of air that are characteristic of an orang on the warpath.

"Again, Lal!" I yelled after the boy had made five or six unsuccessful attempts to get the collar around the struggling ape's neck. Once more Lal tried but again he failed.

"Don't take all year, Blacky!" came from Chips, whose breathing was an indication that the animal was giving him more work than he had expected.

"Hold on, Chips!" I yelled. The carpenter, normally the most talkative fool I had ever encountered, made no reply except a muttered oath. The strain was beginning to tell on me and I knew the carpenter must be feeling it too. I gave Lal a cussing he didn't deserve, imploring him to snap that infernal collar around the animal's neck if he didn't want to be tossed overboard.

Chips was heaving and panting as if he had been running a marathon. Suddenly I saw him go white. Instantly I knew he was going to let go. He did. I lost no time in following suit. It would have been silly to try to hang on alone.

I jumped back, the orang coming after me with those great arms outstretched. I'm keen for affection but I didn't want one of those embraces. The orang's method of fighting, described elsewhere in these pages, is to draw his victim to him in one of those great hugs and then tear him to pieces with his teeth.

As I cautiously backed away I could hear Chips yelling, "This'll fix him, boss!" He was holding up the crowbar with which I had opened the cage. The idiot was trying to hand it to me, nervously edging up.

"Get to hell out of here, you—!" I yelled.

This boob was committing the added crime of trying to get my attention while the animal was closing in on me. As if he hadn't sinned enough in letting go that arm.

The orang, as I kept scrambling for position, made a sudden

rush at me. He had the advantage of a longer reach but I knew more about boxing. As he spread out his arms to grab me he gave me a beautiful opening. I waded in and let him have it smack on the point of the jaw. It was one of those uppercuts that get results, a wallop that had all of my beef behind it. The collision with the enemy's chin came just as the arms were about to enfold me. Shrimpo kissed the deck with a bang while some sailors who had run over to see the scrap broke out into applause like fans at a prize-fight.

It was a clean knock-out. The orang, landing flat on his back, slept the sleep of the kayoed.

After Lal had snapped the collar around Shrimpo's neck, we fastened the ape to a stanchion by a short length of the chain. When we brought him back to consciousness by dashing a bucket of water over him, that was where he found himself.

Chips spent the rest of the voyage making excuses. One day his story was that his hands were perspiring so freely he had been unable to hold on. "No man," he bellowed, "could 'a' held on with his hands soppin' wet." His listeners—fellow sailors who taunted him for the rest of the trip, no longer fearful of his bullying—broke into a horse laugh.

The next day the carpenter's story was to the effect that he had shifted his fingers to get a better grip, the animal eluding his grasp as he did. This story was also greeted with derisive howls.

Chips ceased to be the bully of the forecastle. He had been unable to change the opinion of his mates that the reason why he let go was that he was scared. What really broke his heart, however, was the fact that Osgood ("that roach!") had witnessed his disgrace. Osgood was his hated rival, having once come close to licking the carpenter. Now Osgood acted as if he'd enjoy another chance at the champ. I often wondered whether the fight took place.

Shrimpo soon discovered that there was a lot of fun to be had basking in the sunshine on the deck. We had fine weather practically all the way back and my orang got the benefit of most of it. There were one or two minor flare-ups and when the animal discovered that these weren't getting him anywhere he decided to behave himself.

By the time we arrived in San Francisco he was conducting himself in such mannerly fashion that I was able to lead him over by his chain to where Al Barnes came up to meet me. The showman was greatly pleased with the animal and the deal was closed then and there.

Man-Eater

THIS is the story of a man-eating tiger, probably as vicious an animal as I'll encounter if I continue in my chosen field for another fifty years. I captured him alive; but that would hardly have been possible without the Sultan of Johore.

So I'd better start by telling you something about the Sultan. In fact, I may tell you a good deal about him. In addition to helping me get my man-eater, he is probably the most interesting ruling prince in Asia.

No prince ever got off to a worse start. He was labelled a playboy at the very outset. Prophecies were made that once he became sultan the state of Johore would quickly and surely go to the dogs,—that is, in the event that he didn't dissipate himself to death before he had a chance to reach the throne.

Educated in England, the Sultan-to-be got an early taste of Europe and liked it. Paris was convenient and there he maintained a luxurious apartment where he had one uninterrupted good time, wine and women being featured on the program. Known as a Wild Young Man, no one took him seriously. Everyone liked him—(it was difficult to feel otherwise about him)— but even his best friends shook their heads and declared that so unstable a youth would never go very far.

He spent money at a terrific rate, in the process driving to distraction those back home in Johore Bahru who had to provide the coin. The country was declining rapidly and it was becoming increasingly difficult to provide funds for the unreasoning young spendthrift they were maintaining in splendor in Europe,— who was supposed to be getting his education in England but was really getting it in France.

When finally the ruling sultan died, the young man was practically dragged back to Johore to take his place as reigning prince of an impoverished people.

The government was hard up, the young man's reckless expenditures in Paris having helped more than a little to bring about this condition.

The young ruler took in the situation and decided he didn't like' it. The country was poor and that meant that there wasn't any money for the Sultan to spend on his favorite pleasures.

One day the Sultan got an idea. It was a very simple idea. He would go to work! Perhaps that doesn't sound like a very unusual piece of thinking but only a man who knows this strange part of the world can fully realize what an upheaval has to take place inside a royal idler of the East before he is ready to announce rolling up his sleeves and doing some honest labor.

Of course, I am speaking figuratively. The Sultan of Johore had no intention of turning coolie. This would not have accomplished anything. What he had decided to go in for was a little planning for the future of his country.

The young man had a quick intelligence. Equipped with a lively brain, he had real ability as an organizer but he had been so used to indulging himself that the thought of work of any kind was decidedly unpleasant. Still, it was the only way out. The rehabilitation of Johore was the only means of securing the precious dollars he liked to spend, so he would rehabilitate Johore. Damned if he wouldn't! He swore it by all that was good and holy and much that was neither.

This decision of the Sultan to put his country back on its feet came a few years after the twentieth century had been ushered in. Rubber had been planted successfully in Ceylon, and in some of the neighboring Malay states, and the young man fresh from Paris did not see why the same commodity could not be successfully produced in Johore. He went to the leading bank of Singapore (which is a short trip across the channel from Johore Bahru) and tried to borrow £200,000. They were very polite. It was very good to see the Sultan. They felt flattered by his visit. No one who had entered their portals in years had given them such a thrill of satisfaction. It was the Ultimate Thing. It was not likely that they would ever forget the honor. BUT—£200,000 was a great deal of money. And one could not be sure that rubber would be a success in Johore. The bank had implicit faith in His Highness—(as a matter of fact, they completely distrusted him)—but it would be unfair to expect any man to make a success of an enterprise that was entirely new to him, and therefore it would be unfair to let the Sultan borrow £200,000. It was the Singapore version of the ancient and honorable method employed since the year one by bankers of all nations in turning down an influential would-be borrower.

The Sultan grinned, displaying his diamond-studded teeth,—(despite his education in England he was a Malay at bottom, and jewelled teeth were a part of his ritual)—and went on his way without a word of protest. He was a good sport.

His Highness was not easily discouraged. He tried another bank, a smaller one. They decided to take a chance on the young Sultan. They knew of the wild life he had led but they were intelligent enough to forget that. The young man had a plan, one that was well thought out. He had obviously made a real study of rubber-growing. They were convinced that he was in earnest, that he was really going to work. They liked him. The possibilities of rubber in Johore sounded good to them. If they turned the prince down and he got the money elsewhere and the rubber industry thrived in Johore, they would be completely out of the picture. They had the common sense to see these things. They decided to take a flier. They backed the young Sultan to the limit.

I'm not going to tell you the story of rubber in Johore. It would take a whole book to do that. Let me confine myself to saying that the young ruler made a tremendous success of his rubber-growing scheme. In doing so he staged the greatest comeback I've ever seen a human being make. Discredited, not taken seriously by his best friends, written down as an incorrigible playboy by most, he reared an industry so vast and so profitable that today Johore is one of the richest countries in the world for its size (the Sultan's private income alone being in excess of sixty thousand Straits dollars a month, or over $34,000 in American money.) The bank that decided to take a chance on the untried youngster fresh from his Paris revels today handles millions of dollars of the Johore government's money, profits from rubber and other government enterprises; and the larger bank that politely edged the Sultan out of the door secretly wishes it had not laid such great store by the homely virtues and that it had taken the trouble to investigate, from a purely business stand-point, the rubber project of the brand new ruler whom they un-inquiringly wrote off the books as a crack-brained wastrel.

Today the Sultan, a man of about fifty-five, likes to joke about the days when his wildness had all of Johore worried. Instead of being bitter toward the bank that turned him down, he devotes himself to extolling the sportsmanship of the outfit that backed him. "I had a good idea, of course," he has told me more than once, "but such a bad record, Buck! Such a bad record!" Then he would break into a laugh, displaying two rows of dental sun-shine in the form of frontal uppers and lowers of solid gold which had replaced the diamond-studded front teeth that the Sultan one day decided were a bit too garish.

In the days when the young Sultan first took over the cares of office, Malay Street in Singapore was the worst red light dis-trict in the world. It was a Loose Ladies League of Nations, Turkish, French, Japanese, Armenian, Polish, Spanish, Portu-guese and Italian girls (and a scattering of others) being rep-resented in the brothels. His Highness, in those youthful days, frequently made the rounds of that notorious street, not in quest of women,—for women are no novelty to a Sultan—but to buy drinks for those he liked and to revel in the comradeship of these battered purveyors of themselves whom he considered a race of good sports.

Years ago there was a rule, invoked by the British authorities in Singapore, requiring the royal cut-up to leave the island before night-fall. "How they kept an eye on me, those clever English!" he exclaimed more than once. "And I didn't blame them either. I used to raise hell."

"Those clever English!" Consider one aspect of Malay Street if you doubt the aptness of the phrase. No one, to my knowledge, had ever seen an English girl among the women available in this international array of sporting houses. The English saw to that. They wanted a full measure of respect from the natives for the wives of Britons stationed in Singapore and they were smart enough to know that this would be easier to secure if England was without representation in the Street of All Nations. So that, while hundreds of English tarts hawked their wares in Piccadilly Circus, in Singapore the Foreign Office was building up the picture of a one hundred per cent virtuous British womanhood. In citing this I am not trying to prove anything,—except perhaps that England overlooks nothing by way of making things easier for her sons and daughters in far-away places that she owns or controls.

"Those clever English!" By skillful manœuvering they contrive to exercise control over Johore's foreign affairs, taking so many problems off the native government's hands in the process that their presence is not resented, and is in fact a recognized benefit to natives and foreigners alike. In local affairs, however, the Sultan is supreme. For instance, if he should want to have one of his countrymen beheaded, off would go the luckless head. But the Sultan exercises these extreme powers sparingly, having the good sense to handle his subjects as tactfully as England handles him. It is all a hard-boiled proposition of not treading on the other fellow's feet for fear he may rise up and poke his big toe in your eye. All things considered, it is one of the best ways of getting along with people.

I have known the Sultan of Johore since 1918. I met him in the course of my work as a collector and we became good friends. We don't stand on ceremony in our relationship. The Sultan doesn't want it.

The greatest treat I can think of when I am in this part of the world is to be invited to the Sultan's house for tiffin; and when one of the courses is Malay curry, as prepared in this epicurean household, I become so enthusiastic that H. H. (the nickname which His Highness likes to have me use) kids me unmercifully. One day he accused me of plunging into my curry like a man-eating tiger.

This gave me an opportunity to change the subject, and to pick up one of my favorite themes: man-eating tigers. In my work as a collector I had brought back to the United States many unusual specimens, including animals and birds never before seen in America, but I had never knowingly brought in a tiger that had eaten human flesh. The subject of man-eaters fascinated me, the vaguest reference to it setting me off on an orgy of questions, recollections of what I had heard from others on the theme (little of it involving first-hand experience), and speculation on what I should find if I should ever realize a long-standing ambition to come face to face with one of these eaters of human flesh.

"You would run," opined H. H. one day when we were discussing the subject. "Very fast you would run. That is what you would do. Like a deer you would run. Swiftly,—as you do when I invite you to my house for curry."

Twice I have referred to the Sultan's "house." The Sultan has a beautiful palace but he does not choose to live in it. Tourists have practically driven him out of it, but he went willingly for he does not care for the pomp that is an inevitable part of living there. He lives in a big house on the outskirts of Johore Bahru, despite which enthusiastic tourists, returning from a visit to the palace, which has become a show-place, have been heard to give detailed descriptions of the Sultan, of how he greeted them, etc. The palace, more a museum today than anything else, is the place where visitors flock to see the famous relics of old Johore: the marvellous gold plate, the great collection of jewelled swords from which enough diamonds, rubies and emeralds could be plucked to start a good-sized jewelry shop, and other reminders of the splendor in which former sultans of this picturesque little country lived.

"Some day, H. H.," I told his joshing majesty, "I'm going to land a man-eating tiger and then the joke'll be on you."

"Have some more curry," replied the Sultan with a chuckle.

"Wait and see! The first time I get a chance to go after a man-eater I'm going to bring him back alive. And if it happens anywhere near Johore, I'll bring the beast right to your house where you can look at him."

"You are eating hardly any curry." (I had had three help-ings.) "Have some or I will not believe you like it as much as you say. It will give you the strength to fight man-eating tigers." With this, the Sultan blew himself to another laugh.

"How will you be able to prove your capture is a man-eater?" he added, with a twinkle in his eye. "You forget how difficult it is to make me believe anything."

"If necessary I'll stick an arm or a leg through the bars of the cage and let him chew it off."

"That will be fine," replied H. H. "Then I will know it is not a tame tiger. It is necessary to put you Americans to such tests. You are all such bluffers." Then he roared his enjoyment of his playful dig at me.

In less frivolous moments the Sultan discussed the serious menace of man-eating tigers. The presence of one of these killers would demoralize a whole rubber district, putting the workers on edge and rendering them practically useless.

Perhaps more rot has been written about the tiger than about any other wild animal. Certainly no one will deny that the tiger has come in for its share. Much of this silly stuff has had to do with the subject of man-eaters.

In one year, more than fifteen hundred people were killed by tigers in British India, and the average annual mortality from this cause has not been much below this figure. In most cases the tigers responsible for these deaths are man-eaters, it being an established fact that it is an unusual thing for an ordinary tiger, no matter how ferocious a specimen, to attack a man. In fact, he finds the smell of human flesh repulsive and will lose no time in vacating the spot where this offensive odor reaches his nostrils. Once in northern Perak I practically stumbled over a female tiger with a pair of sizeable cubs. We were not more than six or seven yards apart when we spied each other. She and her youngsters snarled and slunk away without any loss of time.

Man-eating in a tiger is a form of perversion. A normal tiger, cornered by a hunter and killing him in a fight, will seldom give a thought to eating the body. In isolated cases a tiger, in killing a man who had tracked it down and cornered it, has been known to develop a liking for human flesh in the process of mangling the enemy. Once this happens, the animal becomes a confirmed man-eater and may account for a dozen or more human lives before its wild career is checked.

The tiger is decidedly not a man-eating animal. Its normal rôle is to keep out of man's way. Man-eating is a depraved taste, developed under unusual circumstances. A tiger that sustains so severe an injury in combat with another animal that it is not strong enough or fast enough to knock down game will attack a native if opportunity arises, simply because it's easier. Most jungle beasts are too fast or too tough for a badly maimed tiger. A native that is unfortunate enough to stray into the path of a hungry tiger that is incapacitated is likely to be knocked down and devoured.

It would be appropriate to cite here the case of a hunt for a man-eater organized by the Sultan of Perak and a British government official stationed there. The Briton headed the expedition that set out after one of the worst man-eating tigers that ever terrorized a native village. The vicious beast had accounted for several lives when the Englishman, heading a company of Malay soldiers assigned to him by the Sultan, went out into the jungle to get the killer. After a long and strenuous chase, the man-eater was tracked down. The hunting party surrounded him in a little section of jungle and beat him out into an open space. Four soldiers fired and the striped scourge toppled over dead. The Englishman examined the body carefully. The animal was a magnificent specimen, everything indicating perfect condition. There were no signs of incapacitation or impaired strength. "Pretty odd," said the Englishman. "Expected to find some sign of a wound that made the devil take to man-eating." Suddenly one of the Malays cried, "See, *tuan*, see!" Holding up one of the paws he pointed to a great scar across the pad where the foot had once been cleaved wide open. Once there had been a terrible wound there and for at least a month or six weeks that tiger must have hobbled around on three paws. During that period he probably had to subsist on frogs and small rodents, and it is more than likely that he failed to get enough of these to stave off hunger. In his half-starved condition some native might have crossed his path, or appeared in the jungle close to him. Under circumstances of this kind, the animal, desperate for food, would probably attack. It would be an easy matter for a tiger, no matter how badly he was limping, to catch up with a native and knock him down. In all probability this is what happened. The best local students of wild game with whom I discussed the occurrence interpreted it that way, their further belief being that the incident created in the animal a lust for more human flesh.

Old age, strangely enough, is also responsible for the development of the man-eating instinct. A tiger that is getting on in years is faced by a serious problem. His teeth are bad, a thousand fights have left him battered and bruised, he is worn out. He no longer has the strength nor the agility to keep his stomach filled through the normal process of killing game in the jungle. He has to keep alive. Anything will do, even a man. It's meat of a kind, after all, and after a few meals of man-meat, the new diet takes on a peculiar fascination. Nothing else will satisfy. A craving for human flesh is developed and the animal goes on the prowl for this new delicacy. A tiger, crazed by this desire, will enter a village at night, drag a native out of bed, and carry him off into the jungle. There the poor victim is consumed, the killer becoming a more dangerous beast with each mouthful. The more human flesh it eats the more it wants; and when the pangs of hunger again are felt, there will be another man-hunt.

The presence of a man-eater in a district is the signal for much excitement. The natives are in a state of terror, and the local industry, whatever it is, is at a standstill. Soldiers are immediately sent to the spot by the person in authority,—either a British colonial official or the reigning prince.

One night the Sultan of Johore was telling me of the trouble the ruler of a near-by state was having with a couple of man-eating tigers that had become active in his territory. We were standing at the bar of the Raffles Hotel in Singapore (an old haunt of the Sultan's) where he had invited me to have a few drinks with him. "I have no problem of this kind," he told me. "That is

very good, no? Yes, it is very good. Sometimes we have a bad
tiger. He eats a man and we have trouble. But it is no steady
thing. We have not had any for two, three years now. That is
good fortune. Yes."

"The next time a man-eater is spotted in Johore," I said, "give
me a crack at him if I'm in this part of the world, will you? I'd
like to have a try at catching one alive." As I spoke, there was
a crash of glass against the wall. It merely meant that the Sultan
had finished his drink. It is a quaint little feature of his drinking that he will never have more than one drink out of the same
glass, and, not wishing anyone to drink out of the glass that had
touched the royal lips, he would send it smashing against the
wall. This is a pleasant little eccentricity of H. H.'s that nobody
minds. Certainly the management of the Raffles Hotel does not
mind. The Sultan is one of their best customers, putting thousands of pounds into their coffers. Having splintered his glass,
my royal host was ready to resume the conversation.

"It is agreed. The next time I have tiger which eats a man
I send for you. You go up to tiger, say, 'Boo!' tiger say, 'All is
lost, it is Buck,' and lie down on back and cry like baby, and
you go up and throw him over shoulder and swim back to America
with him. In America everybody clap hands and you become
big hero."

The Sultan shook with laughter as he finished this little picture of my exploits with a man-eating tiger. And, while I
dawdled over my last drink, too fascinated by H. H., to do anything but listen, my host drained another glass and sent it spinning against the wall back of the bar to crash and join in a few
gentle tinkles the little mound of broken glass on the floor.

Another time the Sultan asked me if I would like to visit de
Silva's jewelry shop in High Street with him. He is mad about
jewelry and one of his pet pastimes is to visit de Silva's and
bargain for some particular article that happens to strike his
fancy. The Sultan is the soul of generosity, parting with his
money freely, but bargaining is one of his favorite games, providing him with the same kind of pleasure some men get out of a
game of chess. His first move is to make any offer that he

knows to be low; then it is the proprietor's move. They keep at it, sometimes for more than an hour, good-naturedly trying to outwit each other. When a couple of Asiatics start bargaining they go at it hammer and tongs, the zest that they put into it making them easily the greatest bargainers in the world.

On the particular day to which I refer, the Sultan closed a deal for an elaborate piece of jewelry for which de Silva wanted $19,000 and the Sultan finally paid $16,000. (I recall figuring the thing out in American money.) H. H. put so much ardor into the transaction I thought he must have a new love. It developed that he was buying the expensive trinket for his son's one-year-old girl who was to be taken to church in a few days for a religious ceremony of some kind that royal children in the Mohammedan faith must go through.

"You certainly put a lot of spirit into *that* deal, H. H.," I remarked as we were on the way out. "I've never seen even you pursue a piece of jewelry so relentlessly. Such determination!"

"It is like you and your man-eating tigers. You should see yourself when you are talking, talking, talking, on that subject."

Another time, when I was the Sultan's guest at Johore Bahru, he started questioning me about the collection of animals I had assembled at Singapore. I was getting ready to return to America with them. He wanted to know whether I had collected all the specimens I was after.

"Not all," I replied, "but I've got a good assortment. A collector never feels he's got *all* the specimens he wants. There's always something else he'd like to have."

"I suppose you want some of *my* animals, eh?" The Sultan had a number of animal cages, usually well-stocked, in back of an old jail. Now and then, when a visiting notable comes to Johore, H. H. stages a tiger hunt for him, usually omitting to tell his guest that the striped cat he has just picked off so expertly had been dumped out of a cage before the beaters a moment before. Not that the Sultan cannot offer a rip-snorting tiger hunt to the man he senses to be a real sportsman. This he does when he is absolutely sure of his man. The Johore jungle has plenty of tigers and no one knows more about hunting them than the Sultan, the greatest *shikari* I have ever known.

I have bought many tigers of the Sultan. For years he has made a practice of paying the natives a bounty of $100, for trapping live tigers (that being the reason why he can usually stage one of those phoney tiger hunts on a moment's notice for the benefit of any influential stuffed shirt that he considers it good policy to amuse).

More than once I have bargained with him by the hour for some tiger I particularly wanted. Tigers are always saleable and I would invariably try to bring back at least four or five whether I had orders for them or not. H. H. took the same delight in bargaining with me over a tiger as he did in bargaining at de Silva's for a piece of jewelry, only of course where animals were concerned he was on the selling end.

On the particular day to which I refer here, when the Sultan said, "I suppose you want some of my animals, eh?" I decided he must be in the mood for playing that game of his of trying to see how much he could get out of me for an animal.

I told him I'd like to see what he had. I'd be glad to buy anything I could use.

"To hell with you," came the unexpected reply. "There is nothing for sale. Do you hear? Nothing." He wore a strange expression that I couldn't quite fathom. I tried to figure out whether I had done something to offend him.

"Let us go and see what there is," he went on.

I was puzzled. If nothing was for sale, why take me over to the cages?

I said nothing. We walked along in silence till we had reached the cages. There H. H. suddenly became very talkative. "How would you like a snow-white porcupine? And an albino monkey? And a pair of black apes? Very rare, these four, very rare. And a pair of leopard cats. (Small wild-cats with spots like leopards.) And a crocodile? And a tiger? No, I suppose you do not want the tiger. Buck does not like tiger unless he have eaten of the flesh of man."

"How much?" I asked.

"How much!" he echoed. "Have I not said there is nothing for sale today. They are all yours—for nothing. Send Ali over with some boxes tomorrow and get them out of here!"

H. H., when he did not have his bargaining clothes on, would have real bursts of generosity like this. In this particular instance, he had disguised his mood so well that I didn't know what was coming. He was really outdoing himself in including the crocodile, which had been in his garden for at least fifteen years.

"I can't take that, H. H.," I protested. "It wouldn't be fair."

"Why do you not want him?" he asked. "Ah, I know! You think he is not man-eater. But there you have made mistake. You do not know that every day we give him to eat five boys. He will not eat anything else. Take him!" I did. There was nothing else to do. H. H. would have been offended if I had done otherwise.

Again the Sultan had seized an opportunity to kid me about man-eating tigers. Let me point out that what amused him was my wanting to catch one alive. He would have understood my wanting to hunt one down and kill it. But to catch one alive! It seemed such a needless risk. And besides, why prolong the life of one of these killers?

Some time after this session with the Sultan when he made me this handsome present—in 1926, to be exact—I was again in Singapore putting the finishing touches to a splendid collection. My compound was fairly bursting with fine specimens. I had brought back from Siam a fine assortment of argus pheasants, fireback pheasants and many small cage birds. Out of Borneo I had come with a goodly gang of man-like orang-utans and other apes. From Sumatra I had emerged with some fat pythons and a nice group of porcupines, binturongs and civet cats. Celebes had yielded an imposing array of parrots, cockatoos, lories (brush-tongued parrots of a gorgeous coloring),—one of the biggest shipments of these birds I had ever made. My trip to Burmah was represented by a couple of black leopards (more familiarly known as panthers), several gibbons, and a sizeable army of small rhesus monkeys. In addition, I had a number of other specimens picked up along the line.

I was to sail for San Francisco in a couple of weeks. This meant that I would have to make a thorough inspection of my crates and cages to make sure they were all in shape to stand the rigors of a thirty-five or forty-day trip across the Pacific.

With Hin Mong, the Chinese carpenter who had served me for years, I made the rounds of the various boxes, he making notes of new cages and crates that were needed, the ones that required repairs, etc. Mong always seemed to me to be a true genius. A teak-wood tiger-box made by him with the crudest of implements is as fine an example of cabinet work as one could hope to find anywhere.

His cleverness knows no bounds. Working with a home-made saw, a crude chisel made out of a scrap of iron shaped and sharpened on a grind-stone, and a few other primitive tools, he does carpentry that is as finished as if it came out of an up-to-date shop equipped with the finest of tools. Some of it, in fact, is finer than any carpenter work I have ever seen done anywhere. With a couple of chow-boys (apprentices) to assist him, Hin Mong would pitch into any task to which I assigned him and when it was done it was a piece of work to be proud of.

The owner of the house in Katong where I usually lived when in Singapore had sold it, making it necessary for me to move out, although I still maintained my compound there. After the sale of the house I invariably stayed at the Raffles Hotel when in Singapore. I had just returned to my room there, after an early morning session with Hin Mong in the course of which we made a final check-up of the crates and cages, when I was informed that the Sultan of Johore was on the telephone and wished to speak to me at once. Whenever the Sultan telephoned, the information that he was on the wire was passed on to me with much ceremony, sometimes my good friend Aratoon, one of the owners of the hotel, announcing the news in person.

As the morning was still young I was puzzled, for it was most unusual for H. H. to telephone so early. It was a very serious H. H. that spoke to me. He got to his business without any loss of time. Did I still want a man-eating tiger? Well, here was my chance. Breathlessly he told me that a coolie on a rubber plantation twenty-five miles north of Johore Bahru had been seized by a tiger while at work and killed. The animal, a man-eater, had devoured part of the body. Work, of course, was at a standstill on the plantation. The natives were in a state of terror. He (the Sultan) was sending an officer and eight soldiers to war on the killer. It was necessary to show some action at once to ease the minds of his frightened subjects. If I thought I could catch the man-eater alive he would be glad to place the officer and soldiers under my command, with instructions to do my bidding. If, after looking over the situation, it became apparent that in trying to capture the killer alive, we were taking a chance of losing him, he expected me to order the beast immediately shot. He wanted no effort spared in locating the animal. There would be no peace in the minds and hearts of his subjects in the district where the outrage was committed until the cause was removed. In a series of crisp sentences the Sultan got the story off his chest. This was an interesting transition from his lighter manner, the vein in which I most frequently saw him.

Needless to say I leaped at the opportunity to try for a man-eater. H. H. asked me to join him at the fort over in Johore Bahru, which I agreed to do without delay.

At the fort, which is the military headquarters for the State of Johore, the Sultan introduced me to the officer he had selected to assist me, a major with a good record as a soldier and a hunter. He was a quiet little chap, so well-mannered that his courtesy almost seemed exaggerated. (The Malays, by the way, are the best-mannered people in Asia.) His soldiers were a likely looking contingent. It was obvious that H. H. had picked good men to help me with the job.

The major was not in uniform. He was dressed in ordinary rough clothes of European cut. I was interested in the rifle he carried. It was a Savage .303, which most hunters consider too small a gun for tiger-shooting. This capable Malay, however, had killed several tigers with this weapon, the Sultan told me. It took a good man to do that.

The major's command were dressed in the khaki shirts and "shorts" affected by Malay soldiers. They wore heavy stockings that resembled golf hose. If not for the little black Mohammedan caps on their heads and their weapons—(each was armed with a big sword-like knife and a Malayan military rifle)—they might have been taken for a group of boy scouts. A cartridge belt around each man's waist topped off the war-like note.

The major bowed two or three times and announced in his fairly good English that he was ready to start. We departed, the officer and his men piling into a small motor lorry, Ali and I following, in my car. The asphalt roads of Johore are excellent—many of them the work of American road-builders who did a wonderful job of converting stretches of wilderness into fine highways—and we were able to motor to within three miles of the killing. The rest of the journey we made on foot over a jungle trail.

I had requested the Sultan to order the body of the slain coolie left where it was when the killer had finished his work. When we arrived we found a group of excited natives standing around the mangled remains. One leg had been eaten off to the thigh. The animal had also consumed the better part of one shoulder, and to give the job an added touch of thoroughness had gouged deeply into the back of the neck.

Other groups of natives were standing around not far from the body, some of them hysterically jabbering away, some making weird moaning noises, others staring down at the ground in silence. One has to have a good comprehension of the wild world-old superstitions of these natives to appreciate fully what happens inside them when a man-eating tiger appears. All the fanaticism that goes with their belief in strange devils and ogres finds release when a tiger, their enemy of enemies, kills a member of their ranks. They act like a people who consider themselves doomed. Going into a delirium of fear that leaves them weak and spiritless, they become as helpless as little children. Under a strong leadership that suggests a grand unconcern about man-eating tigers, they can be rallied to work against the striped foe; but, until there are definite signs of a possible victory, this work is purely mechanical. The most casual glance reveals that each member of the terrified crew is staring hard at the jungle as he perfunctorily goes through the motions of doing whatever it is you assign him to.

An investigation revealed that the victim of the tiger had been working on a rubber tree when attacked. His tapping knife and latex cup (in which he caught the latex, or sap) were just where they had dropped from his hands when the poor devil was surprised, mute evidence of the suddenness of the assault. Then he had been dragged fifteen or twenty yards into some near-by brush.

Bordering along the jungle wall—as dense and black a stretch of jungle, incidentally, as I have ever seen—was a small pineapple plantation. This was not a commercial grove but a modest affair cultivated by the estate coolies for their own use. An examination of the ground here revealed marks in the dirt that unmistakably were tiger tracks. The tiger's spoor led to a fence made by the natives to keep out wild pigs whose fondness for pineapples had spelled the ruin of more than one plantation. Through a hole in this fence—which could have easily been made by the tiger or might have been there when he arrived, the work of some other animal—the killer's movements could, without the exercise of much ingenuity, be traced in the soft earth across the pineapple grove into the coal black jungle some fifty yards away.

It is no news that a tiger, after gorging himself on his kill, will return to devour the unfinished remains of his feast. If there is no heavy brush within convenient reach he will camouflage those remains with leaves and anything else that is handy for his purpose and go off to his lair. Confident that he has covered his left-overs skillfully enough to fool even the smartest of the vultures, jackals, hyenas and wild dogs, he curls up and enjoys one of those wonderful long sleeps that always follow a good bellyful and which I have always believed to be as much a part of the joy of making a good kill as the actual devouring of it.

I felt, as I studied the situation, that when the tiger returned for the rest of his kill—assuming that this creature would follow regulation lines and re-visit the scene of the slaughter—he would again make use of that hole in the fence. It was a perfectly simple conclusion. Either the animal would not return at all or if he returned he would re-travel his former route.

"*Changkuls! Changkuls! Changkuls!*" I yelled as soon as I decided on a course of action. A *changkul* is a native implement that is widely used on the rubber plantations. It is a combination of shovel and hoe. With the assistance of the major I managed to make it clear to the natives what it was I wanted them to do.

My plan was to dig a hole barely within the borders of the pineapple plantation, so close to the hole in the fence through which the tiger had travelled on his first visit that if he returned and used the same route he would go tumbling down a pit from which there was no return,—except in a cage.

I specified a hole four feet by four feet at the surface. This was to be dug fourteen or fifteen feet deep, the opening widening abruptly at about the halfway mark until at the very bottom it was to be a subterranean room ten feet across.

Soon we had a sizeable gang of natives working away with the *changkuls*. The helpful major, to whom I had given instructions for the pit that was now being dug, bowed a sporting acquiescence to my plan when I knew full well that this accomplished *shikari* who had brought down many tigers with the rifle was aching to go forth into the jungle in quest of the man-eater.

The pit finished, we covered the top with nipa palms. Then we made away with the pile of dirt we had excavated, scattering it at a distance so that the tiger, if he returned, would see no signs of fresh soil. The body was left where it was.

Ali then returned with me to Johore Bahru where I planned to stay overnight at the rest-house adjoining the United Service Club. Before leaving I placed the soldiers on guard at the coolie lines with instructions to keep the natives within those lines.

The coolie lines on a rubber plantation correspond to the headquarters of a big ranch in this country. There is a row of shacks in which the natives live, a store where they buy their provisions, etc. My idea was to give the tiger every possible chance to return. Too much activity near the stretch of ground where the body lay might have made him over-cautious.

Early the next morning the soldiers were to examine the pit. If luck was with us and the tiger was a prisoner, a Chinese boy on the estate who owned a bicycle that he had learned to ride at a merry clip was to head for the nearest military post—(there is a whole series of them, very few jungle crossroads in Johore being without one)—and notify the authorities who in turn would immediately communicate with the fort at Johore Bahru.

The next morning no word had been received at the fort. At noon I drove back to the rubber plantation to see if there was anything I could do. The situation was unchanged. There were no signs of the tiger. No one had seen him, not even the most imaginative native with a capacity for seeing much that wasn't visible to the normal eye.

The body of the mangled native was decomposing. Though I did not like to alter my original plan, I acquiesced when the natives appealed to me to let them give their fallen comrade a Mohammedan burial (the Malay version thereof). They put the body in a box and carried it off for interment.

The major did not conceal his desire to go off into the jungle with his men to seek the killer there. He was characteristically courteous, bowing politely as he spoke and assuring me that he had nothing but respect for my plan. Yes, the *tuan's* idea was a good one,—doubtless it might prove successful under different circumstances—but it was not meeting with any luck, and would I consider him too bold if he suggested beating about the near-by jungle with his men in an effort to trace the eater of the coolie?

What could I say? My plan had not accomplished anything and we were no closer to catching our man-eater than when we first got to work. I readily assented, stipulating only that the pit remain as it was, covered with nipa palms and ready for a victim—though if the animal returned after the number of hours that had elapsed, it would be performing freakishly.

There was no point in my staying there. So, when the major went off into the jungle with his men, I left the scene, returning to Singapore with Ali. I still had considerable work to do before the big collection of animals and birds in my compound would be ready for shipment to America.

I felt badly all the way back to Singapore. Here was the first chance I had ever had to take a man-eating tiger and I had failed. Perhaps I was not at fault—after all, the business of capturing animals is not an exact science—but just the same I was returning without my man-eater and I was bitterly disappointed. Ali did his best to cheer me up but all he succeeded in doing was to remind me over and over again that I had failed. Using words sparingly and gestures freely, he tried to communicate the idea that after all a man could worry through life without a man-eating tiger. In an effort to change the expression on my face he grinned like an ape and made movements with his hands designed, I am sure, to convey the idea of gaiety. He wasn't helping a bit. Feeling that I was too strongly resisting his efforts to buck me up, he grew peeved and resorted to his old trick of wrinkling up his nose. This drew from me the first laugh I had had in several days. Seeing me laugh, Ali broke into a laugh too, wrinkling up his nose a few times more by way of showing me a thoroughly good time.

When we returned to Singapore I kept in touch with the situation by telephone, the fort reporting that though the major and his men had combed every inch of the jungle for some distance around, they found no trace of the killer. The major gave it as his opinion that the beast had undoubtedly left the district and that further search would accomplish nothing.

"Well, that's that," I said to myself as I prepared to busy myself in the compound with the many tasks that were waiting for me there.

The third day, very early in the morning, just as I was beginning to dismiss from my mind the events that had taken place on that rubber plantation, I received a telegram from the Sultan of Johore which, with dramatic suddenness, announced that the tiger had dropped into the pit! No one knew exactly when. "Some time last night." Would I hurry to the plantation with

all possible haste? He had tried to reach me by phone and failing this had sent a fast telegram.

Would I? What a question! Perhaps it is unnecessary for me
to say how delighted I was over the prospect of returning to
the plantation to get my man-eating tiger. Ali ran me a close
second, the old boy's joy (much of it traceable to my own, no
doubt, for Ali was usually happy when I was) being wonderful
to behold.

We climbed into the car and set out for the plantation at a
terrific clip. At least half the way we travelled at the rate
of seventy miles an hour, very good work for the battered bus
I was driving.

When we arrived the natives were packed deep around the
sides of the pit. Never have I witnessed such a change in
morale. There was no suggestion of rejoicing—for the natives
endow tigers with supernatural powers and they do not consider themselves safe in the presence of one unless he's dead or
inside a cage—but they were again quick in their movements. A
determined-looking crew, they could now be depended upon for
real assistance.

In addition to the crowd of coolies, the group near the pit
included the major and his soldiers and a white man and his
wife from a near-by plantation. The woman, camera in hand, was
trying to take a picture. Even in the wilds of Johore one is
not safe from invasion by those terrible amateurs to whom nothing means anything but the occasion for taking another picture. I
distinctly recall that one of my first impulses on arriving on the
scene was to heave the lady to the tiger and then toss in her
chatterbox of a husband for good measure. This no doubt estab-
lishes a barbarous strain in me.

I ploughed my way through the crowd to the mouth of the pit.
The natives had rolled heavy logs over the opening, driven heavy
stakes and lashed the cover down with rattan.

"*Apa ini?*" I inquired. "*Apa ini?*" [What is this?]

"Oh, *tuan! harimu besar!*" came the chorused reply, the gist of
it being that our catch was a "great, big, enormous tiger." I
loosened a couple of the logs, making an opening through which

I could peer down into the pit. Stretching out on my stomach, I took a look at the prisoner below, withdrawing without the loss of much time when the animal, an enormous creature, made a terrific lunge upward, missing my face with his paw by not more than a foot.

This was all I needed to convince me that the natives had shown intelligence in covering the mouth of the pit with those heavy logs. I did not believe that the beast could have escaped if the covering was not there; yet he was of such a tremendous size that it was barely possible he could pull himself out by sinking his claws into the side of the pit after taking one of those well-nigh incredible leaps.

The business of getting that tiger out of the pit presented a real problem. This was due to his size. I had not calculated on a monster like this, a great cat that could leap upward to within a foot of the mouth of the pit.

Ordinarily it is not much of a job to get a tiger out of a pit. After baiting it with a couple of fresh-killed chickens, a cage with a perpendicular slide door is lowered. An assistant holds a rope which when released drops the door and makes the tiger a captive as soon as he decides to enter the cage for the tempting morsels within, which he will do when he becomes sufficiently hungry. A variation on this procedure, though not as frequently used, is to lower a box without a bottom over the tiger. This is arduous labor, requiring plenty of patience, but it is a method that can be employed successfully when the circumstances are right. When you have the box over the tiger and it is safely weighted down, you drop into the pit, slip a sliding bottom under the box and yell to the boys overhead to haul away at the ropes.

It was obvious that neither of these methods would do in this case. I simply could not get around the fact that I had under-estimated the size of the man-eater and had not ordered a deep enough pit. Our catch was so big that if we lowered a box he could scramble to the top of it in one well-aimed leap and jump out of the hole in another. Ordinary methods would not do. They were too dangerous.

I finally hit upon a plan, and, as a good part of the morning was still ahead of us, I decided to tear back to Singapore for the supplies I needed and race back post-haste and get that striped nuisance out of the pit that day. I could not afford to spend much more time on the plantation. I had so much work waiting for me in connection with that big shipment I was taking to the United States.

My first move on arriving in Singapore was to get hold of Hin Mong and put him and his chow-boys to work at once on a special long, narrow box with a slide door at one end. When I left for my next stop, Mong and his boys had cast aside all other tasks and were excitedly yanking out lumber for my emergency order. Knowing this Chinese carpenter's fondness for needless little fancy touches, I assailed his ears before departing with a few emphatic words to the effect that this was to be a plain job and that he was not to waste any time on the frills so dear to his heart.

Leaving Mong's, I headed for the bazaars where I bought three or four hundred feet of strong native rope made of jungle fibres. Next I went to the Harbor Works and borrowed a heavy block and tackle. Then I hired a motor truck.

When I added to this collection an ordinary Western lasso, which I learned to use as a boy in Texas, I was ready to return to the rubber plantation for my tiger. While on the subject of that lasso, it might be appropriate to point out that the public gave Buffalo Jones one long horse laugh when he announced his intention of going to Africa and roping big game, and that not long afterwards the laugh was on the public, for Buffalo serenely proceeded to do exactly what he said he would. I have never gone in for that sort of thing but my rope which is always kept handy has been useful many times, even a crane, a valuable specimen, having been lassoed on the wing as it sailed out over the ship's side after a careless boy had left its shipping box open.

When the box was made,—and though Hin Mong and his chow-boys threw it together hastily it was a good strong piece of work—I loaded it and the coil of rope and the block and tackle onto the truck and sent this freight on its way to the rubber plantation, putting it in charge of Ali's nephew who was then acting as his uncle's assistant at the compound. I gave him a driver and two other boys and sent them on their journey after Ali had given his nephew instructions on how to reach the rubber plantation. Four boys were needed to carry the supplies the three miles from the end of the road through the jungle trail to the plantation.

My own car, which had carried Ali and me on so many other important trips, carried us again. Our only baggage was my lasso which I had dropped on the floor of this speedy but badly mutilated conveyance of mine that for want of a better name I called an automobile.

As I had not seen the Sultan since the day he turned his major and those eight soldiers over to me I decided to drop in on him on the way to the rubber plantation.

Having learned he was at the fort, I headed for these glorified barracks, where H. H. greeted me effusively. He came out of the fort as we pulled up, leaning over the side of the car. Two or three times he congratulated me on my success in getting the tiger into the pit. Then, very solemnly,—(and for half a second I didn't realize that he had reverted to his bantering manner)—he said, "Glad you stop here before you go take tiger from pit. I would never forgive you if you did not say good-bye before tiger eat you."

Laughing, I told H. H., whose eyes were resting on the lasso at the bottom of the car, "You don't seem very confident, do you?"

"Confident?" came the reply. "Sure! You going to catch tiger with rope like cowboy, no? Very simple, this method, no? Very simple. Why you don't try catch elephant this way too? Very simple." Then the Sultan broke into one of those hearty roars of his, slapping his thighs as he doubled up with laughter.

"Don't you think I can do it, H. H.?" I asked.

Tactfully, he declined to answer with a yes or a no. All he said was, "This is tiger, not American cow." This was more eloquent than a dozen noes.

"I'll tell you what, H. H.," I said. "I'll make a little bet with you, just for the fun of it. I'll bet you a bottle of champagne that I'll have that tiger alive in Johore Bahru before the sun goes down." H. H. never could be induced to make a wager for money with a friend; that's why I stipulated wine.

"I bet you," he grinned. "But how I can collect if tiger eat you?" (Turning to Ali with mock sternness.) "Ali, you do not forget that your *tuan* owe me bottle champagne if he do not come back!" Then he blew himself to another one of those body-shaking laughs of his.

We were off in a few minutes. Clouds were gathering overhead and it looked like rain. I wanted to get my job over with before the storm broke. Stepping on the gas, I waved a good-bye to H. H., and we were on our way.

I was worried by the overcast skies but I did not regard the impending storm as a serious obstacle. It looked like a "Sumatra," a heavy rain and wind-storm of short duration, followed by bright sunshine that always seems freakish to those who do not know the East. The chief difficulty imposed by the storm, in the event that it broke, would be the slippery footing that would result. A secondary problem would be the stiffening of the ropes. Rope when it has been well exposed to rain, hardens somewhat, although it can be handled. If it rained, my job would be so much tougher.

We tore along at maximum speed, my engine heralding our approach all along the line with a mighty roar. Considering the terrific racket, I had a right to expect the speedometer to indicate a new speed record instead of a mere seventy an hour. My bus always got noisy when I opened her up, reminding me of a terrier trying to bark like a St. Bernard.

The skies grew darker as we raced along and when we were a short distance from the point where it was necessary to complete the journey on foot a light rain started to fall. By the time we were halfway to the plantation it was raining hard and Ali and I were nicely drenched when we arrived.

The rain had driven many of the coolies to cover but at least a score of them were still standing around when we pulled up. The major and his soldiers, soaked to the skin, stood by faithfully, the major even taking advantage of this inopportune moment to congratulate me again—(he had done it before)—on my trapping of the man-eater. I appreciated this sporting attitude after the failure of his search in the jungle. However, I didn't feel very triumphant. The tough part of the job was ahead of me. Getting a tiger out of a pit into a cage in a driving rain-storm is dangerous, strenuous work.

I got busy at once. Taking out my knife, I began cutting my coil of native rope into extra nooses. This done, I knocked aside some of the stakes that secured the pit's cover, rolled away some of the logs, and, stretching out flat with my head and shoulders extending out over the hole, began to make passes at the roaring enemy below with my lasso rope. One advantage of the rain was that it weakened the tiger's footing, making it impossible for him to repeat the tremendous leap upward he had made earlier in the day when I took my first look down the pit. As I heard him sloshing around in the mud and water at the bottom of his prison, I felt reassured. If the rain put me at a disadvantage, it did the same thing to the enemy.

With the major standing by, rifle ready for action, I continued to fish for the tiger with my rope, the black skies giving me bad light by which to work. Once I got the lay of the land I managed to drop the rope over the animal's head but before I could pull up the slack—(the rain had made the rope "slow")—he flicked it off with a quick movement of the paw. A second time I got it over his head but this time his problem was even easier for the fore-part of the stiffening slack landed close enough to his mouth to enable him to bite the rope in two with one snap. Making a new loop in the lasso I tried over and over but he either eluded my throw or fought free of the noose with lightning-fast movements in which teeth and claws worked together in perfect coordination as he snarled his contempt for my efforts. The rain continued to come down in torrents. When it rains in Johore, it rains,—an ordinary Occidental rain-storm being a mere sprinkle compared to an honest-to-goodness "Sumatra."

By now I was so thoroughly drenched I no longer minded the rain on my body; it was only when the water dripped down into my eyes that I found myself growing irritated.

After working in this fashion for an hour till my shoulders

ached from the awkward position I was in, I succeeded in loop-
ing a noose over the animal's head and through his mouth, using
a fairly dry fresh rope that responded when I gave it a quick
jerk. This accomplished my purpose, which was to draw the
corners of his mouth inward so that his lips were stretched taut
over his teeth, making it impossible for him to bite through the
rope without biting through his lips. I yelled to the coolies who
were standing by ready for action to tug away at the rope, which
they did, pulling the crouching animal's head and forequarters
clear of the bottom of the pit. This was the first good look at
the foe I had had. The eyes hit me the hardest. Small for the
enormous head, they glared an implacable hatred.

Quickly bringing another rope into play, I ran a second hitch
around the struggling demon's neck, another group of coolies
(also working under Ali's direction) pulling away at this rope
from the side of the pit opposite the first rope-hold. It was no
trouble, with two groups of boys holding the animal's head and
shoulders up, to loop a third noose under the fore legs and a
fourth under the body. Working with feverish haste, I soon had
eight different holds on the man-eater of Johore. With coolies
tugging away at each line, we pulled the monster up nearly even
with the top of the pit and held him there. His mouth, distorted
with rage plus what the first rope was doing to it, was a hideous
sight. With his hind legs he was thrashing away furiously, also
doing his frantic best to get his roped fore legs into action.

I was about to order the lowering of the box when one of the
coolies let out a piercing scream. He was No. 1 boy on the first
rope. Looking around I saw that he had lost his footing in the
slippery mud, and, in his frenzied efforts to save himself, was
sliding head first for the mouth of the pit. I was in a position
where I could grab him but I went at it so hard that I lost my
own footing and the both of us would have rolled over into the
pit if Ali, who was following me around with an armful of extra
nooses hadn't quickly grabbed me and slipped one of these ropes
between my fingers. With a quick tug, he and one of the soldiers
pulled us out of danger.

The real menace, if the coolie and I had rolled over into the pit was that the other coolies would probably have lost their heads and let go the ropes. With them holding on there was no serious danger, for the tiger was firmly lashed.

I've wondered more than once what would have occurred if the native and I had gone splashing to the bottom of that hole. Every time I think of it, it gives me the creeps; for though the coolies at the ropes were dependable enough when their *tuan* was around to give them orders, they might easily have gone to pieces, as I've frequently seen happen, had they suddenly decided that they were leaderless. It wouldn't have been much fun at the bottom of the pit with this brute of a tiger.

The coolies shrieked but they held. The rain continued to come down in sheets and the ooze around the pit grew worse and worse. Self-conscious now about the slipperiness, the boys were finding it harder than ever to keep their feet.

The box would have to be lowered at once. With the tiger's head still almost even with the surface of the pit, we let the box down lengthwise, slide door end up. Unable to get too close, we had to manipulate the box with long poles. The hind legs had sufficient play to enable the animal to strike out with them, and time after time, after we painstakingly manœuvered the cage into position with the open slide door directly under him, our enraged captive would kick it away. In the process the ropes gave a few inches, indicating that the strain was beginning to be too much for the boys. If we were forced to let the animal drop back after getting him to this point, it was a question if we'd ever be able to get him out alive.

Quickly I went over the situation with Ali. I was growing desperate. With the aid of the major and three of his soldiers we got the box firmly in place, the tired boys at the ropes responding to a command to tug away that lifted the animal a few inches above the point where his thrashing hind legs interfered with keeping it erect. I assigned the three soldiers to keeping the box steady with poles which they braced against it. If we shifted the box again in the ooze we might lose our grip on it, so I cautioned them to hold it as it was.

"Major, I'm now leaving matters in your hands," I said. "See

that the boys hold on and keep your rifle ready." Before he
had a chance to reply I let myself down into the pit, dodging
the flying back feet. Covered with mud from head to foot as
a result of my dropping into the slime, I grabbed the tiger by
his tail, swung him directly over the opening of the box and fairly
roared: "Let go!" Let go they did, with me leaning on the box
to help steady it.

The man-eater of Johore dropped with a bang to the bottom
of Hin Mong's plainest box. I slid the door to with a slam,
leaned against it and bellowed for hammer and nails. I could
feel the imprisoned beast pounding against the sides of his cell
as he strove to free himself from the tangle of ropes around him.
His drop, of necessity, had folded up his hind legs and I didn't
see how he could right himself sufficiently in that narrow box for
a lunge against the door at the top; but the brute weighed at least
three hundred pounds, and if his weight shifted over against me
he might, in my tired condition, knock me over and—

"Get the hammer and nails!" I screamed. "Damn it, hurry
up!" I leaned against the box with all my strength, pressing it
against one side of the pit to hold the sliding door firmly closed.

No hammer! No nails!

Plastered with mud, my strength rapidly ebbing, I was in a
fury over the delay.

"*Kasi pacoo!* [Bring nails!]" I shrieked in Malay, in case
my English was not understood. "Nails! *Pacoo!* Nails!" I
cried. "And a hammer, you helpless swine!" There weren't any
swine present but that's what I called everyone at the moment.
I felt the tiger's weight shifting against me and I was mad with
desperation.

The major yelled down that no one could find the nails. The
can had been kicked over and the nails were buried in the mud.
They had the hammer. . . . Here she goes! I caught it. . . .
What the hell good is a hammer without nails?

"Give me nails, dammit, or I'll murder the pack of you!"

It was Ali who finally located the nails, buried in the mud,
after what seemed like a week and was probably a couple of
minutes. Over the side of the pit he scrambled to join me in a

splash of mud. With a crazy feverishness I wielded the hammer while Ali held the nails in place, and at last Johore's coolie-killer was nailed down fast. Muffled snarls and growls of rage came through the crevices, left for breathing space.

Then I recall complaining to Ali that the storm must be getting worse. It was getting blacker. The *tuan* was wrong. The storm was letting up. Perhaps I mistook the mud that splashed over me as I fell to the floor of the pit, too weak to stand up, for extra heavy rain drops.

Ali lifted me to my feet and my brain cleared. I suddenly realized that the job was all done, that the man-eater of Johore was in that nailed-down box. I was overjoyed. Only a man in my field can fully realize the thrill I experienced over the capture of this man-eating tiger,—the first, to my knowledge, ever brought to the United States.

Ropes were fastened around the box,—(no one feared entering the pit now)—and with the aid of the block and tackle, our freight was hauled out of the hole.

Eight coolies were needed to get our capture back through the slime that was once a dry jungle trail to the highway leading to Johore Bahru. More than once they almost dropped their load, which they bore on carrying poles, as they skidded around in the three miles of sticky muck between the rubber plantation and the asphalt road which now reflected the sunlight, wistfully re-appearing in regulation fashion after the rain and wind of the "Sumatra." There we loaded the box onto the waiting lorry, which followed Ali and me in my car.

About forty minutes later as the sun bathed the channel in the reddish glow of its vanishing rays, I planted the man-eater under the nose of the Sultan in front of the United Service Club in Johore Bahru.

With more mud on me than anyone that ever stood at the U.S.C.'s bar, I collected my bet, the hardest-earned champagne I ever tasted.

The Sultan was so respectful after I won this wager that once or twice I almost wished I hadn't caught his damned man-eater. H. H. is much more fun when he's not respectful. I enjoyed his pop-eyed felicitations but not nearly so much as some of the playful digs he's taken at me.

The man-eater of Johore, by the way, eventually wound up in the Longfellow Zoological Park, in Minneapolis, Minn.

Baby Boo

IT all started when an animal dealer in Los Angeles cabled me in Singapore asking me to secure for him a female baby elephant under three feet in height. The animal was wanted for work in the movies.

This may not sound like a very difficult assignment. It was every bit of that, however. In fact, I was being asked to produce an elephant shorter in stature than any in the whole United States. If the cable had read, "We want elephant smaller than any now in captivity," it would have meant exactly the same thing as asking me to secure one less than three feet tall.

Some years before, I had brought back from Asia as small an elephant as I had ever known to find its way to these shores,—a little lady named Mitzi who became quite a famous vaudevillian. Mitzi stood three and a half feet high. For years she played with the well-known vaudeville act, Singer's Midgets, travelling with the troupe till she outgrew the midgets.

I couldn't for the life of me figure out how I was going to produce a baby elephant smaller than Mitzi, the most diminutive member of the species I had ever secured.

However, an order is an order and I was more than willing to make a determined effort to secure what the Los Angeles dealer wanted. I had hundreds of other specimens to collect, and, in the process of gathering them together, I planned to make inquiries wherever I went—(my program promising to carry me practically all over the map of Asia)—in an effort to locate a trunked shrimp short enough to meet the specifications.

Ali, who accompanied me on this trip, was instructed to be on the lookout for small elephants and to give me any and all information he picked up. I've been at this business of collecting animals and birds so long that I am known to scores of Asiatic traders, *shikaris*, headmen and others and wherever I go people come to me, and the boy who's travelling with me, with information about specimens of all kinds that are available.

In Siam we heard that the *keddah walla* north of the town of Alostar, with whom I had traded in the past, had some very small elephants in his sheds. However, when I arrived to inspect his stock, I found that he had nothing under four feet eight inches. Wherever I went it was the same. Small elephants were available but nothing under four or four and a half feet.

Collecting activities brought me back to Calcutta and while there I heard that a work elephant at Silaguri had given birth to a calf. As soon as I could get away, I made the trip to Silaguri, only to find the youngster had not survived.

All in all, I investigated at least a dozen different tips, none of them yielding what was wanted.

It was now necessary for me to go to Singapore with the various animals and birds I had collected on these trips. While there I wired the Los Angeles dealer that I had had no success but that I would keep on trying. I wasn't very hopeful of securing the Lilliputian he sought, and, while I was perfectly willing to continue the search, I didn't want this dealer to be too optimistic about the prospects.

A few weeks later Ali and I were in Sumatra scouting around for pythons, gibbons, binturongs and other specimens for which I had orders. We were at Domji, a port on the west coast of Sumatra, north of Palembang. The news of my arrival had spread and several native trappers sought me out with their wares, most of them specimens that were undesirable.

After I had turned down a number of animals, reptiles and birds that I did not want, I was approached by a Batik native who had a few specimens that were worth picking up, although they were not important contributions. Setting down in front of the nipa house where I was staying the two baskets that he bore on his shoulder on a carrying pole, he proceeded to show me his wares. One basket contained a pair of fine big hornbills, the other housed a big monitor lizard, a five-foot creature that was rolled up in the container with its feet trussed up over its back.

These specimens were in excellent condition, and, as I knew I could dispose of them, I was glad to pick them up.

"Berapa?" I asked, pointing to the hornbills. ("How much?")

The reply was a question. Did the *tuan* have any tobacco?

I nodded my head. I always carry plenty of tobacco, not only because I smoke a good deal but because it is frequently very useful in trading with the natives.

With the aid of Ali (my own knowledge of the Malay dialect this fellow spoke proving inadequate) I learned I could have the birds for eight ounces of tobacco. The tobacco available in that part of the world comes in twisted sticks, three ounces to the stick. I would have gladly given him three sticks, or nine ounces, but I was afraid he might decide there was something wrong with the tobacco,—something of the sort having happened to me before—so I decided to give him exactly what he wanted. I sent Ali into the house for three sticks of tobacco. Then I took out an old pocket knife and proceeded to cut one of the pieces at the two-thirds mark (two and two-thirds sticks totalling the eight ounces he named as his price).

I handed him his tobacco and he handed me the birds. He was greatly pleased with his bargain, promptly spitting out his betel nut and biting off a mouthful of tobacco to take its place. (Many Asiatics are more interested in tobacco as something to chew than they are in its smoking possibilities.)

Next I asked this native what he wanted for his lizard. He suddenly became very coy, looking down at the ground and putting his hand to his face as if to conceal a blush.

"Berapa?" I repeated.

No answer.

I suggested five guilders.

He shook his head.

I was puzzled. Five guilders was a good price for that lizard. I asked him what he wanted.

Looking up, he beckoned to Ali who walked over to where he stood. Leaning over, he whispered something in Ali's ear.

Ali looked up, grinning.

"What does he want?" I asked.

Ali, still grinning, told me that the native wanted my knife. He had taken a fancy to it when I took it out to cut the tobacco. He didn't feel right about asking for it, Ali told me, but would deeply appreciate it if I could bring myself to part with it for the lizard. He didn't want my five guilders. He knew that he was asking a great deal in suggesting that I part with my precious knife but if I would consent to the deal, he would be so happy. Perhaps some time in the future when I returned to this part of the world there would be some way in which he could reciprocate.

Ten years before I had bought that knife in America for seventy-five cents. Yet this fellow preferred it to the five guilders ($1.80) that I offered him for his lizard. Of such strange turns is the business of trading with natives comprised.

I readily agreed to trade the knife for the lizard. The simple fellow was delighted with his bargain. He eagerly grabbed the knife,—an ordinary bone-handle affair, with a sizeable main blade and two smaller ones—fondling it as if it were something of infinite worth. Finally he put his treasure in his pocket and jauntily started away.

About ten yards off, he turned around and shouted, *"Berapa ada kechil gajah?"* [How much would you give for a little elephant?]

I had ceased to think about my need for a midget pachyderm. Although I had not given up, the subject had slipped out of my consciousness. The press of other business, involving specimens that were more available, was responsible.

Both Ali and I were excited when the subject was so unexpectedly reopened. We called the native back.

We asked him how big the elephant was. With his hand he indicated a height of about four feet. I shook my head and Ali, resorting to his favorite method of registering disgust, wrinkled up his nose.

That was too big, we told him. Whereupon the obliging soul started protesting that the animal he had in mind wasn't that big at all. It was only so big (indicating a height of about two and a half feet which he gradually decreased until finally his hand was not more than ten inches from the ground).

I was so amused by this exaggeration that I started laughing. Ali was not ready to be as amused as I was, having his private opinion of natives that lied so outrageously, but he did decide that the occasion did not call for too much seriousness for he actually stopped wrinkling up his nose when my laughter reached his ears, confining himself to spitting at the ground, his method of registering fair-to-middling displeasure. When, as I continued to eye the Batik liar who was still stooped over indicating with his hand a height of ten inches, I continued to chuckle, Ali even smiled faintly.

I started questioning the native about his ten-inch elephant. Pressed for a description of the animal, he mentioned the fact that there was hair all over it. This had the effect of making us take the fellow seriously. Regardless of the beast's exact measurements, if it was covered with hair it was bound to be a fairly recent calf and might easily be under three feet. Another thing that encouraged me was the fact that in answer to my question he told me, without hesitation, that the animal was a female. He had no way of telling that what I wanted was a female.

I decided to take a chance and investigate. The Batik's village, it developed, was about fifteen miles off. He had walked all that distance to dispose of his hornbills and his lizard.

Within half an hour Ali, the Batik and I were seated in a bullock cart on our way to investigate the little elephant with the fuzz on it. A baby elephant, when born, is covered with hair, this gradually wearing off as the animal grows up.

Ali was suspicious of our new acquaintance. He even hinted that this native was holding out the promise of a rarity merely to get us so excited we would want to make the trip at once, thus enabling him to get a ride home and rest his weary bones after his long walk to Domji. A rascal capable of promising you a ten-inch elephant was capable of anything, he insisted.

I'm all for taking chances. I've secured some of my finest specimens that way. Needless to say, I've been hoodwinked too, but I always set forth on a mission of this kind willing to trust to luck. If I get the breaks, fine; if I don't, what of it? I know one man, a German collector who might have made a reputation if he had been less suspicious, who very often failed to investigate tips from natives for fear that someone might be trying to put something over on him. He was so careful not to let anyone send him off on a wild goose chase—(he'd show those natives whether they could fool him!)—that on several occasions he just missed picking up some very rare specimens. I know because I beat him to it on more than one of those occasions.

My Batik tipster was wreathed in smiles all the way back to his village. The pleasure he got out of acquiring my knife was almost incredible. He would turn it over in his hand, hold it out and regard it ecstatically, turn it over again and finally put it away. Then he would suddenly think of it again and out it would come, this time perhaps for a few minutes of whittling, or for use in cutting off a piece of tobacco. In fact, he got so much fun out of keeping the implement in use that he cut and chewed more pieces of tobacco on that trip than he probably used in the course of two or three normal days.

After a journey of four hours we arrived at our destination. The native took us to a tapioca garden in back of the village headman's shack. There, with a rope around its neck, and looking terribly thin and emaciated, stood the smallest baby elephant I had ever seen. With the carpenter's rule I had taken with me I measured it and found it to be just two inches under three feet, at the shoulder, which is how elephants are measured. As my informant had told me, it was a hairy little tot, and couldn't have been over ten or twelve days old.

Weak and wobbly, the little babe—(a female, as the native had said)—seemed to be supporting herself with difficulty, her trembliness and starved appearance suggesting that the headman and his four partners, who owned the elephant jointly, had not had much success in feeding their captive. The task of getting food inside a baby elephant that has been suddenly taken away from its mother usually presents real difficulties.

I said to the headman. "What good is your elephant? She's going to die of starvation." I'd have given the creature two more days to live under the conditions that prevailed when I found her.

I was mistaken, the headman insisted. The animal was in excellent condition,—the finest, strongest, best-nourished baby elephant he had ever seen. The fellow evidently thought I was a greenhorn. Never had I seen a baby animal in worse shape.

Yes, the baby was in splendid condition. (The gist of what the headman was feelingly shouting.) Hadn't she been eating bananas? (His four partners nodded their heads.) And was there anything more nourishing than bananas? (Again the four yes-men did their stuff.) Wasn't it a heart-warming joy to see the sweet little thing take a banana in its trunk and eat it? (This time the ever-ready quartet chorused their affirmation, struggling for a note of wistfulness as they O.K.'d the tender picture projected by the spokesman.)

The more the headman spoke the worse his story got. An elephant as young as the one that stood tottering before us doesn't know what its trunk is for. It is so much loose flesh limply dangling from its head, and it has a tough time getting it out of the way when it sucks its mother.

"All right," I said, "let's see you feed her a banana." I got tired of hearing the old dodo tell me that the elephant could take *pisang makan* (banana for food) and I decided to call his bluff. A banana was secured and the headman proceeded to demonstrate. This consisted of an effort to wrap the end of the animal's trunk around the fruit. The bewildered little pachyderm was unable to give the faker any cooperation, having no control over her floppy little trunk. Time after time the banana would fall to the ground.

After five or six failures, in the course of which Ali and I swapped winks, one of the partnership quartet came to the rescue. The animal had eaten six bananas just before my arrival! He'd forgotten all about it. Then his comrades came to life and they remembered the incident too. Why, of course! That explained everything. One couldn't very well expect a little elephant like that to eat a banana so soon after it had consumed the other six.

"You see?" smiled the headman after the convenient four had Explained All.

I nodded (restraining a smile, for I didn't want these rogues to know how much fun I was getting out of their crude efforts to fool me). Yes, I saw. (The headman beamed happily, thinking he had convinced me.) I was dealing, I quickly added, with a cheat who was trying to sell me an animal that he knew to be doomed on account of his inability to get food into its stomach. (The headman's expression changed. Again he took on his protesting manner, vowing by all that was sacred that he was an honest man who was being grossly misunderstood.) He turned and asked his partners if it wasn't a fact that he was an honest man. (They almost nodded their heads off.) Was there a more honest man in the whole district? (Four emphatic shakes of the head.)

"See?"

I still didn't see.

I wanted the elephant. It was in very bad condition but I felt I might be able to save it. Naturally I did not feel like paying a good deal. The risk was too great. It wouldn't have surprised me if the shaky little creature had curled up and died that very day. It was as frail as a Christmas tree ornament and about as valuable unless I could devise some means of making it eat.

The headman's object, of course, was to establish that he was selling me an elephant in perfect health and to be paid accordingly. I didn't know what the market price that day was for food-refusing, half-dead baby elephants, so I was forced to consult my own index of values. I quickly decided what was a fair price to pay for this wobbly little pachyderm and resolved that once I made my offer I would stick to my story.

The headman, switching tactics, decided to feign independence. If I was unwilling to buy the animal as a perfect specimen, he knew someone that was. He and his associates were rattan gatherers and they were anxious to return to the jungle to resume their work. If he did not get his price from me, he would have to start negotiations with another prospect that was in the district.

I decided to call his bluff. "All right," I said, "go ahead. . . .

Come, Ali." We started to go. As we left, a violent argument broke out among the headman and his four partners. Evidently they were accusing him of gumming up the deal. There was much name-calling and for a while it looked as if they would come to blows. Ali, looking over his shoulder, told me that the native who had brought us there was trying to pacify them, evidently in an effort to earn the commission that would be his if a deal took place.

Suddenly the headman started running after us, inspired no doubt by the words of our Domji friend. With the four partners following him, the spokesman pulled up alongside me and pantingly pleaded with me to take the elephant off his hands. I knew he realized full well that anything he got would be so much velvet, for the animal could not survive much longer in the state it was in. None of them knew enough about the species to figure out a way of making a food-declining baby elephant eat; and there was apparently no one in the district that could or would help them solve this problem of providing nourishment.

I decided to close the deal without wasting any more time. Taking out ten ten-guilder notes (I had fixed on one hundred guilders as the maximum that a half-dead baby elephant was worth) I handed them to the headman, saying: *"Bagi lima."* [Divide this among the five of you.]

The headman counted the money and smiled, apparently greatly pleased with the deal. His partners, pleased too, added their smiles to their spokesman's and soon everybody was happy, including the native who had given us the tip, this chap proceeding to collect his commission.

Their problem was over but mine had just began. I had to get some food into that elephant's belly,—and without much loss of time. I sent Ali out to scout around for a milk-goat. He brought one back and hurriedly milked it. I tried to pour some milk down the stubborn pachyderm's throat but I couldn't get her jaws open. Once or twice I managed to get them partly open but before I could pour the milk down she closed them again.

I considered five or six different plans for feeding that animal, dismissing them as impractical as fast as they popped into my head. Then I got an idea that I thought was worth trying. The first step was to send Ali to a near-by clump to cut me a length of bamboo. As is commonly known, a stick of bamboo is made up of a series of joints, the wood being hollow between joints. Ali brought back exactly what I had sent him for, a piece of bamboo about two inches in diameter. I cut off a piece about nine inches long, leaving the joint to form the bottom. This gave me a device which I planned to use as a feeding tube. I sharpened the opening till it came to a point, and, satisfied that I was on the right track, I proceeded with the next step.

Before this could be carried out we had to get our elephant— (we practically carried her)—to the shack where we had arranged to spend the night. I instructed Ali to boil some rice in water. When the rice was cooked I mixed some goat's milk with it, the result being a thin but nutritious gruel. Then I proceeded to fill my bamboo tube with this substance.

This done, Ali got his shoulder right under the elephant's fore-quarters till she was almost standing on her back legs. Then I forced the point of the bamboo tube between her tightly closed jaws, gradually working it in until I could tip it up and dump the contents down her throat. Stubborn to the last, she tried to keep from swallowing, giving in after a few seconds of gurgling. A second tubeful was prepared and the operation was repeated, this time the task proving less difficult. In all, I fed her three tubes of gruel that session.

An hour later I put the obstinate little girl to bed, covering her up with some old gunny sacks. The following morning there was a definite improvement in her condition, some of the wobbliness having disappeared. We gave her her breakfast, repeating the performance with the tube. This time it was unnecessary to prop her up.

A little later in the morning we put her on a bullock cart and took her back to Domji, from where she was transported, along with my other specimens to Singapore. We had no trouble feeding her en route, the bamboo feeding tube working perfectly.

As soon as I reached Singapore I cabled the Los Angeles dealer that I had a female baby elephant under three feet, which he could have for $2,000. I received a prompt acceptance.

I installed the midget pachyderm in my compound, and, within a week after her arrival there, she had developed so complete an interest in food that if I took out the bamboo tube she would follow me all over the lot. By the time I was ready to return to America she was in splendid condition, full of life, alert, and a wee bit mischievous. A loveable animal, she became a great favorite on board ship, the crew taking a particular fancy to her.

I exercised her regularly on deck, one of my principal difficulties being to get her past the full-grown elephants I was bringing back. She would try to get chummy with them, nuzzling against their legs and making other friendly advances.

She was an amusing sight when she began to learn to use her trunk. She developed a sudden consciousness of the uses to which this part of her, till now a dangling impediment, could be put. Gaining control of it, she would swing it in all directions, delighted with the discovery that this was something she could make do her bidding, like her legs. All the way across the Pacific she kept it in action, like a child captivated with a new and interesting toy. For the benefit of "company" she would promptly show off, swinging that little trunk till I thought it would come off.

When I arrived in San Francisco the dealer who had ordered this baby elephant was waiting for me on the dock. He was delighted with his acquisition, the little lady from Sumatra being exactly what he wanted. I turned her over to him together with three of my bamboo feeding tubes, instructing him how to use them.

Not long afterwards she became a movie queen, under the name of Baby Boo. Someone gave her this sobriquet in Los Angeles and it stuck.

One day Baby Boo was being filmed in a picture in which Al St. John was the featured player. To create a desired effect, it was necessary for the camera to catch the little elephant on the run. Baby Boo was not in the mood for running. Coaxing availed nothing. Either she didn't get the idea or she had decided that she didn't want to run, as she had once decided that she didn't want to eat.

The cameraman was frantic. The director was in a frenzy of despair. Both appealed to the animal's keeper. Wasn't there something that could be done?

The keeper said he would see what he could do. When Baby Boo had been turned over to him, with her came a magic wand that had proven helpful more than once in handling her: one of my bamboo tubes, which the keeper always carried with him. Getting out of range of the camera, he took out the tube and called to the balking elephant. She caught sight of the bamboo and as she did, he started to run, Baby Boo making a hurried bee-line after him. Once more the tiniest elephant I have ever brought back to America was under the spell of the bit of bamboo that had saved her life.

The cameraman got what he wanted.

Monkey Mothers

I HAD some orders for crocodiles. Not being fond of these reptiles,—a vicious lot at best, with none of the color and imaginative appeal one frequently finds in savage creatures—I had put off securing these specimens until I had gathered most of the other items of a big collection that I had rounded up at Singapore and Calcutta for shipment to zoological gardens, dealers and circuses in the United States.

I was in Calcutta when I decided to land my crocodiles and get this dull chore out of the way, little knowing that these stupid reptiles were going to provide an opportunity to witness as touching an example of the maternal instinct at its heroic best as I have ever seen,—in a species that had nothing to do with my mission.

I left with Lal for the Sunderbunds, that vast lowland studded with innumerable islands and marshes, where the Ganges splits into many rivers and enters the Bay of Bengal. This district is easily accessible from Calcutta and was the ideal place to go for my crocodiles.

Until recently the Sunderbunds were one of the game paradises of Asia. Most of the big game has been killed off, although there are still some tigers and leopards. Thousands of monkeys still inhabit this territory, however, and it is also alive with crocodiles, cobras and wild pigs.

The Sunderbunds cover an area of over 1,000 square miles. Some of this is heavy jungle but in the main it is not the thick black jungle of other parts of India and the Malay country.

There are several light-houses in this district. An old *shikari* who used to get crocodiles and other specimens for me lived with one of the light-house keepers and I was on my way to see him, having notified him of my needs and arranged for a meeting place.

Zoos are the only market for crocodiles. Hardy creatures, they live a long time and practically every sizeable zoo has at least one specimen to round out its reptile exhibit.

The natives have many ways of catching crocodiles, but the one most commonly used is to take a live monkey and tie a stout hard wood stick about the same length as the monkey along its back. The stick is sharpened at both ends. Attached to the center of this stick and set crosswise upon it is another of about half its length. The monkey is then tied out on a leash in the mangrove bushes that grow in the shallow water along the edge of the streams where these creatures are found. When the crocodile grabs the monkey, whichever way it takes its prey, either sidewise or perpendicularly, its jaws clamp down on the two sharp ends of the stick which hold its mouth open. Being unable to close its mouth, the crocodile cannot swim, so it immediately makes for the banks where its tracks can easily be followed by the trappers who have no difficulty in catching the monster on land.

As little enthusiasm as I have for crocodiles, I am always glad to pick one up for a zoo that wants it. It is all in the day's work; and usually it is part of an order that includes more interesting assignments.

I'll say this for crocodiles: once you get 'em boxed for shipment they cause very little trouble. I recall one that I brought back for the St. Louis Zoo that declined food and drink for forty-five days and yet had the good grace to be in perfect condition when I delivered him. I mention this by way of giving an idea of how hardy these strange reptiles are.

Another specimen that I brought back had no interest in food for almost as long a period but in this case the long fast was more understandable as the creature had consumed a native woman before he had been caught. This victim had gone to the river-bank to do the family washing when the reptile dealt her a terrific blow with its tail that felled her. Then the killer dragged her off into the mud and finished the job.

Crocodiles are among the worst of the man-eaters. In some sections the local governments pay a reward for the killing of these vicious reptiles. For instance, in Sarawak, North Borneo, which is ruled by Rajah Brooke, the only white rajah, a bounty of twenty-five cents (Straits money) per foot is paid for all crocodiles killed and captured and for man-eaters a larger bounty is paid. The depredations of these murderous creatures have reached sizeable proportions in that district and for some time past everything possible to stamp them out has been done.

Most of the specimens brought in by those claiming bounty money range from ten to fourteen feet. (The biggest crocodile I ever saw was a sixteen-footer that got into a drain ditch on a rubber estate in Johore and was killed by coolies.)

A native claiming bounty money usually goes through this routine: First, of course, he catches his crocodile. (Experts tell me that is the most important step, and I guess they're right.) Next the question of transporting the captive arises. The reptile's front legs are trussed up over its back and tied, then the hind legs are treated in a similar manner. The prisoner is then lashed to a pole and two men carry it on their shoulders to the nearest village where it is taken before the headman, the local police magistrate or anyone else in authority.

In the presence of the Authorized One the reptile is cut open and then his insides are explored for signs of a human feast. Practically all the natives wear trinkets of some kind, usually pewter, brass or silver bangles. The first object of the search is to look for the bangles which a greedy crocodile does not hesitate to cram down his throat along with the flesh. These ornaments become imbedded in the reptile's insides and apparently do him no harm. I know of one case where a crocodile that was caught and killed was found to have bangles so deeply imbedded in his flesh (which had completely grown over the trinkets) that it was the opinion of the headman that these ornaments represented a killing made twenty or twenty-five years before.

If signs are found indicating that the captured reptile has been feasting on human flesh, the special "man-eating bounty" is paid. If not the smaller reward applies.

Lal and I travelled by bullock cart the last seven or eight miles of our journey to meet the *shikari*, there being no other means of conveyance. If I could have expected something besides crocodiles on my arrival I would have found the trip more enjoyable. As it was, I was bored by the necessity of re-travelling this familiar ground which did not promise to yield anything in the way of a new experience. My one thought was to meet my man, get my crocodiles and return to Calcutta with all possible haste. I couldn't have been less interested in my mission if I were on my way to collect a herd of cows,—although that's an unfair comparison. I find cows more interesting than crocodiles.

As we rumbled along I found myself mentally cussing out the driver for not making better time, although I knew full well that he was doing all that could be expected of him. Suddenly as we passed a spot where there was a small clearing on one side of the jungle, the driver let out an excited yell in his best exclamatory Hindustani. As he did I heard crashing sounds near the side of the road. Then I saw a monkey jump frantically from a gnarly twisted tree trunk that leaned out over the roadway and scramble across the trail some ten or twelve yards ahead of us. Obviously the frightened creature was making for the trees on the other side of the clearing. When the monkey was halfway across the road I could see what was happening. There was a yellow streak in pursuit . . . a leopard! The pursuer had no doubt dashed up the sloping tree after the little rhesus, and having failed to make its capture there, was now after the elusive simian on open ground. The unlucky monkey had barely reached the other side of the road when the big cat, coming on in a great rush, pounced upon it. There was an agonized screech and in a fraction of a second the monkey population was reduced by one.

Just before the leopard seized the shrieking monkey and disappeared with it into the jungle on the other side I thought I saw a small dark object drop to the ground a few feet away. I had no idea what I had seen,—in fact, I wasn't sure I had seen anything—but my curiosity was aroused. I halted the driver and with Lal went over to investigate.

Lal wasn't sure what I was looking for,—which wasn't surprising since I wasn't either. He had kept his eyes on the leopard.

For several minutes I looked around on the ground, my search yielding nothing. I was about to give up the hunt and decide that I had been imagining things when I suddenly spied something in the grass, a baby monkey not more than four inches long. I picked it up and examined it. It couldn't have been more than a few days old. Its head was about as big as a good-sized marble, its face and hands were pink and its very thin hair was a further indication that it had only recently arrived on earth.

I wrapped the little baby in a handkerchief and placed it in one of the pockets of my jacket. Then we were off again.

What had happened was obvious. With the breath of the leopard on its back, the last thought of the doomed mother was to throw her babe to safety. This she had done.

A monkey mother carries its babe in a peculiar way. The infant, facing the parental stomach, puts its little arms, as far as they'll go, around the body from which it sprang, and hangs on for dear life in this fashion. The mother moves from place to place, on the watch for food and looking after its other concerns, knowing that its babe will instinctively cling to her. When the heroine of the episode I have just described realized that she was faced by certain death, she tore the young one loose and threw it to a place on the grass where she hoped it would be safe. I hadn't any doubt that this is what had happened.

At the nearest point along the line, I stopped and got some goat's milk which I fed with difficulty to the little child of my favorite jungle heroine.

I met my *shikari* and picked up my crocodiles but they received scant attention from me. I assigned to Lal the job of looking after them. My little monkey was my primary concern.

When I returned to Calcutta I found it easier to feed the little infant, for there I was able to secure an eye-dropper, a device to which I have frequently resorted as a means of getting milk into the stomachs of tiny animals. The little fellow thrived and I made a pet of him all the way back to America, and for some time afterwards. I didn't like to part with him as I had grown very fond of the tiny cuss,—as amusing a handful of rhesus monkey as I'd encountered in some time—but eventually it became inconvenient for me to keep him.

His best chance of surviving was to put him in a place where there were attendants to look after his needs, so I gave him to the San Diego Zoo, where I knew he would have excellent care. On only a few occasions have I parted with an animal more regretfully.

Ali and I were in Pontianak, Dutch Borneo, where I found myself bargaining with a Malay trader for some specimens he had on display in front of the nipa shack where he made his headquarters.

I had heard from a member of the crew of one of the boats that ply between Singapore and the Borneo coast that this trader had recently come down from the jungle with a pair of orangs and a number of other interesting catches. Tips of this kind having resulted profitably in the past, I decided to investigate. It is a short trip from Singapore, where I was at the time, to Pontianak. The boat remains only one day,—long enough to pick up a cargo of rattan which eventually finds its way to Grand Rapids, Michigan,—then goes directly back to Singapore.

So here I was in Pontianak, looking around for bargains,— and more particularly for something unusual. Your dyed-in-the-wool collector is ever on the lookout for something that has never before been seen in the country where he disposes of his specimens. There is no bigger thrill in the game than bringing back rare "firsts" and on every trip I've ever made since I got started in my chosen field I've always kept my eye peeled for novelties. Nothing delights me more than to place under the nose of an eminent zoologist a bird or a beast or a snake he has never seen before,—something that up to then had only been a name—perhaps a ponderous Latin one—in the natural history books or the zoological dictionary. A phlegmatic scientist suddenly come alive is always a treat to me. There is one—a chap who normally seems as devoid of emotion as a flounder—who, when I show him a rare zoological specimen, becomes so animated I begin to fear that the quick transition from his usual state of bloodless calm may prove too much for him. He jumps up and down, waves his arms, shouts and acts for all the world like an astronomer who has discovered a new planet. These bursts of scientific joy are one of the real compensations of my work.

The Malay trader had a fairly interesting collection but nothing that I had not brought back many, many times. Still, I had orders for most of the species he showed me, and as his specimens were in good condition I started bargaining with him for the lot. The exhibits on display constituted his entire collection, he told me, and he preferred to sell the whole business for a flat price. As I was about to close the deal, Ali, who had been snooping around, came over and whispered something in my ear.

The information Ali gave me was decidedly important. Instantly I turned and went up into the house, the trader chasing after me protestingly. There, in the place where Ali told me to look, I found as unusual a sight as I'd witnessed in years of collecting—a pair of proboscis monkeys! These are the rarest of simians and had never been seen in the United States. It was the first time I had ever beheld the species.

The male was about three feet high, its nose sticking out from its face about two and a half inches. The female was somewhat smaller in size, but she too had a very prominent proboscis. The animals were tannish brown in color.

Ali had done an excellent piece of detective work, a very necessary part of the business of dealing with native traders. Very often they hold out their best specimens. When I buy out a man's stock I feel entitled to a look at everything he's got. As these traders can seldom be depended upon to tell the truth, it was part of Ali's job to snoop around and see what else he could find while I bargained for whatever I selected.

With more indignation than I really felt—for the trickiness of natives was something that I had grown accustomed to—I demanded to know why he had been holding out on me. What was the idea of telling me he was showing me everything when he knew full well that the pair of monkeys in the house would interest me more than anything he had shown me?

He was sorry. But the proboscis monkeys were not for sale.

Not for sale? Then he could keep his other stuff. . . . Come, Ali. . . . Together we started walking away. (Of course we were bluffing. It is all part of the business of dealing with a native trader.)

The trader ran after us, needless to say. Would I please return? He would explain.

Yes, I would return for a moment but he was wasting his time. How could I believe anything that came from the lips of a man who said he was selling me everything and then held back his best goods? Bah! (I did my best to restrain a chuckle as I made this show of disgust with having encountered the appalling trait of deception. No, not until I had come to Pontianak did I realize there were people who were capable of such dastardly conduct.)

Would the *tuan* please listen. I nodded, shrugging indifferently as I did. . . . The *tuan* would soon see that he, the trader, had not been trying to practise deception. He had merely been following the advice of the Dutch resident who had told him that the proboscis monkeys were very valuable. If they could be got to Batavia, there they could be sold to the Amsterdam Zoo for a handsome price. Surely the *tuan* understood. He might never again acquire another monkey like that pair. He would have to have at least fifty guilders ($21.00) apiece for them.

To close the deal in a hurry I offered the Malay a thousand guilders for his whole collection, including the proboscis monkeys. He was overjoyed. This was a fortune to him. He had probably secured that pair of rare simians from the Dyaks for five cents' worth of salt or a few ounces of tobacco. I know of one instance where a trader left a group of Dyak savages in a delirium of joy by giving them a dozen yards of cotton cloth and a hatchet for a fine collection of animals and reptiles. When he threw in a little salt and tobacco for good measure they decided they had been dealing with the most generous man in the world.

Often the original price I pay for an animal represents only a very small percentage of what it costs me to deliver it to a zoo or a circus in the United States. I am always willing to pay a decent price for a specimen, confining my slashing of prices to those occasions when I am asked to pay sums that I know to be well above the market.

In this particular case I was willing to boost the price on everything in order to get the proboscis monkeys, the sum of a thousand guilders, as little as it seems, giving the trader more money for his other specimens than he originally asked.

Ali and I departed, with the blessings of the Malay ringing in our ears. A few hours later my purchases were at the dock; and when the little inter-island packet heaved anchor at Ponti-anak, I was having a much-needed sleep on a pile of loose rattan under the shade of a matting awning which had been rigged up for me, while Ali sat upon the poop-deck peacefully chewing his ever-present betel nut surrounded by two orang-utan cages, four baskets containing argus pheasants, a crated leopard cub, two gibbon apes looking out of crude native containers, a box containing a twenty-four foot python, and the cage housing my rare "firsts."

The trip back to Singapore was a happy one, for I couldn't help revelling in the fact that I had picked up the only proboscis monkeys, with one exception, brought out of Borneo in several years. The single exception I knew of—(I kept in close touch with such matters, having been on the hunt for this species for some time and having failed to find one after consulting prac-tically every trader and trapper along the Borneo coast)—was the proboscis monkey captured for the Prince of Wales on the occasion of his visit to India and the Straits during 1921-1922, when a good-sized zoological collection was presented to him by both the Indian and Straits governments for the zoo at Regents Park in London. This specimen, however, died a few days after arriving in Singapore.

When I got back to Singapore, this rare pair of apes was not installed in the compound with the balance of the collection. Ali, who was almost as pleased over securing them as I was, decided he could take better care of them and keep a closer watch on them by taking them out to his own house. So the two quaint little long-nosed simians became members of his household. A roomy cage was built for them on his nipa-thatched veranda and they were made as comfortable as if they were in their jungle home. Ali fixed up the cage with log perches and swings and watched the pair's diet and general welfare as carefully as a mother might look after a delicate child. A couple of weeks after they were installed at the Malay house, a little baby proboscis was born to the female, so when I went up to Calcutta some days later I left quite a family on Ali's front porch.

Ali's main problem, and it was this that I stressed more than anything else before leaving, was to find a steady palatable substitute for the food these strange creatures were accustomed to. In their wild state they live mainly on three or four varieties of thick, waxy jungle leaves obtainable only in Borneo. A sudden change of diet is dangerous in handling animals, especially in the case of monkeys, with the exception of the hardy little rhesus chaps that eat practically anything.

Ali finally fixed on a thick-leaved water-plant, used by the natives in salads. My long-nosed simians soon grew very fond of it. The faithful Malay daily had his army of grandchildren out gathering these plants. Raw carrots also proved popular, and occasionally a meal of bread and boiled rice.

All went well until we transferred my lucky finds to my compound, just before I returned to the United States with my entire collection. At the compound Ali continued his careful supervision of these odd little creatures from Borneo. Our first mishap took place when, without warning, the male decided he had seen enough of this world, and died. Only a few hours before he had been as gay and chipper as could be. It was one of those sudden casualties about which it is possible to theorize at length but which are never fully explained.

The female, of course, was affected by the loss of her mate but her little baby kept her so busy and filled her life so completely that she had no difficulty in retaining a very healthy interest in life. Spry and energetic, she kept fussing over her little child, obviously as proud of it as any human mother could be of her offspring. It was a charming little infant, about the size of a marmoset, and very much like a human baby. Its long nose had not yet formed, which made it impossible for me to tell the mother, regardless of how much I wanted to flatter her, "Your child takes after you." Without the long nose of its species, it looked like anything but the child of the female that was nursing it so tenderly.

Along with the rest of my collection, this proud mother and her babe, hale and hearty in a brand-new roomy cage, were placed aboard a small freighter bound for Hong Kong where I was trans-shipping. There the twain from Borneo were placed in a protected place on the aft main deck of the *President Wilson*, the boat on which I was returning to the United States, alongside other monkey boxes which housed, among others, some rare Wanderoo monkeys, those queer black fellows with manes and tufted tails like lions. Rare, yes, but not "firsts" like the long-nosed lady from Borneo.

I've seen a great many monkey mothers,—(good ones too)— but never have I seen one nurse her little one with such tender solicitude as my Pontianak purchase displayed. When strangers came to have a look at her she would draw to the back of her box, pulling the babe over with her and encircling it with her arms as if to prevent someone from stealing it. A contented look on her face, she would sit by the hour hugging her little treasure, feeding it, gently stroking it, and showing it every conceivable attention. More than one passenger, come to visit Lady Cyrano, the name by which this monkey came to be known, was moved by the demonstrations of affection.

One morning, a few days after we sailed, I noticed that most of the cages in the monkey sector, including the one that housed the proboscis, were water-soaked. In washing down the decks, an early morning ritual on board ship, the crew had been careless and some of my best specimens had received a dousing which didn't do them any good.

I complained to the boatswain in charge of this gang, an officious Filipino who strutted about like an admiral. Give a Filipino of the working class a little authority and there's more than an even chance that he'll swell up till there's no dealing with him.

In all my years of sea travel I have had very little trouble with ship people. Usually they're easy to get along with, a reasonable, good-natured, understanding lot.

I did my best to convince that boatswain that he'd have to tell his men to be more careful with the big hose that was used in washing down the deck. I didn't want my collection to get any more salt water baths. All I succeeded in getting out of him was a shrug of the shoulders and a stupid statement to the effect that his men were doing the best they could and that if any damage was being done, he couldn't help it. This didn't sound very reassuring, so I decided to keep an eye on the fool.

When I got a good look at my long-nosed monkey and her babe I was fighting mad. Both were shivering after their soaking with the hose. The mother, who had grown to know me and would get chummy when I looked in on her, deciding at last that I had no designs on her young one, made no response when I approached her now. She sat slumped back in a corner of the box, eyeing me sluggishly as she wrapped her trembling arms around the cuddling infant in an effort to keep it warm. I promptly replaced the wet straw in the cage and threw over the barred opening the canvas covering that normally was put into use only at night. My prizes from Borneo were soon warm again but I was worried about them. Animals that are used to tropical warmth don't thrive on treatment of this kind.

Every morning I was on deck at five o'clock, the hour the washing-down was started. The boatswain, realizing that I was watching him, would eye me sourly, striding past me stiffly without a sign of recognition as he ordered his men about.

One morning the man at the hose let it go wild, the water shooting straight at my monkey cages and giving a number of my specimens, including the proboscis and babe, another thorough soaking. After the first experience, this certainly did not look like an accident. If ever an act had the ear-marks of de-liberateness, this was it.

Angry enough to throw him overboard, I tore over to where the boatswain stood. I called him fifteen kinds of a lowdown skunk, consigned him to hell and promised to knock his front teeth out, upper and lower, if that hose squirted another drop of water on any of my animals. If I didn't know what serious business it is, rightly or wrongly, to strike a member of a ship's personnel while at sea I'd have knocked that idiot as cold as last week's soup.

"Speak to *him*," said the boatswain, pointing to the man with the hose, "he's the one that did it." Then he grinned crazily and strode away. I afterwards learned that this numbskull was making his last voyage with the ship,—(other complaints had resulted in a decision to dispense with his services)—this un-doubtedly accounting for his defiant manner. He was quitting the vessel anyhow. To hell with me and my animals.

I called the mate as soon as I had seen to it that my dripping monkeys were again dry and comfortable. I told him what had happened, making the air blue with various opinions I expressed of the conduct of that damnable boatswain. The mate was a decent chap. He volunteered an opinion of that Filipino besides which even my most violent outburst seemed tame. He called him a —— but perhaps I'd better not set it down here. The mate reported the matter to the Captain and shortly afterwards that boatswain was up in the "old man's" quarters hearing some plain language which of course fell on deaf ears.

Even if the boatswain had decided to behave himself, it would have been too late. That night the baby proboscis died.

This was the start of one of the saddest animal tragedies I have ever witnessed. The mother of the dead infant started pining away. I'll never forget her grief. As I approached her cage, after the death, she was shaking the lifeless body, not yet ready to believe what had happened and striving to stir it into being. I stepped back a few paces, too touched to violate the privacy of Lady Cyrano's suffering. After shaking the body for a few minutes, she picked it up and embraced it as I had seen her do a hundred times when it was alive. The idea, I suppose, was to hug it back to life.

Convinced, finally, that her efforts were useless, she slumped back in a corner of her cage, spiritless and heart-broken. As I removed the body she looked up at me pathetically in a manner that seemed to say, "I'm dead too. Better dispose of me also."

From then on Lady Cyrano was a real problem. Her chin down in her chest, she would sit motionless by the hour. She lost interest in everything, including food. Even such dainties as raisins and fresh bananas, which normally would have been joyously received, were ignored.

When I visited her she did not even look up. We had become such good friends that usually when she heard my voice she would run to the bars of her cage to meet me. Now there was no response when I greeted her. Chin buried in her chest, she sat silently mourning her bereavement. It was a pathetic sight, this picture of an animal tortured by the sudden death of the babe that comprised her whole life. With her mate gone too, she was now all alone, and hour after hour, without budging an inch, she sat brooding over the cruel fate that had befallen her.

After she had skipped several meals I began to grow worried. Starvation was hardly the right program for this rare animal with which I hoped to delight the zoological world. Coaxing availed nothing and I was finally reduced to forcing a little food down her. Mechanically she swallowed a few mouthfuls, again sinking her head in her chest and forlornly staring down at nothing as soon as the brief unwanted meal was over.

Lady Cyrano got over her dousing—(I carefully watched her temperature for signs of fever which did not develop)—but she never recovered from the loss of her youngster.

I figured that if I could keep her alive until I arrived in America and put her in a big busy zoo where new and interesting surroundings would help her take her mind off her troubles, she had a good chance of developing a new interest in life and of taking her place among the rarest exhibits in the world.

All the way back to San Francisco I worked on her. I arranged her cage so that when the weather was good she was sure to get the benefit of all the sunshine there was. When the weather was bad I took the necessary precautions to keep her cage warm and comfortable. I continued to ransack the galley for choice morsels in the hope of finding something so exquisitely tasty that she would eat voluntarily. But her interest in food was gone. Practically everything she ate for the rest of the voyage had to be forced down her.

Her brooding continued. Day after day she sat in that one position till her chin and her chest seemed to have merged and her bowed head suggested an attitude she had been ordered to strike and must not change for fear of punishment.

Poor Lady Cyrano was having a tougher time than any animal I had ever handled. I was having a pretty tough time myself. It is no fun to have to witness the slow pining-away of a fine, sensitive animal,—and when that animal happens to be a rare specimen whose safe delivery means the enhancing of your reputation, it comes all the harder. (Not being in business for my health, I might also add that I did not like the prospect of losing so valuable an animal; but financial considerations were far outweighed by the others I have mentioned.)

We finally arrived in San Francisco, and viewing the trip in retrospect it is no exaggeration to say that of my many Pacific crossings none provided more worry. There were far more exciting crossings but none that occasioned quite so much mental anguish. The sufferings of Lady Cyrano got under my skin to such an extent that the whole trip took on an air of tragedy.

A careful physical examination of my mourning proboscis monkey revealed, curiously enough, that she was in good physical condition. I had managed to do enough forced feeding to provide ample sustenance. Sometimes, on a trip of this kind, an animal fares better if it does not eat too much. Physically Lady Cyrano was in better shape than some of my monkeys that had had far more to eat. It was the old girl's mind that was sick. She was as listless as ever when we docked, showing no interest in anything.

I wired the Bronx Zoo in New York that I had this rare specimen. Did they want her?

Did they! I received an immediate reply asking me to ship the animal at once and guaranteeing me a handsome price for it.

I never collected. Lady Cyrano was dead within an hour of the time I received my acceptance.

This is the only instance I have ever encountered, in all my years as a collector, of an animal dying of a broken heart. This monkey mother never got over the loss of her child.

Ghost of Katong

EARLY one morning a man clad only in a knee-length white union-suit was seen tearing down the Katong Road at a terrific rate of speed. Katong is the suburb of Singapore where I lived and maintained an animal compound when in this part of the world.

This early morning sprint was variously interpreted. A facetious American would have it that the gentleman in the undergarment was an athlete in training to represent Singapore in the next Olympic Games. The town gossip—as common a phenomenon in the East as anywhere else—gave it as his opinion that only one thing could have happened: the runner was simply putting distance between himself and an enraged husband who had surprised him in the act of collaborating with an unfaithful wife. While such occurrences are as common as mosquitoes in the East, the theory did not hold water, as no pursuer had been seen. The race was a solo affair. Superstitious natives found in the happening material for one of their wild ghost stories. A phantom had visited Katong and had dashed through the town to notify everyone of his presence,—a subtle way of telling the populace that anybody who didn't behave himself would be haunted. With fantastic embellishments that included a list of punishments the spectre would mete out to the unruly, this became quite a story among the more gullible natives, providing them with conversation for many days.

Later in the morning the ghost was seen riding into Singapore in a *gharry* or native horse hack,—(many had witnessed him) —and this gave rise to another series of rumors, ranging from the supernatural to the hard-boiled. The Chinese interpretations—(he was observed in Katong mainly by Chinamen)—laid most of their emphasis on the weirder side of life or the life to come, while Europeans and Americans who took in the show indulged in more materialistic comments. An engineer from Connecticut said he hoped that by this time he was familiar with the spectacle of a man paying off an election bet. He hadn't attended Yale for nothing. There were other theories, including a flippant one to the effect that this was just another one of those absent-minded professors, come to study Asia and so absorbed in what he saw that he had forgot to put his trousers on.

When all the evidence was in—(it was easy to secure as it was from the house in which I lived that the ghost of Katong made his provocative dash)—the events of the morning clarified themselves. This evidence, plus what I was privileged to witness myself, makes it possible for me to tell what actually took place.

If Mack hadn't gone and got himself stewed again there simply wouldn't have been any ghost.

When I took my house in Katong I found it would be too expensive for me to operate alone. I entered into an arrangement with two Singapore friends whereby they were to "mess" with me. The three of us shared the house and got our meals together, and we split the expense.

The soaring prices of Singapore real estate had made it necessary for me to move to Katong. My old compound in the Orchard Road section of Singapore had become a costly piece of property,—much too valuable for use as an animal shelter. I had heard of a place in Katong where I could get a decent house and three acres of ground at a figure that suited my purse better than my Singapore compound which was rapidly becoming prohibitive. What with the hazards of animal collecting, even the Katong property involved too heavy an expense and I was glad when Andy Mack and Joe Beckwith decided they would like to "mess" with me.

Mack was a Scotch engineer with a Singapore firm and Beckwith an Englishman in the Singapore Harbor Department.

Both were good sports. I had been warned about Mack— (he was reputed to be the heaviest drinker in Singapore)—but I paid no attention to those who were rushing to my aid. Heavy drinking is so prevalent in Singapore that one accepts it as a commonplace.

Besides I liked Mack for the contradiction he was. He gave the lie to the familiar stories about the stinginess of Scotchmen. The soul of generosity, a few minutes after he pounded his way into a bar—(he was a big heavy-set fellow who brought his enormous shoes down with a bang when he walked)—he would buy a drink for everyone in sight, sometimes, in his mellower moments, frightening the timid kowtowing Chinese help with the impossible invitations he roared at them to join the gang in a tipple.

"Mack's a good sort," more than one Singapore comrade told me, "but you'd better not try to live with him. You don't know what it means to try to live with a man who drinks the way he does. He'll drive you crazy."

I soon found out what it meant to live with Mack. More than once I wished I had listened to the advice of friends. I can be bull-headed when I want to, and I paid no more attention to those who warned me about him than I did to the well-meaning individuals who would try to talk me out of exploits in connection with my work as a collector that they considered too dangerous.

I never seriously regretted living with Mack,—(he was one of the most genuinely interesting men I had met in the East)— but more than once I was tempted to sock him one.

Mack was thorough. In his work as an engineer he never missed a trick, and he was the same in his drinking. When he set out to get drunk he got drunk. He despised compromise. At four-thirty, the day's work done, he would concentrate on the business of taking on a load. He would start at the Cricket Club, go from there to the Raffles Hotel or the Hotel Europe, and keep going indefinitely.

One of Mack's specialties was looking for "good drinkers." Whenever he found a man whom he felt he could call a "good drinker"—(and Mack's standards were high, for only the most thoroughgoing sot ever earned the compliment)—he would hang on to his find until they had both drunk themselves into a state of boozy helplessness. Mack's definition of a "good drinker," when you analyzed it, was a man who didn't fall on his head more than an hour earlier than he, Mack, did, and who in falling didn't hurt himself. Once Mack completely reversed himself on his discovery of a "good drinker,"—the best, he had announced, that he had met in some weeks—when the poor fellow, in falling out of a *gharry*, cracked a rib. Mack said that proved beyond a doubt that he had made a mistake. The chap was a bad drinker. "Good drinkers" never hurt themselves.

He had other ways of detecting bad drinkers. For instance, in a mellow moment he once greeted me in this fashion: "Buck, I just heard you tell the bartender you wouldn't have another drink. Don't deny it. I heard you."

"Well, what of it?"

"What of it? That's a fine question! You're not a good drinker! That's what of it!"

Mack's specialty was disorganizing the schedule of our house in Katong. He was rarely on time for dinner. I see no harm in occasionally wrecking a schedule,—in fact, I consider it a healthy thing in the United States, where there's entirely too much living by the clock—but Mack went too far. He didn't give the help a break. On one of those nights when he'd meet a "good drinker" and come in late for dinner,—anywhere from two to five hours after the table had been cleared—if he and his discovery chanced to be hungry he'd rout out the servants, sometimes pulling them out of bed, and order them to throw a meal together.

It was on such occasions as this—and there were many of them—that I was all for pasting Mack on the nose. I'd call myself a fool for ignoring the advice of the people who had warned me, and, in the privacy of my mind, cook up a red hot speech with which to greet him.

Then I'd face him and something would disarm me, either his utter helplessness (and after all it isn't very sporting to wallop a wobbly drunk) or some tipsy observation that would make me laugh against my will.

We had three house servants,—a cook, a *tukenia* (a boy who did such rough jobs as scrubbing, emptying the slop jars, etc.) and a No. 1 boy, who served our meals and bossed the other two. These servants were "Straits-born" Chinese. They had the typical slant eyes of China, the chief point of variance from their China-born brethren being in the matter of complexion. They were almost as dark as the Malays. They dressed in the regulation Chinese fashion.

Thanks to Mack, these boys led a very irregular life which involved many tasks out of the regular line of duty. For instance, when Mack brought home his latest "good drinker" it was their job to carry the paralyzed pair out of Mack's car into the house.

The night before the historic morning to which I refer here, Mack brought home what he considered (so he said for many weeks afterward) his greatest find—the best of all the "good drinkers" he had ever encountered. Mack had run into this genius in the bar of the Raffles Hotel. There they started one of the most thorough drinking bouts in the history of Singapore, visiting bar after bar until they had broken all records for plain and fancy drinking.

The house in Katong in which Mack, Beckwith and I lived was one of the familiar bungalows of the district. Built slightly over three feet off the ground, it rested on cement pillars.

At the time of the episode of the Ghost of Katong, the sheds of my compound were filled to over-flowing with birds and animals. A new tiger, fresh from the jungle, had just arrived from Ipoh, in the Malay Peninsula. It was a ferocious specimen, one of the wildest I had handled in some time. Whenever anyone went near its cage it would lunge at the bars and let out blood-curdling screams of rage that could be heard a half mile off. No cry is quite so piercing as that of a tiger that has decided to raise a commotion. It is well-nigh indescribable,—a combination of shriek and snarl suggestive of a whole army of infuriated common cats yelling in deafening unison. At its full-fledged best it has made more than one strong man blanch and shiver.

There being no other place for my new tiger, I had him shoved under the bungalow, his cage resting under the unoccupied spare room.

I frequently stored animals under the house. It was an excellent shelter. I found it particularly useful in housing birds of paradise, orang-utans and other specimens that required careful watching. It was a place where I could constantly keep an eye on them.

Mack, when he arrived with his latest version of The Best Drinker on Earth, arrived with a bang. It was an entrance that couldn't very well be lost on anyone within fifty yards unless he happened to be deaf.

Having heard Mack make grand entrances in the past, I didn't place any new valuation on the occurrence. From my room I could hear him thundering out commands to the servants whom he had wakened with one mighty roar. It took the combined efforts of the three of them and Mack's chauffeur to get the tipsy pair into the house.

I could hear the bad boy of Katong cussing out the chauffeur. He was asking this faithful slave wheninell he was going to learn to drive straight: "You damned near knocked the house over!" bellowed the king of drinkers,—"What are you trying to do— wake up everybody?" As Mack's chauffeur was the soul of carefulness, one of the sanest drivers I'd ever seen, this was a sure sign that we were all in for a large night.

Mack installed his new drinking hero in the spare room. Not more than three inches beneath the legs of his bed was a cage containing a vicious tiger, but he couldn't have been safer if he were sleeping in a rabbit hutch. The fact remains, however, that he was sleeping directly over one of the jungle's wildest specimens.

The boys put Mack's Drinker of Drinkers to bed. By this I mean that they took his clothes off (down to his B.V.D.'s), heaved him into bed and threw a mosquito guard over him.

As safe as he was, if Mack's friend had known how close he was to a cageful of tiger, perhaps he would not have wanted to sleep there. He was practically on speaking terms with the beast. A quaint feature of Eastern houses such as this was that there was an open space of about a quarter of an inch between the boards of the floor. This facilitated the dreary business of sweeping. Each movement of the broom sent the dust flying through the cracks onto the cement below. It was a good arrangement, providing permanent floor ventilation and facilitating the work of the servants.

Mack was put to bed shortly after his friend was disposed of. As was usual with him under such circumstances, he accused the servants of trying to bully him, charged them with drunkenness and threatened to fire them unless they sobered up and learned how to look after a gentleman. He bellowed these choice bits for the benefit of all Katong, kicking the furniture around for emphasis.

It was about three-thirty in the morning by the time peace was restored to our troubled household.

About six o'clock in the morning Ali's duties began. He would launch his program by making a round of the cages, with an assistant. Together they would clean the cages and put everything in order.

One of his most important responsibilities was my tiger underneath the house. He reached this at about six-thirty. His first task was to unbuckle the "front" that is used to shut a cage of this sort for the night. Then, while the other boy aimed buckets of water at the floor, Ali would quickly work an iron scraper through the bars and clean out the cage.

Ali had hardly got the front off the cage when the occupant let out one of the most ear-splitting tiger cries—(shriek, snarl, howl and roar, all in one)—that ever threatened to ruin a man's ear-drums. Then there followed a whole series of these blood-curdling screams, accompanied by a racket that made it plain that the beast was making terrific assaults on the bars.

I was dressing at the time. In the East I make a practice of early rising as I like to get in as much work as possible in the morning so that I may do my share of loafing in the afternoon.

At the height of the rumpus in the tiger cage, another commotion could be heard,—this one coming from the living-room. It developed that Mack's friend (who hadn't the faintest notion of where he was, having entered the house thoroughly plastered and being still in a more or less groggy state) had jumped out of bed when the tiger underneath him had started to raise hell, and dashed out of his room as if pursued by every animal in the jungle, through the living-room, where he collided with the center table, sending books and tobacco jars crashing to the floor. He also got tangled up in some chairs before he was out of the house onto the porch, sending these pieces over on their backs. By this time I was out of my room, half-dressed, to see what was going on.

I arrived in time to see Mack's friend negotiate the porch steps in a leap that was more of a flop, the gentleman not having completely recovered from his jag. He had not bothered to put on any clothes, a white union-suit being his only apparel. It was of the type that has a flap in the back that buttons over the seat. The flap was unbuttoned and it waved back and forth like a flag of truce notifying the enemy that he was for peace at any price, uncovering a pink posterior in the process. His leap proved top-heavy, as post-alcoholic acrobatics often do, and he landed in a heap. He picked himself up instantly and was off again, the flag of truce slightly soiled and the pink complexion underneath furiously red after his fall, as if blushing for having left the house uncovered. I reached the porch as the Ghost of Katong picked himself up and made for the front gate about 150 feet off. There was nothing between him and his objective but the *caboon* (our native gardener) who was out cutting the grass with hand-shears. If the startled *caboon* had remained where he was, all would have been well. But in his needless effort to get out of the way he got directly in the ghost's path and they collided, *caboon*, spectre and hand-shears flying in all directions.

But Mack's friend was a determined phantom. He was up and off in a twinkling, the rumpled flag of truce still flapping back and forth but with less spirit. Soon he hit the driveway and after that the Katong Road, down which he dashed with a new burst of speed. I followed him as far as the road, hurdling the sprawled-out *caboon* as I followed the union-suited spectre.

The rest of the story I had to piece together, the ghost, Beckwith, Ali, the manager of the Raffles Hotel and others supplying the necessary information.

About a half mile down the road Mack's friend caught up with a native *gharrywalla* (hackman) driving his *gharry* into town. When he spied the pop-eyed figure dressed only in an undergarment he whipped up his bony nag but it didn't do him any good. The resolute phantom already had a firm hold on one side of the hack and he swung himself up.

The *gharrywalla* yelled to him to get off, brandishing his whip in the air. Mack's friend tried to make the fellow understand his predicament but after all what can an American—(the ghost was an importation from California)—do with a chap who understands nothing but Malay? The ghost's frantic supplications got him nowhere until, inspired, he shouted, "Raffles Hotel!" This means something to the stupidest *gharrywalla* of the district,—and most of these chaps are pretty dull, there being some who have dealt with Americans and Englishmen for ten years without picking up a dozen words of English.

With the mention of the Raffles Hotel the driver beamed. A *tuan* who lived at the Raffles Hotel was worth accommodating. The ghost was invited to sit down and make himself comfortable.

Mack's friend hadn't the faintest notion of where he was. He happened to be eight miles from his hotel, which meant that he was in for a ride of at least an hour and a half, in the course of which there was no way of hiding his union-suited plight from the gaze of the populace.

First the phantom rode through the bazaars and markets of Katong village. In this part of the world, activities of all kinds get going at an early hour, for everyone tries to get as much work done as possible in the cool of the early morning. Native men and women, in the market place to buy and sell, stood rooted in their tracks and salaamed superstitiously as the *gharry* bearing Mack's latest "good drinker" picked its way through the crowded streets.

Then the vehicle passed the driveway of the Seaview Hotel

where quite a few people were up, some of them getting ready to go down-town in their motor cars. No little sensation was created by the informally attired figure seated behind the shabby *gharrywalla* who, at the earnest behest of the ghost, was trying to coax some speed out of the winded nag.

Then the unusual trio—(horse, *gharrywalla* and spectre)— entered the European residence section of Singapore where there are many fine homes. Not a few residents were stirred into unusual early morning activity by the strange sight that went past, the first and only thing of its kind ever to greet their startled eyes.

The next thing along the line of march represented temporary relief from the stares and grins of the amused. It was the stretch of tidal marsh that one encounters at this point, a desolate spot where there are small crocodiles to laugh at one but practically nothing else.

Coming out of the marsh, one gets closer to the more thickly settled section of Singapore, the Chinese section where, at the hour the ghost of Katong made entry, there are hundreds of Chinamen, many of them merchants, seated at the tables of street restaurants eating their morning rice. These quiet breakfasters broke into cackles of emotional chattering as the *gharry* with its strange freight bobbed into view. Other Chinamen, mostly curious idlers, crowded round the hack, making it necessary for the *gharrywalla* to pound furiously at his horse's rear (meanwhile heaping imprecations on the celestials) in order to make any progress.

Next the ghost of Katong found himself passing through the great Malayan markets of Singapore, which are thick with Chinamen bearing everything conceivable on carrying poles. Added to these are hundreds of bullock carts, come to market loaded with produce, and hordes of women with loads on their heads, scurrying in all directions. It is, and has been for years, one of the world's greatest traffic jams, and you can readily visualize the surprise, the amazement, the chorused outburst of astonishment, in this dense mob through which the driver had to find a lane.

Once out of this jam, Mack's friend, still acutely conscious of his union-suit, found himself passing Bunbee's Store, an old Singapore institution where the women, including many of the English and European residents, do their shopping. These ladies were diverted, shocked, annoyed or merely astonished, according to each one's particular outlook on life. But a goodly percentage of them, their sensibilities acclimated to Eastern unconventionalities, broke into hearty laughter.

The next stop was the Raffles Hotel. Curious throngs surrounded the ghost of Katong as he alighted from the *gharry* and made for the entrance.

There, though the phantom with real tears in his eyes pleaded for admittance, the *jager* (doorman) wouldn't let him in. This, the *jager* contended, was no sight for the virginal eyes of the women in the lobby.

A heated argument took place in front of the hotel, part of the crowd favoring the *jager*, some siding with the pantsless passenger whose *gharrywalla* hung around anxiously for his fee.

The *gharrywalla*, more anxious to collect his money than concerned over Mack's friend, finally succeeded in convincing the *jager* that the ghost should be admitted. The doorman got a gunny-sack, discreetly wrapped it around the phantom while the crowd pressed forward and howled its delight, and at last let Mack's harried "good drinker" in.

Later in the day Mack, hearing what had happened, rushed forth in his car to join his drinking companion and offer his sympathy. When Mack told him of my tiger under his bed, he jumped to the conclusion that he had been the victim of a practical joke and vowed to beat me up. He cooled down, however, when he learned that I was an animal collector and that the tiger was there for better reasons than to scare him out of his wits.

Elephant Temper

IN my business a tame-sounding order often makes the most trouble. When Herbert Fleischhacker, well-known banker and President of the Park Board in San Francisco, told me that he wanted a big elephant for presentation to the wonderful children's playground he founded on the city's ocean front, I naturally classified the assignment as routine business. It eventually proved to be far from routine.

Mr. Fleischhacker had made Golden Gate Park a present of two smaller elephants that were in constant use. Each of these pachyderms carried six children at a time (in howdahs which I designed). The animals developed such popularity that it was growing difficult to accommodate all the children that wanted a ride.

Mr. Fleischhacker, pleased with the success of his elephants, asked me one day if I couldn't bring back an animal capable of accommodating more children than the medium-sized elephants he had. He wanted one on whose back a much roomier howdah could be placed so that the little boys and girls of San Francisco would not have to wait in line too long for a ride. He discussed the matter as gravely as if it were an important banking problem and I couldn't help feeling that the children of the city had a marvelous friend in this wealthy citizen who had not forgotten his boyhood days,—who, in fact, revealed so much knowledge of what children consider good sport that you'd have thought it was only the day before yesterday that he was twelve himself.

I suggested that a good way of accommodating several children at a time would be to build a big ornamental wagon, as colorful as a merry-go-round, and capable of carrying twenty little passengers, or more. I would supply the right elephant to pull them around.

Mr. Fleischhacker was delighted with the suggestion and I was commissioned to deliver a good-sized elephant (for the sum of $3,000).

Up in northern Burmah an influential Burmese went to the British Colonial Forest officials in the district in which he lived and made a contract with them to keddah (or corral) the elephants in that district. This meant, among other things, that he had to visit native villages throughout this territory and make a thorough canvass of the various stretches of jungle with a view to determining where the different herds of wild elephants were and approximating the number of animals in each herd.

The Burmese *keddah walla* had many things to bear in mind. Only elephants of a certain size could be taken and only a fixed percentage of those from each district in the territory covered by his contract. There were other taboos that stipulated that the male leader of a herd could not be taken nor a full-grown breeding female. ("Male herd leaders" are mentioned here with reservation. A big male is the real boss of every herd of elephants though an old female actually leads the herd as it moves from one feeding ground to another.)

Males that were not herd leaders and young females comprised the main group of allowable captures,—the size range taking in animals between four and eight feet in height, although sometimes the keddahing of bigger specimens was permitted.

When he had the lay of the land—when, in other words, he had taken a reliable census of the elephants in the area of jungle covered by his contract and had a good idea of how these animals were distributed over the stipulated territory—he fixed upon the best location for centralizing the beasts and here he built an enormous corral known as a keddah.

Elephants being a government concession, the Burmese had an arrangement with the government whereby he was to pay a fixed price for each animal he selected that came under the head of allowable catches.

Had he been in Siam or the Malay country, the Burmese gentleman would have gone through practically the same operations to get his pachyderms. The points of variance would have been few. Siam being an independent country, he would have dealt of course with the King instead of a British Colonial official but the rest of the procedure would have been practically the same.

Siam, by the way, has as well organized an elephant industry —(the operations are on so big a scale they may fairly be described as an industry)—as there is in all of Asia. Its Forestry Department is one of the best regulated government bureaus I know of. They can tell you almost the exact number of wild elephants that are to be found in any section of Siam you are minded to name.

All his arrangements made, the Burmese proceeded to build his *keddah*. Huge posts were driven into the ground a few inches apart and firmly lashed with rattan and wire cable. These posts covered an area of several acres that comprised the main *keddah*. Connecting with this, by means of a gate, was a smaller corral.

At one end of the big corral was a huge sliding door or gate that, for want of a better name, might be designated as The Main Entrance. It was into this opening that the elephants were to be driven, some of them never to return to the jungle.

When the *keddah* was finished, an army of native trackers, expert in the business of keeping elephants on the move, was sent out to drive the pachyderms in. By the time the drive began, the checkers had provided a reliable map indicating the approximate location of the different herds and an accurate census of each of them.

Hundreds of natives, in charge of lieutenants appointed by the *keddah walla*, or chief, take part in an elephant drive. Too much is at stake to permit of any but wholehearted methods.

My Burmese, a big man in his district, had secured financial backing for his elephant enterprise in Rangoon. A tremendous investment (certainly in terms of Burmah) was involved. It was up to him so to conduct his drive that he would be able to round up the elephants he wanted with as little loss of time as possible. He had a big pay-roll that must not get out of hand. While each man received a very small sum for his services there were so many trackers and checkers that it would not be difficult to get "in the red" if the enterprise was sloppily conducted.

Disposing of his elephants was the least of the Burmese's problems. His main job was to round them up at a minimum of expense.

Export sales—(orders like mine, for instance, regardless of how extensive my operations as a collector)—are a drop in the bucket. The local market for elephants—a considerable one—was what the Burmese was figuring on to make his big investment pay. Every tea estate has one or two elephants to do hauling and other rough work. Many elephants are also used in India for road building and other work. Then there is the "ceremonial trade," scores of elephants being regularly sold to princes, rajahs and sultans for use in court functions. The teak business is another important outlet for elephants. Hundreds of them are used in this important industry that supplies the fine hardwood that goes into the decks of practically all ships that sail the seas.

His army of trackers and checkers in motion, my Burmese was receiving bulletins at his headquarters on the progress of the round-up as a general receives communications on the progress of a battle. One messenger would come tearing in to report that this herd, consisting of so many elephants, was working in this direction; another courier would come on the run to report that such and such a herd had veered off the path that had been set for it but that the trackers, beating on their tin-pans and making the other noises that were expected of them, were again in back of the off-course group and could be depended upon to work them back to the path that would lead straight to the *keddah*.

I have been asked many times whether other animals do not interfere when a herd of elephants is being rounded up. The answer is no. To all other animals in the jungle, a herd of elephants in motion is regarded as an elemental force that is not to be disputed. The thing to do is to get out of the way as when a storm comes.

There are few sights stranger than that of an army of trackers working behind a herd of elephants. . . . No weirder combination of noises ever reached human ears, no more fantastic sight ever greeted human eyes. Gesticulating wildly and moving along like figures in an unearthly dance, the tin-pan pounders pummel their discordant instruments into masses of dents. Some of the panless boys pound anything else that will give off a noise. A few of the elect, natives with old muzzle-loading guns, superiorly brush past their unarmed comrades and shoot holes in the air by way of making their presence felt. Other natives, bearing firebrands and depending exclusively on lung-power for their contribution to this Jungle Movie with Sound, shriek and scream and screech and howl like so many demons out of hell.

Forward, forward move the elephants. Closer and closer to the *keddah* they come, their movements in most instances as accurately controlled as if someone were working a giant steering wheel that sent them now to the right and now to the left. The helmsman—the lieutenant selected by the *keddah walla* to direct the din barrage—directs his forces by signals, swinging the tumult this way or that to suit the needs of the moment.

Usually the elephants are rounded up one herd at a time. This may mean anywhere from ten to twenty animals. Sometimes two herds are brought in together, the deafening armies behind them converging and driving the double catch in together.

In their joy over participating in a holiday-like swing through the jungle that means money in return for noise, the natives sometimes forget that rounding up elephants is not without its dangers. My Burmese has had many proofs of this.

In the course of the drive that netted him the wild herd from which my Fleischhacker specimen was selected an over-aggressive native was wiped out so quickly his comrades hardly had a chance to realize what had happened. In fact, it was over so soon many of them didn't know about it until afterwards.

The herd had been driven to a position directly in front of the huge open door of the *keddah*. In a final assault on the ears of the all-but-trapped pachyderms, tin-pans, guns, lungs and what not were called upon for a last epic outburst designed to stampede the frantic beasts through the opening of the great prison.

The demoniac hullabaloo had its effect, most of the elephants tearing forward madly according to the lieutenant's plan. They stirred a real breeze into being on a hot and windless day with their headlong rush into captivity, knocking against one another as they came on in a mass formation. It would have been a clean job of *keddahing* the whole lot if not for a female elephant that lagged behind with her calf, keeping three others from going in, including a fine young specimen that was particularly wanted.

An overzealous native—the poor devil I just mentioned—conceived the foolish notion of using a long bamboo pole to prod the lagging lady, who was half-crazy with the din and in a panic lest something happen to her little one.

Normally that native would have known better than to do anything as foolish as that. Emboldened no doubt by the fact that the other elephants were in the pen, signifying one more victory for man over beast, and with the absence of fear that is common among natives at such a moment, the reckless one advanced with his pole and let the elephant have it. With a tremendous shrill trumpeting that gave voice to all the rage in her being she whirled around and charged her tormentor, grabbing him and raising him up and stamping on him with her forefeet as she swung him back to earth. Before anyone could interfere she had pounded him into an unrecognizable mass, her trumpeting achieving a piercing high falsetto as she broke every bone in that luckless body. In record time the population of Burmah had been decreased by one.

After some clever manœuvering by the lieutenant and a picked squad, the stragglers, including the killer and her calf, were driven into the *keddah* and the great door was locked.

The elephants were then worked from the big corral into the small pen where the *keddah walla* gave the whole herd a careful inspection (there were seventeen in all) to see how many of the animals complied with the clause of his contract with the British officials governing purchasable specimens and how many of these eligibles he wanted. He selected seven out of the lot, healthy young specimens that would fetch good prices at Rangoon where he marketed most of his elephants.

Four *mahouts* (keepers), on tame elephants accustomed to participation in such work, were sent in to perform the ticklish task of tying up the ones that were wanted. Cautiously they worked their mounts in among the herd, selecting the first animal to be tied, and carefully avoiding the tusks of the old bull herd-leader that acted as if he had a burst of indignation coming on. They sifted their way through the captives, cleverly surrounding the elephant that was to be No. 1 of the seven nominees to be put through the process of taming. Jockeying for position with the skill that only a trained *mahout* possesses, the expert four continued their manœuvers until they had their prisoner's side against the pen, two of them getting alongside, lining up parallel to him, a third lining up in front at right angles to the side pair, and a fourth lining up in the rear and completing the square. Thus the captive was unable to move forward or backward or to either side. One of the *mahouts*—the most skillful and fearless of the quartet—then quietly slipped off his elephant, and, with a chain that he carried so deftly that it didn't rattle once as he alighted, got a quick hold on the back leg nearest the fence. A long stout rope was quickly tied to the chain and thrown out between the posts of the corral to a group of natives in charge of a pair of heavy work elephants. Speedily the rope was manipulated so that the elephants outside were tugging away until they had brought the wild specimen inside flush against the wall of the pen. The captive's other hind leg was then quickly tied and his front legs hobbled.

The six other prisoners were put through the same process until there were seven fine elephants tied up in the corral.

The gates were then thrown open and the rest of the herd were driven back into the jungle to breed more elephants to be *keddahed* in future years.

A man schooled in the art of handling wild elephants was assigned to each of the seven. The captives were nicely treated, food and water being regularly brought to them.

As soon as one of the captives showed signs of becoming manageable he was lashed to two tame elephants with ropes and chains and taken out of the pen to a near-by shed that was divided into stalls. Here his keeper put him through a further process of taming. With his front legs hobbled (and a rope tied to the back legs as a safeguard in case he tried to make a getaway) he was taken for an occasional walk, at the start for a very short distance, this being increased as the animal grew tamer.

It was not long before the animal was resigned to his lot and doing whatever his *mahout* was asking of him. The same was true of the other six. There were a few rebellions but these were minor and quelled without any serious consequences. Once subdued, the rebels decided that they had more to gain by behaving themselves, which they did. By this I do not mean to say that these seven elephants, comparatively fresh from the jungle, could be classified as tame specimens. They were moderately manageable, responding to the as yet simple commands of their *mahouts*.

While this taming process was going on other wild herds were being driven up to the *keddah* to be handled in the same manner.

Two of the seven were purchased by buyers representing teakyards located at Moulmein, two others were bought by representatives of interests at Bangkok and three were picked up by the Rangoon Zoo.

I came down to Rangoon from the interior about the time the three elephants were brought in and installed in the zoo. They still showed signs of wildness but they were not hard to handle for animals that were practically fresh from the *keddah*, permitting themselves to be led about without much coaxing.

Not long before, I had delivered to the Rangoon Zoo an American buffalo, or bison, which they had ordered of me. This was the second animal of its kind ever seen in Asia. The first was one that I had presented to the Sultan of Johore, who for years had been anxious to secure a specimen to keep in his deer park adjoining the palace in Johore Bahru. The Sultan had read a great deal about the American buffalo, and when I finally secured one for him he was delighted with it, this species having captured his fancy the very first time he had heard about it.

The officials of the Rangoon Zoo had offered me a worth-while trade for the buffalo and now that they had something I wanted, I decided to collect. One of those three new elephants, after the process of taming had been carried further, would be ideal for the Fleischhacker Playground. The zoo officials agreed to let me have one of them in an even swap for the buffalo. I selected a fine healthy young lady that stood about eight feet in height. The animal I picked, with a little more training, would be just right for the job of hauling the kids around in the ornamental wagon that I had suggested to Mr. Fleischhacker.

The deal closed, I arranged with the British India Steamship Company at Rangoon to take the elephant (she afterwards became known as Babe) to Singapore where I would install her in my compound. Little Ali, nephew of Old Ali, my No. 1 Malay boy, accompanied me on the trip.

In loading an elephant onto a ship a big canvas sling is used that is fastened around the belly, the hold on the animal being further secured by ropes passed around the neck and under the tail. We had a hard job getting the sling around Babe on the dock at Rangoon. There was nothing in her conduct to indicate rebelliousness or a mean disposition but it was hard to get her used to the idea of something new. We finally got the sling around her and hoisted her on board but she trumpeted plenty of displeasure over the business of being swung through space. She didn't like it a bit.

However, once we got her installed in her place on deck, she was again herself and gave all the signs of being the manageable animal I knew her to be. We reached Singapore without mishap and Babe was walked out to the compound, conducting herself en route in lady-like fashion and behaving very well for so new a captive on being placed in the temporary home which she shared with four smaller elephants that I had secured from a *keddah walla* in Siam. The Siamese pachyderms were more used to captivity, having been caught several months before Babe was driven in from the jungle. They required less attention than the lady from Burmah, who was naturally friskier, her jungle freedom being still a recent memory.

But Babe made no trouble for us beyond the normal difficulties involved in completing the adjustment of a wild elephant to the idea of captivity. By way of preparing her for her career on the Pacific Coast I had a breast-band and traces made and hitched her to a heavy log that she pulled around daily. After a while she was going through this performance with a good deal of zest, starting to pull without waiting for the command by way of showing what a smart girl she was. So good-natured was her response that I was surer than ever that she would be perfect for the rôle of pulling little children around the Fleischhacker Playground in the gay wagon that was to be made for her.

Big Ali came out to assist me, and, by way of rounding out Babe's education, he taught her to lie down and get up; and with Little Ali on her back he walked her around the compound daily till she had done about a mile. She seemed to enjoy these workouts, responding with a good will as soon as she understood what was wanted of her.

When all the specimens I had collected at Singapore were ready for shipment to the United States I arranged for passage on a cargo boat that was lying out in the bay about three miles from shore. This meant loading my collection (many varieties of animals, birds and reptiles) onto lighters from which we would transfer to the ship.

We loaded all my crates and boxes into motor lorries and bullock carts and started for the dock. The elephants, some led and some ridden by boys, brought up the rear.

At the dock we quickly transferred the crates and boxes to the lighters, saving the elephants for last.

It was then that I made a mistake. I should have loaded Babe first. Instead I started with the other four elephants.

When the first of the four was lifted into the air by the dock's gear she started squealing and trumpeting. By the time she was lowered onto the lighter she had made quite a commotion. The other three were just as noisy, kicking up a big fuss the second they were lifted off the ground. There are few elephants that do not yell blue murder when you suddenly lift them into the air.

It was Babe's turn next. Not only had she demonstrated at Rangoon that she didn't enjoy being swung through space but she had also been listening to the protests of her predecessors. The others were too small to cause much trouble but Babe was a big husky lady, with a capacity for making trouble if sufficiently frightened. Having seen her balk at Rangoon, I should have loaded her first instead of giving her a chance to remember that this was a business she did not like.

The Girl from Rangoon had made up her mind that she was not going to be swung aboard the lighter. She balked the second we tried to get the sling around her belly. She would not have any of it. That was her story and she stuck to it.

We struggled and we struggled but we could not get the sling around her. She'd either raise up a foot and push the device away or get down on one side to keep us from slipping it under her. Over and over she repeated the performance, first fighting the sling with her feet, then getting down on her side. She had a chain tied to one front leg and a rope fastened to a back leg but there was enough play to enable her to go through this performance, which she did until I found myself perspiring and cussing freely.

The captain of the freighter (the only sea captain I've ever wanted to choke) kept yanking out an enormous watch and shouting that if I didn't hurry he'd have to leave without me. At the height of his peevish outburst Babe decided to get down on her belly and stay there, thrashing around with her trunk and trumpeting angrily as a warning that she wasn't enjoying this business at all.

By way of aiding me the captain kept bellowing that he was getting tired of waiting. So far I had held him up about twenty minutes, and I was sorry; but I was doing everything I could to speed the loading of that stubborn elephant and the foolish skipper wasn't helping any with his repeated wail that we were losing time. I wouldn't have minded that, however, for I knew that he had to leave while the tide was high, but I felt like aiming for his jaw when he said, "I thought you knew your business. I wouldn't have let you ship with me if I thought it was going to be like this."

Having loaded scores of elephants onto lighters and ships without mishap I had a right to resent this; also his superiority about carrying my freight,—several thousand dollars' worth of business that his company was glad to get.

We finally managed to get Babe off her belly and back on her feet. Ali and I took counsel. We agreed that the chances of getting the elephant harnessed in the regular manner were slim. We would have to try something else. The captain continued to storm and swear that he wouldn't wait another minute. No, sir! Not for a damned elephant.

With that infernal skipper, a lanky sour-faced Yankee, behaving like a lunatic there was no chance to work out a careful plan. I would have to take a long chance—and be quick about it.

I figured that if I could get between the animal's front legs, Ali could throw me the end of the sling quickly and we could get it on her. Ali got close to her on one side, two Siamese boys, experienced elephant hands who had helped me get my group of five to the dock, getting on the other side so they could grab the sling as I passed it through to them.

When everyone was in his appointed place—it was a tense moment, only the captain's curses breaking the silence—I got ready to dive between Babe's front legs. Having successfully played crazier and riskier rôles in my dealings with animals, I thought there was a pretty good chance of accomplishing my purpose now.

I rushed in and as I did Babe reached down with her trunk and raised me straight up in the air over her head as if to say, "Well, how do *you* like being lifted off the ground?" I was about ten feet up in the air but not for more than a second. She let go, throwing me straight forward with every bit of strength she had, which was plenty, sending me a distance of ten to twelve feet. I landed smack on my bottom, sitting down with enough vehemence to dislocate a less battle-tried posterior, and sliding forward four or five feet on the loose gravel with which the dock was covered. Good upholstery is all that saved me. If there were ribs in that part of the human form all of mine would have been broken.

Above the shouts and screams of the boys who came running over to pick me up, I heard a laugh. For the first time the captain was enjoying himself. Anyone who can laugh when a man is heaved violently into space by an enraged elephant has a queer sense of humor. I got a few laughs out of the whole business later myself (as, for instance, when the gravel that had imbedded itself was painstakingly picked out of my stern) but I could not understand the show of captainly mirth that reached my ears as the ground and I collided. With less luck I might have suffered a broken neck or snapped my spine.

While the boys bent over me to see how much damage Babe had done, the bad girl from Burmah was struggling to free herself. Ordering the boys to look to the elephant, I got up with difficulty and hobbled over to join them. As I came up, Babe, having managed to shake herself loose from the rope that had held her hind leg fast, came running forward. When she reached the end of the twenty-four-foot play she had now that she was no longer held from behind, the impact of her forward rush snapped the chain on her foreleg, nine or ten feet of it remaining fastened to the foot.

The chain dragged along after Babe as she ran, annoying her and slowing her up. When she was about ten yards ahead of us she stopped to pick it up with her trunk; and as we came up she started whipping it around like a big bull whip.

It was not my lucky day. As I stood there telling the boys what to do with their elephant hooks (I was too wobbly to wield one myself) the whirling chain struck me on the leg, wrapping itself around me in a rattle of metal. With the chain around my leg, Babe started to run, dragging me on one knee across the gravel that seemed all at once to become a series of saw-like points.

Luckily the two Siamese boys, as good a pair of elephant hands as I've ever known, didn't forget what to do with their hooks. Keeping in front of the would-be runaway they kept jabbing her in the trunk and forehead until they stopped her, after she had dragged me some fifty or sixty feet. The flesh was off my knee and I was a wreck, unable to stand up, when I was released from the chain that had crazily bound me to the elephant. I don't mind adding that I had had a bad scare and that this, added to my physical troubles, left me shakier than I had been in some time.

The captain, waving his watch in the air in a frenzy of despair, called upon heaven to witness that this was my last chance to leave with him for his boat three miles away. He would give me five minutes more and would go without me if I was not ready then.

I was licked. It was the first time in several years that I was faced by the prospect of leaving behind an animal that I had set out to bring back to America. There was nothing else to do. All my crates and cages had been loaded on the freighter and my four elephants were in the last lighter below, the only part of my collection that had not been taken down the bay and hoisted on board.

I would have to leave; but I had no intention of abandoning that elephant. She was a fine animal, her erratic conduct having proven nothing except that fear of dangling by a sling in mid-air, a sensation that probably gave her a sickish feeling the first time she experienced it, was capable of making her seem like a vicious pachyderm.

As soon as she saw that no further efforts would be made to put a sling around her and lift her off her feet, Babe quieted down. The Siam boys, keeping their hooks handy, had her well in hand by the time I had used up only half of the captain's five minutes. I ordered Babe back to my compound, adding that I would send instructions later telling what I wanted done with her.

We reached the boat with time to spare, the condition of the tide being such that we could have left a half hour later without doing any damage to the jumpy captain's schedule. I might have been able to overlook his time-craziness if he had taken the trouble, even once, to drop in at my quarters to see how I was getting along. After all, I had boarded his vessel too weak to negotiate the ladder,—so helpless in fact that it had proven necessary to swing me over the side like one of my animals; and it wouldn't have done the old fool any harm to look in and say hello. I didn't exactly miss him. But I'd have thought more of him if he'd showed himself to be that human. As it was, I was unable to decide whether he was a fish or a reptile.

"What's the matter with that damned captain of yours anyway?" I asked the mate the day after we sailed. I got to know him quickly for on a boat of this kind there is no doctor, the mate (who is required to know something about first aid and some of the other fundamentals of healing, such as ministering to a gravel-inlaid posterior, etc.) acts as medical officer.

"You asked a question?" said the mate, a likeable chap with an amusing habit of repetition, as he dislodged from my right lower cheek the tenth bit of gravel in five minutes.

"Yes, I did," I replied.

"I believe you asked, 'What's the matter with the captain?' "

"That's right," I said.

"Yes, that's right," he echoed. "That's what you asked." He dug out another bit of gravel as he solemnly made this statement.

"Well, sir, if you ask me I'd say—"

"Yes, I'm asking you."

"Well, sir, it's a question. What's the matter with anything? Take, for instance, a mud-turtle. What's the matter with a mud-turtle? Take a bedbug. What's the matter with a bedbug? Or take something simple. Take a dead fish. An old dead fish. One that's good and ripe. What's the matter with it? It stinks, sir. That's what's the matter with the captain."

His work on my bottom concluded, the mate turned his attention to my knee, replacing the neat bandage he had made the day before with a fresh one.

"That's what I thought," I said.

When the mate left I found myself thinking of Babe. I was determined not to lose her. She was a valuable property and I had no intention of letting her remain in Singapore. If I had considered her capable of running amuck under ordinary circumstances I'd have felt differently. I had had enough experience with the species to know that the gentlest of elephants will act badly if sufficiently scared. For an animal fresh from the *keddah*, Babe had made wonderful progress. She was not to be judged by an erratic performance involving her pet prejudice: belly slings.

To this day my right knee bears Babe's trade mark. Perhaps it seems strange that, with the wound still fresh, I should have been so tolerant of her misconduct. The answer is that I had seen so much freakish conduct in animals mistaken for viciousness. I had a hunch about Babe and I was going to play it.

I was soon busy putting into effect a plan that I considered worth trying.

I sent a wireless to a close friend in Singapore asking him to give Ali these instructions: The boy was to see Hin Mong at once and order the Chinese carpenter to build a platform strong enough for Babe to stand on. He was then to lead the elephant on to the platform, keeping her standing there while Hin built a crate around her out of heavy timbers with iron reinforcing bars, using the platform as the floor of the crate. If the elephant could be quickly crated, she was to be shipped to Manila on the first boat sailing, with ample food for a six-day trip. My friend Captain Yardley was due at Manila with the *President Cleveland* a few days after my boat was scheduled to arrive; so, in sending the animal to Manila, the thing to do was to have her consigned to the Dollar Line, which I did.

When I arrived at Manila I found a telegram from Singapore advising me that the elephant was on its way aboard a Spanish boat. This vessel was due in Manila a few days after our departure and about the time the *President Cleveland* was scheduled to arrive. I arranged with the Dollar Line to ship the elephant from Manila to San Francisco, leaving a long letter of instruction for Bill Morris, mate of the *Cleveland*, as likeable and intelligent a seaman as a man would want to know. I arranged for Bill to get at Hong Kong the food that Babe would need for the trip, this to be charged to me at a local ship's chandler where I carried an open account.

At Manila I had another job to do. I had been unable to pick up sufficient hay at Singapore, a commodity difficult to secure there in large quantities. I needed more than I was carrying to keep my elephants fed on the long trip across the Pacific in a cargo boat. I had arranged by wireless to secure some hay at Manila that was to be brought in from an army post fifteen miles in the interior. When we arrived the hay was not at the dock. There was a message for me saying that there had been some delay but that the hay would be delivered.

A half hour before the time set by our Yankee skipper for our departure from Manila the hay had not arrived. I telephoned the army post and learned that the trucks were on their way and would arrive in an hour.

I asked the captain if he could not wait a little longer, telling him that if I did not pick up this hay I wouldn't have enough food for my elephants.

"You should have thought of that before," he told me.

I told the old sour-belly that I had, adding a few details about the difficulty of buying hay in Singapore. All I had been able to secure there was a small quantity of Australian hay that I was able to divert, after much effort, from the racing stables which had ordered it.

Although I learned in confidence from the mate that another hour's wait was perfectly feasible, the captain was unrelenting. He raved about the unreasonableness of landlubbers. (At the time of this occurrence I had crossed the Pacific over thirty times and was rated a pretty fair sailor by some hard-boiled sea captains.) No, he would not wait. Not for any danged hay! I had held him up long enough at Singapore. He'd be blowed if he'd let me delay him again.

We left without my hay, which gave me a real problem. I would be without anything to feed my elephants toward the end of the trip.

My problem was complicated when we got up into the North Pacific. The captain received a wireless from the owners instructing him to cut down to the most economical cruising speed, which in the case of this freighter was eight knots an hour.

This meant several more days on the ocean and, of course, aggravated my food problem. The situation was now serious. I had to find some way of getting more food for my elephants or face the prospect of losing them.

I discussed the matter with the engineer, with whom I had struck up quite a friendship. In the course of our conversations it developed that we had many mutual friends on the sea and we spent a good deal of time getting reminiscent about them. After we'd been out four or five days we were calling each other by our first names.

The engineer was sympathetic. The captain was a dirty thus and so for not waiting a little longer at Manila. But what are you going to do with a skipper like that? Nobody liked him. In all his experience he (the engineer) had never known so unpopular a ship's captain. Mean, that's what he was, mean. Why, do you know, Frank . . . and then he launched a series of stories that more than proved his point.

"What are you going to do?" he asked me when he had concluded.

"Damned if I know. But I've got to figure out something. I don't intend to let those elephants die. There's too much money tied up in them. If they pass out on me, I'll lose money on the trip. Months of hard work with nothing to show for it."

Suddenly the engineer brightened. "I've got an idea," he said. "It may work and it may not. But it's worth trying."

"Swell! Let's hear it."

Then the engineer, a great scout, if I ever knew one, told me his scheme. He would let some fresh water out of the tanks and report to the captain that with the ship's speed reduced to eight knots an hour the fresh water on board would not be sufficient for the rest of the trip. We were about two hundred miles off the Japan coast and the following morning we would be just opposite Kobe. He would suggest that we put in there for water. This would give me a chance to get my hay. I could wireless ahead for it. We would be at Kobe three or four hours if the captain fell for the scheme, giving me plenty of time to load my hay.

"I know what the louse will tell me. 'Ration each man's water and use your condenser.' But I've got an answer. The condenser is in bum condition. I have my doubts as to how much fresh water could be made with it. I've been trying to get the owners to buy a new one but they're a stingy lot. That's why we're crawling along this way. They're trying to save a dollar's worth of fuel oil."

There was much feeling in this outburst, despite which I found myself smiling through it. The idea of putting one over on the captain appealed to me.

The engineer didn't lose any time putting the scheme into effect. The tanks tapped, he left for the bridge to report the water shortage to the captain.

I saw the engineer an hour later. "What's the verdict?" I asked.

"Not sure yet," he replied, grinning. Forgetting to be indignant, as before when his peevishness over the line's stinginess got the better of him, he was now enjoying himself. "But it looks pretty good."

"That's fine."

"When I showed him what the gauge registered he blew up. 'I don't understand it!' he roared. 'There ought to be more water than that.' 'It *is* kind of funny,' I said. 'I could have sworn there was more water in that portside tank only a little while ago.' He nearly had convulsions. Told me I was a hell of an engineer. If I was any good I could fix the danged condenser so she'd work right. 'Don't stand around doing nothing!' he wound up. 'Go and have another look at it.' So I went and had a look. That's what he told me to do, wasn't it? Having looked the condenser square in the eye for twenty minutes, I'm now on my way back to report that after trying everything, I've decided it's hopeless. If he doesn't like it, he can get a new engineer. I'm sick of this old tub anyhow."

Before I could reply he was off.

Twenty minutes later the engineer announced his victory. The captain was boiling mad,—ready to kill someone, in fact— but that didn't mean anything. All I was interested in was that we were going to stop at Kobe.

I lost no time in getting off a wireless to the Japanese port ordering plenty of hay. This commodity is easy to secure there and I knew that my supply would be on the dock when we arrived.

A few hours after I got my message off, I bumped into the skipper. "I see you're taking on some hay at Kobe," he said. On a freight boat all wireless messages have to pass the captain, —which is why Old Belly-ache knew that I had ordered the hay.

"That's right," was all I could bring myself to say.

"Why don't you figure out before you start on a trip what you'll need in the way of supplies and carry that much?" (This after all I had told him about the difficulty of securing hay in Singapore.)

"I understand you're going to take on some water at Kobe," I replied. "One of the sailors told me."

"Yes," came the irritable retort, "we're stopping for some danged water."

"Well," I responded, "why don't you figure out before you start on a trip what you'll need in the way of water and carry that much?" The effort to say this with a straight face was almost too much for me.

The captain stomped off in a rage, saying unprintable things about the ignorance of landlubbers. I caught a few phrases to the effect that if I knew anything about the sea I'd understand such emergencies, these phrases mixing with a jumble of oaths in as weird a cocktail of angry words as my much assailed ears have ever been called upon to drink in.

We stopped at Kobe. The captain got his water and I got my hay. Also a good laugh. So did the engineer.

A week after I reached San Francisco, rested and almost entirely mended, the *President Cleveland* arrived, with Babe on board riding on top of the poop deck. The only elephant I had ever shipped by crate (and the only one, to my knowledge, ever transported in this fashion) made her American début in splendid condition, furnishing one more proof of the hardiness of her species.

Not long afterwards, harnessed to the glittering wagon which I designed, reminiscent of the circus, Babe, the most mannerly of elephants, was pulling the children of San Francisco up and down the Fleischhacker Playground—and enjoying the work. She's doing it to this very day, and if there is a better behaved elephant anywhere in the country I'd like to know its name.

Every day of the year Babe goes through her paces, delighting hundreds of children. The last time I saw her at work I couldn't help enjoying the comment of an ecstatic mother who said, "Isn't she the gentle dear!" as she watched the Lady from Burmah pull her little boy around along with several other children. It was a warming confirmation of my own belief in the fundamental good nature of this animal even after she had almost blotted me out.

Not the least amusing phase of this experience was the way the story of my encounter with Babe on the dock at Singapore spread. I'll never know who started it but it certainly got under way. All along the coast of Asia the newspapers carried stories to the effect that I had been fatally injured in a tussle with the biggest and most ferocious elephant ever seen on the island of Singapore, —probably the most terrible animal of any kind ever seen anywhere, capable of wiping out a dozen tigers with a butt of the head or a stamp of the foot.

Proving once more the truth of the Hindu proverb which says, "If a man sneezes in Bombay it's a typhoon by the time it reaches Calcutta."

Monkey Mischief

I'VE brought back to America over five thousand monkeys. That's a lot of monkeys.

More than once I've marvelled at the fact that they didn't cause me more trouble. If my luck had not been good, that army of simians could have got me into more trouble than any one lifetime ought to know. That's because monkeys are full of cunning and mischief.

If two particular experiences I had with these impish creatures that enjoy man's discomfiture more than any other animals had been typical I should have cheerfully retired from the monkey industry and let someone else take my place.

In speaking of "the monkey industry" I refer to the business of supplying the steady demand for this strange commodity which, on a smaller scale, of course, clears through organized channels of trade just as tea and coffee do.

Monkeys are imported not only for sale as pets and for exhibition purposes in zoos and circuses, but also for use in scientific research. There are dealers that regularly supply these demands.

The monkeys most commonly used in supplying scientific bodies are the rhesus monkeys of India, the hardiest of all the small simians. They are less subject than any other species to the two scourges most common among the creatures: lung trouble and dysentery. These little animals (which weigh only 6 to 10 pounds full-grown) bring about $850 a hundred.

The Indian rhesus monkey is also the variety used in supplying the pet-shop market, the same price applying. I usually sell to jobbers who in turn sell to the shops in dozen and half-dozen lots.

Mother monkeys with babes are a staple line in the monkey trade. These are great attractions in carnival shows and circuses, making a big hit with women and children. I've sold hundreds of them, my price averaging about $40 a pair. The mother-and-babe circus trade, like the business with pet shops, is practically confined to the small rhesus species.

The biggest shipment of rhesus monkeys I ever gathered together was a consignment of 750 to a dealer who had an order for that quantity from one of our great medical research institutions. Even this big shipment didn't seriously deplete the population, for there are millions of rhesus monkeys in India. This is one branch of my business where there is no danger of the demand exceeding the supply.

A monkey commonly used in pit-shows and carnivals is the pig-tail rhesus, a much larger variety, the males weighing as much as thirty-five to forty pounds. I've brought about 800 of these out of Borneo, the price secured for them ranging from $35 to $50. This type of monkey has to be handled very carefully, what with the big canine teeth that they bring into play in settling arguments. The males are particularly savage and require considerable taming.

One of these Borneo pig-tailed chaps,—a big ill-natured male—once raised the devil on board ship in a manner I'll never forget. I was on the Pacific, several days out on my way from Asia to America. The boat was the *West Caddao*.

The pig-tailed rhesus to which I refer managed to get out of his cage by working away cleverly at a loose slat. Regardless of all the precautions one takes, an occasional specimen will escape. Alongside the total of tens of thousands of birds and animals I have brought back to America, the number of escapes I have had to combat is small indeed. But most of them caused me so much trouble I'm not likely ever to forget them.

A man who collects live specimens on as big a scale as I have for several years can't inspect and test all his crates and cages himself. Some of the work has to be done by others, and sometimes this assistance isn't as thorough as it might be. Invariably I order a new box when I know it is needed,—Hin Mong has made hundreds of them for me at Singapore—and I have old boxes repaired when they show signs of needing it. Even so, faulty cages get aboard. Careless inspection is not the only cause either. Sometimes, in the process of loading, a sound cage is handled roughly, and weakened. This does not always come to light in the inspection I make on shipboard before putting out to sea.

Other things happen—freakish occurrences that can defeat the best job of packing and loading—and all one can do is to be philosophic about them and accept them as part of the business of collecting live specimens, just as black eyes and swollen lips are part of the boxing profession.

When my pig-tail rhesus got loose aboard the *West Caddao* he did a thorough job of messing things up. At the outset, by staging some quick killings among my birds, he established that he was no mere playful monkey out for a lark. Reaching into one of the cages, he strangled a Shama thrush, one of the most valuable birds I had on board, and by way of showing that he wasn't fooling he killed off a few other feathered specimens which I had secured after much difficulty.

By the time I arrived on the scene—I was in the dining-room when the cyclone from Borneo started his career of crime— several birds were loose and three were dead. Overhead a quintet of Shama thrushes, released from their bamboo cages, flew round and round in nervous circles and a brush-tongued parrot squawked weird sounds of protest or triumph,—it was hard to tell which.

With escaped birds circling above me and a loose monkey raising hell on deck, I was not in an enviable position. My first impulse was to concentrate on capturing the birds, which were more valuable than the pig-tail rhesus but I downed that quickly. A monkey like this rascal from Borneo was too dangerous to leave to his own devices, even for a short time. Assigning to little Ali (nephew of Old Ali whom I had left in Singapore) the job of working on the loose birds, I gave myself the task of re-capturing the monkey. Sailors volunteered to handle the monkey chase for me but I didn't think it fair to let them handle the job alone, as anxious as I was to recapture my birds. An inexperienced person trying to grab one of these treacherous Borneo tree-dwellers has a fair chance of coming off with a badly torn wrist. The vicious canine teeth of the pig-tail rhesus have done plenty of damage of this kind—and worse—in their time.

Recruiting some sailors as assistants, I set out after the most troublesome forty pounds of monkey I've ever encountered. Our ambitious idea was to corner the wretch. He didn't think much of our efforts, scampering all over the deck and easily eluding us. He'd get about ten yards ahead of us, and turn around and eye us contemptuously over one shoulder; and as we'd come up on him he'd be off with a burst of speed. The sailors were more willing than helpful, confining themselves in the main to tossing pieces of dunnage, not especially well-aimed, at the simian foe.

We weren't getting anywhere this way, so I instructed my lumbering aids to reverse themselves and meet the monkey head on, the idea being to make the creature turn and run straight at me. I waited at the appointed place on the deck. The scheme was a success up to a certain point. The boys managed to drive the little villain toward me where I was prepared to stun him with a stout stick and drag him back to captivity; but the wily cuss had a plan of his own. He took a flying leap against my chest, hitting me with such force he knocked the wind out of me and almost spilled me. Then he disappeared for five or ten minutes and when he returned it wasn't hard to guess that he'd paid a visit to the galley coal hole. The *West Caddao* is an oil-burner but she carries a bunker of coal for the galley stoves where the cooking is done. Covered with coal-dust, the monkey, with a perfect instinct for making the maximum amount of trouble in any given situation, had a sudden inspiration to mess up the mate's nice new paint job. During the last two weeks of a trip like this on a cargo boat, all hands are assigned to cleaning the ship and painting her spick-and-span for arrival at her home port. From forecastle to poop the *West Caddao* was being painted till she started looking like a brand new vessel. My sailor assistants had been recruited with the mate's permission from among the renovating crew.

What an opportunity for a monkey black with coal dust! The scamp from Borneo, even if he had had the capacity for figuring such things out, couldn't have done more damage. In a flash he was all over the poop deck, seeming to run in four directions at one time. It wasn't long before the freshly painted funnels and rails were smeared here and there with coal dust and it wasn't long before the mate's curses,—and I didn't blame him—were ringing in my ears.

At this point, spurred on no doubt by the mate's cussing and a fervent desire to earn his blessings, the sailors resumed the target practice they had started on the main deck. With tin cans, lumps of coal and other odds and ends they fired away at their elusive target, one of them, the star marksman of the group, actually coming within a foot of the monkey's head. Then, to show that if he couldn't hit the roughneck from Borneo, he could hit something else, this fusilier sent a lump of coal crashing through a port window. As if I wasn't already sufficiently in bad with the mate!

If groaning was in my line I would have groaned then,—although I suppose I did give off a couple, mentally.

The interesting thing about that monkey was the fact that he was entirely unafraid. Curiously enough a much more savage animal in a similar situation might have been full of fear on account of the strangeness of his surroundings. This was true of my leopard that got loose aboard the *Granite State*. He was frightened because he was at a disadvantage, and though this didn't mean that he wasn't dangerous, I had the upper hand because it was a tip-off on how to handle him.

No monkey is at a disadvantage where there is scampering space and there are things to climb up, over and around. Instead of being scared, this little pest actually seemed to be laughing at us. As he'd duck a grenade tossed by one of my marines, he'd suddenly right his head and stand still, as if to say, "Well, here I am. Let's see you hit me!" Then there'd be another barrage, and the monkey, with what almost seemed like a grin of triumph, would scramble off to another point.

After he'd done a pretty thorough job of transferring the coal-dust on him to the ship's fresh paint, we managed to get the tantalizing imp off the poop deck onto the main deck again. I suspect he came willingly, just to show how little he feared us. And then, as we chased him, he added the final insult by dashing right back among the cages, and, before we could stop him, pulling the head right off a valuable Impeyan pheasant.

A quick reach through the slats and this worst of all the pigtail Borneos I've ever handled had killed a bird that was worth over twice as much as he was. It was pretty rough on the bird too, a rare fellow that was on his way to a zoo where he'd have had a good home and many admirers.

I had had quite a job landing that pheasant and it was tough to lose him after I'd carried him all over Asia and more than halfway across the Pacific. As I pulled up to the scene of the slaughter I heard a series of crashes. The vandal had knocked over a stack of bird cages but fortunately these were so stoutly built and so securely shut that no more of my feathered freight escaped. The jolting, however, didn't do the birds any good.

I came up in time to corner this destructive little demon against the side of the tarpaulin thrown tent-fashion over the hatch that served as a shelter for my cargo of birds. One of the sailors, in a sudden burst of usefulness after his failure as a marksman, got in and around, and drove the monkey toward me. Before he could leap at me as he had done earlier in the chase, I brought down on his head the capable stick I was carrying. I put enough force behind the blow to knock the little terror cold but not enough to injure him. Back to his box he went and this time he stayed there. The slats were reinforced and in vain he worked all the way back home for another taste of life on the open deck where there were men to mock and birds to kill and where every day there was more nice fresh paint that any monkey would enjoy smearing up.

Meanwhile little Ali, working with one of my landing nets, succeeded in capturing three of the Shama thrushes (little birds no bigger than a robin). Two of them, however, refused to listen to reason and shortly after I got my monkey back in his box, the silly little things put out to sea, with as much chance of surviving as a deer has in a fight with a tiger. It was a heart-breaking spectacle, as is always the sight of helpless little creatures battling against forces that are too much for them and against which they have no chance of surviving. I will never forget the picture of these two beautiful little songbirds setting out to conquer the mighty Pacific. It was only a question of how many hours would elapse before, exhausted from the aimless flight deeper and deeper into the wilderness of water, with no place to stop for a rest and nothing to eat, they would drop to a salty grave. I stood watching .the foolish little adventurers till they became tiny specks and disappeared. Once I thought I saw them falling and I found myself, lost in revery, starting forward against the rail and reaching out as if to grab them. Birds were my first love—it was as an amateur collector of them that I got started in the business in which I now find myself—and I have never ceased to be daffy about them. I have brought back over a hundred thousand of them, of nearly every known variety—some of them species never before seen in America like the great black cockatoo, Pasquel's vulture-headed parrot, and the fairy blue-bird of Borneo—and I hope that no one to whom I have sold birds will ask for his money back when I say that the experience has been so full of genuine pleasure, so replete with a kind of thrill that only the plumb crazy bird-fancier understands, that perhaps I should have paid for the privilege of handling these creatures instead of being paid.

The only other fugitive, the brush-tongued parrot, or lory, had perched himself high in the rigging and there he remained for three days and nights. With a grand unconcern about food and drink (we left offerings at places that would be convenient for him to reach if he felt minded to leave his perch) he stayed there in his new-found home over our heads. It would have availed nothing to go up after him: he would only have flown out to sea and perished like the little Shama thrushes.

One day, when we were within a mile of an island (by a curious coincidence, it was Bird Island, the westernmost of the Hawaiian group), an idea involving the future of that parrot occurred to me. I put it into effect with a handful of nuts and bolts. These I hurled at the stubborn bird in the rigging until I drove him from his perch. He circled around a few times till he got his bearings and then he put out to sea, heading for the island. I hope he had a good time when he arrived,—that he found plenty of the kind of food he liked. For all I know he may be alive and squawking to this very day. If he is, I hope he doesn't feel unkindly toward the fellow that threw all those nuts and bolts at him. In my crude way I was trying to save his life.

The smaller rhesus monkeys—the little chaps from India—have also given me samples of the mischief of which they are capable but never has there been anything vicious about it. Natural comedians, they confine themselves to antics that give rise to mirth rather than to wrath,—although I must admit that when enough of them get mischievous at the same time I feel like giving the little devils a spanking.

Which reminds me of something. I was returning from Asia on the S.S. *Santa Cruz* with a big shipment of birds and animals. Among my cargo were several boxes of small rhesus monkeys, twenty-five to a box. These boxes were stacked up in tiers, five to a tier.

We had hit a stretch of fine weather, enabling me to remove the canvas coverings that were used to protect the inhabitants of these containers from the wind. In this way I could give them the benefit of the sun and the balmy air. Without warning we ran into a quick blow which caused the lightly lashed boxes to shift. Before I could get everything firmly fastened, two of the top boxes that had shifted with the sudden lurching of the ship, slid off and landed with a crash on the iron deck, a fall of about nine feet. They broke open and in a few seconds there were fifty monkeys loose on that ship. They scampered off in all directions,—up the masts, into the rigging, onto the cross-beams, into the crow's nest, everywhere. Wherever your eye lit you saw a monkey.

Three of the little mischief-makers got up on the poop-deck where there were some potato boxes. The galley boy, who was carrying potatoes to the cook, had left the top of one of these boxes open, a natural thing to do as he was returning for more. When he returned he found the monkeys throwing potatoes all over the deck. They scurried off, looking back at him in the typical manner of prankish simians, tossing a last few potatoes around by way of making it clear that they didn't take the boy very seriously.

One of the fugitives decided to visit the galley where the baker had laid out some rolls, fresh from the oven, to cool. Before the baker could do anything about it, his unexpected visitor started scattering the rolls around, leaping on a stack of bread loaves in beating a retreat and sending several loaves toppling to the floor. Dodging sundry missiles in the process the happy monkey, revelling in his new-found freedom, proceeded to investigate the work of some galley boys who were preparing vegetables for the cook. He dove right into a pail of cut-up carrots, upsetting it and disappearing with a mouthful before the awkward boys, too surprised to do anything but stare at each other, could do anything to stop him.

Other members of the escaped fifty decided to show their sociability by calling on passengers. There were about forty-five on board, several of them women. Through a porthole one of the monkeys visited a lady who was dressing, scampering off with one of her stockings. As I chased after another one of my runaways I almost ran into this lady, who, shoeless, and wearing one stocking, was pursuing the little chap from India who had stolen the other one. "I want my stocking!" she frantically yelled as we almost collided. I'd have been glad to give her her stocking, having as little need for it as the monkey that had swiped it, but unfortunately there wasn't anything I could do about it. Stocking and monkey were off before anything could be done, and the lady never regained her property. What happened to that stocking I'll never know. I hope the monkey didn't eat it. It didn't look particularly digestible. I tried to pay the lady for a pair of stockings but she refused. She said she would have her own stocking or nothing. Ladies are sometimes like that,— although I refrained from making any such impolite comment for obviously I was in the wrong. After all, I had no business letting those monkeys get loose.

Another of the fugitives, preferring male society, called on an engineer who was returning to America and did his best to make this professional gentleman's trip memorable by knocking over a can of tobacco.

Still another of the sociable monkeys, with a fondness for face powder equivalent to its brother simian's leaning toward stockings, stuck its face into a box of the said powder (after another lady's privacy had been violated) and emerged with a nicely powdered face. Overzealous scientists have claimed the discovery of new species on the strength of less evidence than the powder on that monkey's face, and perhaps I lost an opportunity in not immediately taking a photograph and announcing the finding of the white-faced monkey of the Forest of Singacutta.

All in all the passengers had a thoroughly enjoyable time. There aren't many things that have greater laugh-provoking possibilities than a half hundred harmless monkeys loose on a ship and defying re-capture. A few passengers made complaints. In fact, the lady whose face powder was messed up called on the captain and demanded that "those nasty monkeys" be put off the ship. To which the captain (an old friend with whom I had made several crossings), unfeelingly replied: "I'm afraid we'll have to catch 'em first."

Despite the fact that the captain was a friend and stood by nobly, I didn't feel any too comfortable on account of the glares of those members of the ship's crew whose work was being messed up by my frivolous fifty. To this aggrieved group, I soon had to add the Chinese stewards in the dining salon, particularly their chief. This chap claimed,—and I had the misfortune to laugh as he hysterically voiced his complaint—that some of the monkeys had got into the dining salon and yanked the tablecloths and silver off four of the tables. I agreed that this was a most deplorable state of affairs but the chief steward was unimpressed by my chuckling expression of sympathy, for he dashed off in a huff, announcing that the captain would hear of the matter in short order.

For me the choicest aspect of the whole episode was represented by the activities of an agent of the Standard Oil Company —an American in his early thirties—who started a contest among the passengers to see who could catch the most monkeys. This chap—who came to be known as The Monkey Tamer—got hold of a wooden box which he converted into a trap. Turning the box over so that the opening faced the deck, he placed a wooden peg under one end by way of providing an entrance for his victims. Then he baited the trap with a banana. The idea was to lure a fruit-loving fugitive under the uptilted box, and, just as he snatched the banana, to yank out the peg which was controlled by a string. Down the box would come over the monkey and he would be a prisoner.

Within a few hours of the time he got his trap going, the Monkey Tamer had made his first capture. The fun began when he raised the box and stuck his hand underneath to grab his monkey. The little fellow had no desire to be taken into custody and he scampered around in his prison, which was about the size of an ordinary soap-box, eluding the grasp of his jailer. In working his hand around in an effort to grab his victim, the Monkey Tamer scraped one of his fingers against a nail and suddenly decided that he had been bitten. In his anxiety to get a quick look at the injured member, he raised the box too high and the little animal dashed out, triumphantly carrying off the banana with him.

You'd have thought that young man had been nipped by a cobra. All I could see on his finger was a scratch. There were no marks of teeth. But the Monkey Tamer insisted he had been bitten and within the next twenty minutes he doused his "wound" with three different kinds of antiseptic.

I'm always amused by the myths surrounding what is known as "monkey bite." There are all sorts of stories to the effect that if a monkey nips you, you're in danger. Having been bitten by monkeys hundreds of times, I naturally cannot take these stories very seriously. In fact, I don't know of a single case where monkey bite caused any real damage unless the victim happened to be in bad health. Even then the bite would have to be a real one.

In view of these facts I was unable to summon up much sympathy for the father of the monkey-catching contest who hadn't been bitten at all. I soon reassured him by telling him that every shipment of monkeys I had ever made had involved at least a dozen bites, and that even granting he had been savagely nipped, there was no immediate danger of death. His fears soon disappeared and he was again busy with his trap. His "injured" finger bound up in gauze, I saw him a little later baiting his box with another banana.

His method was again successful for less than an hour elapsed when I heard him excitedly shouting, "I've got another one!" The contest continued merrily. A score-board was rigged up and a record was kept of each monkey that was captured. I caught four of the little rascals with a hook dip-net that I always carried with me but I decided to retire from the contest, letting a zealous passenger borrow my net. After all, my fellow travellers seemed perfectly willing to capture my monkeys, and I saw no reason why I shouldn't let them do my work for me.

At the end of the second day the Monkey Tamer had six monkeys, which left him in the lead, the nearest player to him having a score of two less. The high scorer was becoming cockier by the minute, telling highly colored stories of his captures to any listeners he could summon in the bar. In fact, this chap was becoming so puffed up with his success that he began to annoy the other passengers, a group of them putting their heads together and agreeing to pool their captures the following day and contrive to credit them to the score of an exuberant girl from California who ranked third on the list of contestants.

The contest wound up the following day, the Monkey Tamer winning with a score of eight, the girl from California finishing second with seven.

Only two monkeys were lost. One, in trying to elude a pursuer, went overboard. A second died freakishly of poisoning. A sailor was out on one of the hatches cleaning a pair of pants. Attracted by the picture of two ladies chasing a monkey, he broke into a laugh, and too amused to keep his mind on his work, he watched the spectacle on the deck. As he did, another of the loose fifty quietly paid him a visit. This foolish little fugitive decided to sample the cleaning fluid (an acid of some kind) that the sailor had placed on the hatch, in a saucer. Before the seafaring gent could do anything to prevent the act, the monkey took a good swallow of the fluid, dying shortly afterwards.

When we pulled into San Francisco the local reporters interviewed me as they usually do when I arrive with a sizeable menagerie. One of the reporters, an old friend, called me over to one side and, pointing to the Monkey Tamer, asked, "Who the hell is *that* guy?"

"One of the passengers," I replied. "He represents the Standard Oil Company somewhere in China."

"What's this story he tells about capturing fifty wild monkeys?" he asked.

"I'd quite forgotten," I replied. "He's the hero of the trip. Saved several lives. Better get the story from him. Big stuff."

At this point the Monkey Tamer looked over at me and I broke into a laugh. Discouraged, the ace of monkey catchers walked off.

"Who're you trying to kid, Frank?" asked my reporter friend. As if I'd ever try to kid a newspaperman!

Loose on Board

I HAD just left Calcutta aboard the S.S. *Granite State* with a big shipment of animals and birds. On the way down the Hooghly River we stopped at Budge-Budge, an oil station just below Calcutta, to discharge a cargo of oil.

We remained at Budge-Budge all day. Shortly before we left I negotiated an unexpected deal for a leopard. In fact, the gang ladder was about to be pulled up when a native came tearing up in a small motor lorry (borrowed or stolen) with a crated leopard on it. The box bounced around uncertainly as the driver suddenly applied his brakes and came to a halt.

The native arrived with such dramatic suddenness and gave vent to so much excited chatter that he seemed like the bearer of important tidings or a man on an epoch-making mission and before anyone could stop him he was on deck making more wild noises and gestures there. It seems that he had to see Buck *Sahib*.

This was quickly arranged. In fact, he bumped into me as I hurried over to see who was paging me so frantically. Breathlessly the native told me (partly in broken English and partly in Hindustani which Lal translated for me) that he had heard from Atool Achooli, the Calcutta bird and animal trader, with whom I did considerable business, that I was in the market for another leopard. He had one in the lorry below, an excellent addition to my collection, he assured me. In fact, it was the finest leopard in India, and if I didn't buy it I was making the mistake of my life.

I got hold of the mate (who was really too busy with his preparations for departure to be bothered) and he was good enough to give me a few minutes' grace before pulling up the gang ladder, to inspect the animal that the excited native had in the cage on the dock.

I went ashore, made a hasty examination, saw that the animal was a first-rate specimen,—though not quite the finest leopard in India—and negotiated a quick deal. Lines were thrown over the side and made fast around the cage, and the latest addition to my floating menagerie was hoisted over the side by hand.

My new cat was a full grown male spotted leopard in perfect condition. He was a savage devil, raising a rumpus with his snarling and growling whenever I went near him; and when Lal attempted to pass a few hunks of perfectly good beef into the cage he lunged against the bars with a roar that resounded from the poop deck to the forecastle head in his attempt to get at the boy.

I saw at once that it would never do to keep this screaming cyclone near my better behaved cats. The others, leopards and tigers, were a fairly manageable lot, pretty much convinced that misconduct wouldn't get them anywhere, and I didn't want this rambunctious cuss to destroy the morale I had built up. With this villain to lead the rebellion there was much likelihood that the work I had done on all those other jungle tabbies would be undone. I therefore stowed his cage on the iron deck right down against the rail at the ship's side, a fair distance from the rest of my collection which had been loaded on the tops of No. 1 and No. 2 hatches where they were protected against the weather by a heavy tarpaulin flung tent-fashion over the cargo booms.

I spent a fair amount of my time on the bridge as the guest of Captain Harry Wallis, a friend of many voyages and a skipper with a great record of achievement. Each of us thought the other had the most interesting pursuit in the world and, when the sea was calm and we had easy sailing, we'd swap stories.

During one of these chats a blow came on. Whenever anything like this occurred I would beat a hasty retreat, for no sea captain, no matter how good a friend, wants to be bothered when he has to think about the weather. The best way to be re-invited to the bridge is to know when to vacate it.

As I started to go, I mentioned that it would be a good idea to play safe and move my new leopard to a more protected spot.

With a laugh, the skipper accused me of babying my latest arrival. "How do you expect to make a sailor of him if you coddle him that way?" he asked. "A little spray won't hurt him. That's all he's in for. We won't take any green seas over the forward deck out here at this season." We had left the typhoon area in and about the China Sea far behind us by this time and were somewhere out in mid-Pacific.

About five-thirty o'clock the next morning there was a furious pounding on my door.

"What's the matter?" I yelled, half asleep.

"There's hell to pay!" I heard through the door. "Open up!"

Groggily I stumbled to the door in the semi-darkness. I didn't know whether I was being serenaded by a drunk, or whether we had another one of those practical jokers on board.

Opening the door and blinking, I discovered the third officer there. Pale and trembling, he looked like a man who had been having a bad dream.

"Come in and sit down," I sleepily greeted him. "You look all in."

"No time for sitting, sir," he replied. "There's hell to pay!"

Not having anything specific to worry about yet, and being more asleep than awake, I could think of nothing to do but yawn and drop into a chair. At least, this is what the officer afterwards told me I did. He didn't mind telling me either that this was no way to act when a ship's officer paid you an emergency call. Now I think it over, he was right. But I *was* sleepy.

"Put your clothes on, sir!" he barked. "Captain directs it. There's—"

My principal recollection of that sleepy session was that I had no desire to be told again that there was hell to pay. Fairly awake by now, I revelled in my triumph. I had frustrated the third attempt.

Mechanically I reached for my clothes and started to dress.

"Faster, sir!" I was obviously not dressing very rapidly.

"If you expect any speed out of me," I replied, "you'll have to tell me what's wrong."

The third officer was saving his big news for a grand climax. He was a pleasant little chap on the whole but he was so con-

structed that when entrusted with an important message he liked
to nurse it along, loath to part with it until he had squeezed the
last drop of excitement out of it.

"What's wrong, you ask?" he echoed. "What's wrong indeed!
Plenty's wrong! Your leopard's loose! The one on the iron
deck! That's what's wrong. And, if you ask me, it's a bad
situation, sir. Bad!"

I fairly leaped from my chair. "My leopard's loose? I'll be
damned!" Feverishly I finished dressing, firing questions at the
third officer in the process.

Vicious seas breaking over the forward deck with a sudden
rush had sent the cage on a ten-foot spin and turned it upside
down. The officer on watch evidently thought that a leopard in
a cage bottom-side up was as safe as a leopard right-side up, as
long as he was still inside his cage.

All went well until later when another tremendous sea came
smashing over the upturned cage, pounding it amidships and
completing the damage by dropping tons of water on the top-side
bottom which was never meant to be as strong as the real top.
The roof of the cage was gone. A bewildered leopard scampered
out, mixed a few growls with the roaring of the sea, and pattered
down the iron deck to think things over among some oil barrels
lashed around the mast and against the bulkhead.

I had heard enough,—more than enough. My visitor was
right. There *was* hell to pay, although I'd have shot him if he
had said so again. He turned to go. "Anything I can do, sir?"
He really was a decent sort despite my murderous thoughts.

"Yes, send a quartermaster at once to rout out my boy Lal.
Have him chased here as fast as his legs can travel."

My early morning caller left, looking graver than ever. I could
even hear him run down the hall, a remarkable performance in
so dignified a chap.

The passengers were still abed. There was one thing that had
to be done immediately. The mid-section of the ship, the part
occupied by the passengers, would have to be cut off from the
foredeck and promenade deck.

In a few minutes Lal arrived, struggling to throw some clothes over himself as he entered on the run. I gave him some hasty commands. His principal task was to take a few dozen revolver bullets I tossed at him and pull out the lead noses with a pair of pliers. Then he was to stuff wadding into the empty ends to hold the powder in. He had done the job for me before.

I left on a hurried visit to the captain's quarters. He sportingly agreed to give me a chance to catch my leopard alive. I had to make a promise to shoot to kill if the escaped animal became a menace to passengers or crew. There was small likelihood of danger to passengers whose section of the vessel was quickly shut up, preventing access to open deck space. The crew could be warned to keep out of the way.

"But remember, Buck" (the captain speaking), "I reserve the right to step in whenever I see fit and order the animal killed. I can't let this leopard chase go on forever. The minute I decide you've had a fair chance to catch it, you'll have to submit to my decision. You know enough about the sea to realize I can't let this sort of thing interfere with efficient operation of my ship. Go ahead. But don't take any unnecessary chances. No leopard is worth it. Good luck."

Before leaving, I asked the captain if he would have instructions sent to the ship's carpenter to repair the broken cage at once. He readily agreed. "I don't know what I'll do with it," I said as I left, "but I'll want a place to put that damned leopard if I do catch him alive."

I returned to my cabin where Lal had completed his task. I didn't realize until he started questioning me that I had failed to tell him why I had routed him out of bed. The early morning assignment of castrating the revolver cartridges had puzzled him badly. By now he was used to any kind of instructions from me and he took his orders like a good soldier; but he'd get cross and irritable when he thought I was being secretive. I explained hastily that I had not had a chance to tell him, and pushing him out of the door as I grabbed my rifle, told him that the new leopard was loose.

"*Soure Cabatcha!*" exclaimed Lal. "Better you shoot him quick, master, he's bad lelpid." (This was the closest Lal ever got in his life to saying "leopard.") Then giving me a sort of disappointed look, he displayed the handful of blank cartridges and asked, "Why you want these no good bullets?"

"Never mind," I said, "just hold on to those blanks. I think I'll have some use for 'em in a little while." A grunt which savored of disgust was his only reply as we hurried along the passageway.

As we made for the iron deck I examined my rifle. It was in fine working order. One of Lal's duties on shipboard was to keep it in good shape, ready for immediate use in just such an emergency as this.

I wanted to get in among those oil barrels and gradually work my way back to the spot where the leopard had taken refuge. How near I should get to the savage beast would depend upon his behavior. But before making any definite decision or plans about taking him alive I had to find out just how his new found liberty was affecting his morale. If he proved as ferocious loose on the deck as he had been while in the cage then, of course, he must be shot immediately. While I felt pretty certain that he would be more scared than vicious, my first job was to make sure of this.

Lal was carrying my revolver, which he had loaded with the blank cartridges. He also had with him, in addition to a further supply of blanks, a round of perfect revolver bullets ready for use.

With the boy at my side I began to crawl in among the barrels. I was prepared to shoot to kill. Lal, aware of this, was delighted. His was a typical Hindu view that the animal had sinned grievously and should be punished. The only fit punishment was death.

We crept up closer and closer. I raised my rifle for action, getting a bead on the leopard not more than fifteen feet away. My finger was on the trigger. I had no desire to shoot. But I was prepared to pull the trigger if he gave any signs of springing at me. I crept a few inches closer. All the leopard did was snarl and bare his claws and once or twice make a movement as if he were going to jump up on top of the barrels to get away from me.

Everything in his manner indicated that the thought uppermost in his mind was escape. Of course he would fight unto death if attacked but my guess was—one plays hunches in my business, there being no rule-book by which to judge animals—that here was a badly worried leopard. In surroundings that were more familiar to him, where he would be surer of himself, he might have forced the fight, lashing out with his vicious claws and ripping open everything in sight with his cruel teeth. But my experience told me that here was an animal that considered himself at a disadvantage.

"We can take him alive, Lal," I whispered. I've never seen the boy's face take on a more disappointed look. The animal had caused much trouble and should be shot before he caused more, was the way he felt. On occasions like this the boy would thirst for gore, his primitive instincts asserting themselves.

Dragging Lal along by the arm, I crawled out, leaving the leopard where he was, and made for the steps leading from the iron cargo deck up to the ship's main promenade deck where the officers' mess-room was located. I looked the ground over carefully and decided that it would be possible to drive the leopard up the steps and into the mess-room.

With Lal's assistance—he still thought the animal should be shot but that didn't interfere with his speed and sureness as a helper—I hauled the empty cage, now repaired by the ship's carpenter, up the steps to a space near the door of the mess-room. Leaving the door open, I had all other means of reaching the room closed.

Then I went after my leopard, revolver in hand. It was loaded with blanks but I don't mind saying that I wasn't taking any chances. I am not one of those fearless adventurers who snap their fingers, in their memoirs, at any rate, and step right up to the jaws of death while someone, miraculously on the scene with a camera, takes a picture. After all, a leopard is a leopard. These spotted cats have killed many human beings and I had no desire to be added to the list. My loose leopard, in addition to being worried, was perhaps rather scared (any wild animal, no matter how ferocious normally, is at a disadvantage in a setting

LOOSE ON BOARD   241

that befuddles him) but he was still a leopard; and once he got it into his head that he was fighting for his life, he would become a terror. This is by way of explaining that I wasn't as bold as I seemed when I set forth with my blank-cartridge pistol. I saw to it that Lal was by my side with my loaded rifle, ready to hand it to me any second,—or to blaze away himself if there was not sufficient time to hand me the weapon.

Again Lal and I were among the oil barrels facing the enemy. The leopard, at a loss to know what to do, was approximately where we had left him. My mind was made up. There was nothing for me to do but to chase him from the position he had taken up among these barrels, get him to scamper up those steps leading into the mess-room, drive him into this chamber and then slap the open cage against the door and drive him into that.

Lal and I took up a position where I could fire at the leopard at an angle that would drive him out on the open deck (in the event he was in the mood for being driven). I raised my pistol and blazed away. The big spotted cat, in a series of great leaps— and even if he isn't leaping at you there is something terrifying about those tremendous and seemingly effortless jumps—made for the open deck. Round and round he went, Lal and I in pursuit. After circling the iron deck about half a dozen times I blazed away at the animal three or four times in a row when we were about ten yards from the steps leading to the promenade deck where the officers' mess-room was. Instead of scampering up the steps as I hoped he would the animal stopped in his tracks and whirled around. Teeth and claws bared, he faced me, ready to spring. I let him quiet down. We stood facing each other this way for a full minute. I could not afford to back away, any more than I could afford to advance. The animal started to relax. His lips began to close over his teeth. His claws were receding. This was a good time to shoot. I let him have another blank, the fire bursting close enough to his eyes to frighten him. He turned and ran. I thought I had him cornered so that he couldn't help col- liding with the steps but he swung wide as he ran, and passed my objective. Round he went for two more circuits, making such speed I thought he would lap me. He would have done so in a few more rounds, for by now he was desperate for a means of escape and he had dropped his halting manner of running. As he completed his second circuit he was not many yards behind me. Swinging round, I advanced and opened fire. The suddenness of my attack was too much for him. At a loss what to do, he swung around and started going in the other direction. As he went around the turn, I heard an agonized shriek. The leopard had almost collided with a Chinese boy carrying two buckets of water. What the boy was doing on deck I didn't know. I thought everyone had been warned to keep off.

The buckets went careening crazily down the deck, the water splashing in all directions. The boy scrambled to his feet, frightened out of his wits. Madly he tore for the bulkhead doorway from which he had recently emerged. The leopard, as scared as the boy, ran uncertainly for the same door, neither of them quite sure what it was all about. When the unexpected takes place in this fashion, the animal is as much at a loss as the human being involved. As he neared the doorway the boy saw a rope hanging from a boom above his head. He grabbed the rope and scrambled up it like a monkey.

I took advantage of the animal's confusion, coming up on him suddenly, as he stood still after a few hesitant movements beneath the boy swinging on the rope. The chambers of my gun re-filled with blanks, I blazed away again, and this time succeeded in manœuvering the leopard to a position in front of the steps that led to the deck above. Another series of shots sent him scampering up; and the first stage of my task was over.

In the meantime, the passengers (there were about eighty of them) had awakened, not unaided by the many shots I had fired. The news of the leopard chase had spread and the passengers rushed for the glass-enclosed upper deck above the mess-room to take in the show,—or as much as they could see.

The much harassed leopard made circuit after circuit of the promenade deck, Lal and I in pursuit. Every other lap or so, he would suddenly swing around and face us, teeth and claws bared as before, and ready for action. Again we would stand motionless and give him a chance to quiet down. Once after his teeth and claws relaxed to normal and we thought he was calming down, the cries of passengers startled him and he poised himself for a leap, his eyes distorted with rage and fear.

"The rifle, Lal!"

The boy was so anxious to place it in my hands he almost threw himself at me in handing it to me. He wanted that leopard killed; there was no doubt about that.

I got a bead on the animal about five or six yards away. My finger on the trigger, I was ready to bang away and catch the enemy in mid-air if he leaped.

I advanced a foot to see how anxious the leopard was for a scrap. He started backing away.

"Give him the pistol, Lal!" I had handed Lal the revolver when I took the rifle from him. Lal blazed away and again the animal turned and ran.

It was getting to be a tiresome business. I made up my mind to get that leopard, dead or alive, without wasting much more time and energy.

Fortunately my spotted fugitive was tiring too. Weary of the chase, he would hesitate before the open door of the mess-room and scamper round the deck again, without much assurance,—not quite certain whether he had anything to lose by going in. Finally seeing that there was no other place to go, he entered. I banged the door shut and the second stage of the job was finished.

Lal and I, after a few moments of well-earned rest, removed the bars from one end of the repaired and reenforced cage and shoved it smack against the doorframe, first hastily opening the mess-room door. We took the precaution of blocking in the open space above the cage.

So far so good. This was progress.

With a group of husky sailors holding the cage firmly against the door I decided on the next move.

Going into a hallway from the other side of the deck opening into the mess-room I lowered a dumb-waiter window (through which the mess-boy on duty passed food when a meal was being served) and, with a long bamboo pole, tried to prod the leopard into the box.

My spotted foe would snarl his opinion of these tactics, two or three times grabbing the end of the pole between his teeth and biting off a piece. He'd spit out the bamboo and look up at me in a rage, all the bitterness in his heart reflected in his cruel glare.

After fifteen or twenty minutes of this he decided to mock what he must have considered a feeble effort to get him into the cage. Another leopard, under the same circumstances, might have scampered in. This one expressed his contempt for my methods by stretching out on the floor and ignoring me after he was convinced there was nothing to fear from that pole which he had already chewed to pieces. Perhaps he was taking advantage of a lull in the battle to get a rest. At any rate, he made it clear that it would take more than a bamboo pole to get him inside that cage.

The stubborn beast was beginning to annoy me. It was time to show him who was boss. I sent Lal to my cabin for my lasso. Then I had one of the sailors bring me a long piece of ship's rope, which I securely tied to the end of the lasso. Next I filled my revolver with honest-to-goodness lead-nosed bullets. Then, gun in belt and lasso in hand, I started climbing through the dumb-waiter window.

I heard one of the petty officers yelling: "What's the matter, man? Are you crazy?"

I was too busy to answer. As a matter of fact, I was quite sane. I was doing the only thing that could be done with the facilities at hand to get that mulish leopard into his cage.

Before swinging over the window I threw the end of the rope through the bars of the cage to the sailors outside. "When I tell you fellows to pull," I instructed, "pull for all you're worth."

The mess-room was about seven feet wide and fifteen or sixteen feet long. A stationary dining table with clamped-down chairs practically filled the room leaving just enough space between the chairs and the wall for the officers to pass along to their places at the table. It was an easy step from the dumb-waiter window onto the table. With the loop end of the lasso in my hand ready for action I advanced slowly toward the leopard which was crouched down by the foot of the table at the other end of the small room.

As I made my cautious approach (advancing only a few feet), the animal let out a throaty snarl, one of those ugly low ones that give you the creeps till you get used to hearing them, and suddenly reared up with his forepaws on the other end of the table.

Again I resorted to the simple expedient that has saved me from being clawed any number of times. Standing motionless, I gave the animal a chance to calm down. This he did, slipping his paws off the table and edging back to where he was when I entered. The only sound that came from him was a faint growl, suggestive of muttering, making it seem as if the creature was talking to himself. Now that the animal was fairly quiet I started once more for his end of the room, working my way across the table toward him in tiny steps.

He lay there cringing, his teeth bared. His snarl this time was more of a wail and I felt sure that I had him on the run. It was ticklish business but I was making headway. Only a man who has had long experience in handling animals can get the feel of a weakening enemy in a situation of this kind. Reducing the thing to simple terms, I was making it clear to this foolish beast who was running the show. It is purely a mental proposition, the same psychology entering into it that makes it possible for experienced trainers to tame the jungle's wildest beasts.

Nevertheless, I don't mind adding that I was more than a little comforted by my loaded revolver and the nearness of an open window.

I kept steadily working up to where the leopard was crouching, getting my rope ready as I advanced. With a quick movement as I neared the other end of the table I sent a loop around the animal's neck, taking up the noose's slack in a flash as I yelled, "Pull!" with every ounce of lung power I possessed.

The men responded beautifully, giving a great yank that started the roped leopard sliding toward the door. As he was dragged along he let out a series of spine-chilling snarls, struggling to dig into the floor with his claws, and, when he saw this availed him nothing, striking out with his paws in a desperate effort to get a grip on a table leg or one of the stationary chairs he was being tugged past.

With a final great yank, the men pulled the growling and struggling beast till they could drag him no further. In order to get the animal into the cage he would have to be pulled around a corner of the door-jamb, as he was at right angles to the cage-opening toward which he was being dragged. A trial tug, to see if this miracle could be accomplished,—(what we really hoped for was that at this stage of the game the beast would see he was licked and scamper into the cage himself)—availed nothing. He had braced his back against the chair nearest the door and he couldn't be budged. All the men could do now was to keep him wedged in by holding the rope taut, which they did. It was impossible for the animal to move backward and it was equally impossible for the men at the rope to drag him forward another inch.

For several seconds we remained deadlocked, the animal making a perfect bedlam of the mess-room with his cries of rage. The rope around his neck was uncomfortably tight,—(much tighter than I wanted it to be, but there was no other way to hold him)—and he gave voice to the murder in his heart in as terrible a solo as I've ever heard from a cornered animal.

Hastily I reviewed in my mind possible ways of getting that leopard the rest of the distance to the cage, his head now being only about a foot from the opening.

I shouted my simple plan to the men outside. "And when I swing him round," was my final command, "pull like hell."

Then I proceeded to put my scheme into effect, the only course that could possibly save the situation. It was a risky business, for an infuriated leopard is a menace, even when partly a prisoner.

Jumping off the table I quickly grabbed the animal by a kicking back leg and squared him around so that the men could pull him straight through the door. Considering that it was my first experience at swinging a leopard around a bend by a back leg, I did a good job. The men at the rope did an even better job. The second I surprised the animal with my attack from the rear that placed him directly in front of the open cage he had been so stubbornly resisting, they gave a tremendous yank that sent the spotted mule—(only this cat was more obstinate than a mule)—catapulting headlong through the opening as though he were on the wrong end of a tug-of-war, with an army of elephants working the other end of the rope.

All I heard from the leopard was a strangled gasp as he went whizzing through the opening into the cage. Lal, who was now on top of the box, did a speedy job of dropping the bars that made the animal a prisoner again. With two sailors to assist him in the operation, it was over in a jiffy.

As I mopped the perspiration off my forehead, thinking that my task was over, I was alarmed by the labored breathing that came from the cage. Running around and peering inside, I saw that the animal was choking. For some strange reason that I never could fathom the slip-knot around the neck had not loosened when the sailors at my order slackened their hold on the rope.

Something had to be done immediately. I grabbed the end of the rope and sent the slack twirling through the bars, hoping this would result in slacking the noose. It didn't.

Again I rallied my sailors. I commanded them to grab the end of the rope and jerk the animal forward to the bars. I was no longer interested in the creature from the standpoint of its value. All that the situation meant to me at this moment was that here was an animal threatened by strangulation. To me, an animal dying is as painful a sight as human death and I meant to save that pesky leopard's life if I got clawed up in the process.

I got out a heavy pocket knife I always carry. The agonized breathing of the choking beast rattled me as much as anything ever had in all my experience, and I found myself fumbling with the knife in my feverish efforts to open up the biggest blade, with a powerful cutting edge of over four inches. I got the blade open as the men dragged the animal to the bars with a powerful pull. All I saw in front of me was a couple of hundred pounds of tortured leopard as I reached in and slipped the knife under the rope, quickly cutting it through.

Ironically enough, now that this animal was caged, I was in greater danger in my dealings with him than at any time since I set out to capture him. I took my chances when I stuck my hand into the cage to slit that noose, but this was as nothing compared to the danger I was in during the fraction of a second that elapsed between the time I restored him to normal breathing with a great slash of my knife, and the withdrawal of my hand. He seemed to come alive again instantaneously, making a terrible lunge for me, one paw just reaching the right shoulder and ripping my leather jacket wide open. Fortunately I ducked as I frantically backed away or that vicious paw would have dug down into my shoulder and held me fast while the other paw reaching out through the iron bars got in its deadly work at my throat.

Five weeks later the troublesome creature, considerably tamed though not exactly what you'd call docile, wound up at the Lincoln Park Zoo in Chicago.

Mouse-Deer

A POET in search of a theme could do worse than consider the possibilities of the mouse-deer. Of all the animals in the jungle this is the one that the Malays, a primitive people with a strange sensitiveness to beauty, have selected for their hero. Artistically the selection is perfect; for if there is a more beautiful animal than the mouse-deer or one that makes its appeal more directly to the affections I don't know its name.

Pelandok, as the Malays call this little-known animal that suggests the unreal to the extent of seeming the product of a fertile imagination, is a tiny deerlike animal, which, full grown, varies in height from about ten to twelve inches. (I am discussing the variety that is most common in the Malay Archipelago.) Like regular deer, Pelandok is a browser, eating the same kind of food that serves as fare for the big fellows he resembles. He is almost a perfect replica of these larger animals, one of the few points of variance being that the bucks of the mouse-deer family do not have antlers.

Pelandok is very fleet of foot. His speed is an asset but it is not enough to keep him out of trouble. The jungle is full of enemies, most of them too big and too fast for him. Figuring speed in proportion to size, the mouse-deer is probably faster than anything on legs but that doesn't help him any when he's pursued by a leopard or a wild-cat. When his wanderings take him too close to one of these carnivorous beasts he's as good as eaten and digested. The same is true when he strays too close to where a python lies in waiting for a tasty mouthful. Even the lordly tiger whose appetite is usually stayed by more formidable fare is not above devouring a mouse-deer that has the bad fortune to cross his trail.

Pelandok is a treat to the eye. His little legs are no bigger around than a lead pencil, his little cloven hoofs covering no more space than a ten-cent piece. A shy little creature, walking with a queer, stiff-legged, tiptoeing gait, he seems like something plucked out of a book of fairy tales and given life by some process of magic. He has a beautiful soft coat of a fawn color that sometimes borders on the reddish.

The mouse-deer is also to be found in Ceylon, in southern India, and in Palawan, one of the southernmost islands of the Philippine group. These species are essentially the same, the chief difference being in the matter of markings,—the Ceylon variety, for instance, having more pronounced spots than the Malay type which is only faintly marked.

There is also an African mouse-deer, although I have had no experience with the species (which is found in East Central Africa.) This is not so graceful an animal as the Malayan variety, the principal point of variance being that the legs are stouter and shorter.

The indications are that thousands of years ago the mouse-deer made its home in lands where it is now unknown. For instance, the remains of an identical species, differing only in size (though not greatly), have been found in the Miocene deposits in France.

It is safe to speak of Asia as the home of the mouse-deer as all the indications are that this continent has by far the greatest representation of this beautiful little animal that so few people know about.

Even on the Island of Singapore many of them are to be found. One of my greatest pleasures when in Singapore is to take a drive, toward nightfall, along Mandi Road some ten or twelve miles from town where virgin tropical forest has not given way to orderly rows of cultivated rubber and cocoanut as it has over a greater part of the island. Here I leave the car and walk to the edge of the jungle, where music is to be heard that only the man who has lived in the jungle understands. One minute you hear the peculiar howl of the gibbon. From another point in the blackness—perhaps a half mile away—you hear an answering call. Birds of a dozen varieties can be heard greeting one

another, the whole making up a chorus that falls pleasantly
on the ears of the Texan in Asia (that's me) who is tired of
bargaining with natives for animals. Bargaining can be fun,—
it's given me so many laughs that perhaps I shouldn't complain—
but after you've had weeks of it in a row, it's like walking into
heaven to stroll, alone, to the border of the leafy theatre where
daily the greatest drama in the world is enacted.

On one of these walks I passed a trap in which a little mouse-
deer of surpassing beauty was imprisoned. . . .

The natives are sentimental about Pelandok to this extent: en-
dowing him with supernatural cunning, they make him the god of
all their legends. It is Pelandok that can outwit any other
animal in the jungle; it is Pelandok that brings about peace
when civil war threatens to divide the jungle into factions that
can hope to do nothing better than annihilate one another; it is
Pelandok that comes to the rescue when the life of a native child
is threatened by a venomous cobra or a man-eating tiger; it is
Pelandok who is all things to the native. So perhaps it isn't surprising that one of those things should be food. To the Malay
there is nothing inconsistent about devouring his hero by the hundred, which is what he does.

. . . I passed a trap, as I started to say, from which, as I
stooped over, an achingly lovely little Pelandok looked up at me
appealingly. Eloquently those big (big, yes, for one of these
tiny animals) liquid deer eyes said to me, "Get me out of this,
please. It's awful."

There's only one thing to do when a pair of mouse-deer eyes
speak to you in that fashion. You do what's asked of you. I was
plainly being requested to free Pelandok from the trap that
made him captive. This I cheerfully did. I had no desire to see
this stunning little creature go into some native's curry. In
letting this prisoner out of his cell I was not doing anything
new. Whenever in the past I encountered a mouse-deer in a
trap I released him. If this reveals me as a sentimentalist, I'm
sorry. All I can say is that there are few sensations comparable
to the thrill of raising a trap door and seeing a mouse-deer go
bounding off like a streak in a series of ecstatic leaps (for the

running of Pelandok is really a succession of rubbery bounces.)

The only thing new about the release of the particular mouse-deer to which I make reference here is the fact that the native who owned the trap caught me in the act of freeing his catch. This was a bit embarrassing. After all, it was none of my business, and, had the native told me so, I'd have been forced to agree with him. Instead, he just wrung his hands, and, cringing till the sight was painful, tearfully announced that the *tuan* probably did not realize that there was nothing he and his family so thoroughly enjoyed in the way of *makan* (food) as a Pelandok curry.

I tossed him a coin, suggesting that he buy some *makan* with that. Instantly he was a happy man again and as I walked on I heard him showering me with blessings.

As I strolled along I heard more gibbon cries and bird calls. And then I thought I heard a faint tapping on the ground, followed by an answering series of taps, like faint drum-beats. This is how one mouse-deer signals to another.

It was becoming a mouse-deer evening. Mouse-deer was all I could think of now, and as I walked on and on I found myself musing on some of the legends about Pelandok. To one who is familiar with Asiatic legendry this provides a considerable field for thought, for Pelandok is the Malayan counterpart of our own B'rer Rabbit and of Reynard the Fox, in European child stories; and there are scores of stories about him.

Nothing is stressed quite so much in these native myths as Pelandok's capacity for shrewd and rapid thinking. It is a folklore that glorifies wisdom above all other virtues, the little mouse-deer emerging as the wisest of the wise. No matter how serious his plight, he can think his way out of it. The legendry that has grown up around Pelandok, then, is just another Asiatic monument to sagacity and nimbleness of wit.

One of these fancies tells how Pelandok one day encountered a hungry tiger that was about to pounce upon him. Fervently he pleaded to be spared.

"On what grounds?" asked the tiger.

"Every time a mouse-deer is destroyed," said Pelandok, "the jungle is less beautiful."

"You mouse-deer make me tired," said the tiger. "You always expect to be spared because you are beautiful. Does *my* handsomeness spare *me* from attack? It does not. Only the other day I chanced to step close to where a cobra lay. Luckily I chanced to look down as the poisonous wretch prepared to nip me. If I had not jumped away in time I'd have suffered an injection of the deadly fluid from which there is no recovery. Would that not have been an ignominious death for a tiger?

"The plea you make for your life, then, in the name of beauty, falls on deaf ears. You probably do not know that, in congress assembled, all the tigers in the jungle recently voted me the handsomest member of their species. If the most attractive tiger in the jungle is not immune from attack I fail to see why a mouse-deer should be."

"Are you sure there is not a tiger as handsome as you?" asked Pelandok.

"What a question!" exclaimed the tiger. "I never saw such ignorance! You deserve to be devoured for that alone." With which the tiger prepared to spring.

Turning pale, Pelandok cried, "Accuse me not of ignorance, O Mighty One! I know whereof I speak."

"What do you mean?" roared the tiger. "Out with it!"

"I mean," said Pelandok, "that I know where there is a tiger as handsome as you."

"You lie!" thundered the tiger. "There is no such animal!"

"I speak the truth, O Lordly One," replied Pelandok. "If I show you a tiger as handsome as yourself, will you spare me?"

"That I will!" exclaimed the tiger, confident that the mouse-deer would be unable to make good his declaration. "Now, knave, show me this tiger that is as handsome as I."

"Follow me," said Pelandok.

The mouse-deer led the tiger to the edge of a near-by stream.

"Gaze into the water," said Pelandok. This the tiger did, seeing a reflection of himself.

"Fool!" exclaimed the tiger. "That is I!"

"Are you not as handsome as yourself?" asked Pelandok.

A puzzled look on his face, the tiger, scratching his head to speed his mental processes, said, "I suppose there's something in what you say."

"Of course there is," said Pelandok.

"Still I can't help feeling that you took an unfair advantage of me," said the tiger, a stupid look on his face.

"It would have been taking an unfair advantage of you," declared Pelandok, "not to point out that the only thing in all the world as handsome as your handsome self is your handsome reflection."

This flattery had its effect on the conceited tiger.

"And now may I go?" asked the mouse-deer.

"You have shown me a tiger as handsome as myself, haven't you?" asked the great cat, still somewhat puzzled.

"Of course, O Beautiful One!"

"An agreement is an agreement," said the tiger. "Run along!"

This Pelandok did, chuckling to himself as he bounded away to safety.

(Not the least amusing phase of this story is that it endows the tiger with a sense of honor. He is a man of his word, so to speak, letting his captive go as promised.)

Another of these legends has to do with a mouse-deer that was confronted by the problem of crossing a stream that he knew to be full of crocodiles. It would have been suicide to attempt to swim waters that were inhabited by so many of these vicious monsters.

As he stood on the bank trying to decide what to do, Pelandok's eye lit upon the King of the Crocodiles, an enormous fellow who lay sunning himself near the edge of the stream.

"Good day," said Pelandok, keeping at a safe distance. He was much too fast for this big brute yet he did not see the wisdom of getting too close.

"Why don't you come over and be sociable?" asked the crocodile monarch.

"You can hear me from here, can't you?" asked Pelandok.

"Perfectly," replied the reptile rajah, "but I thought you might want a better view of me. You probably don't get a chance to look at a king very often, do you?"

"So you are the king!" exclaimed Pelandok with a courteous bow. "I hope you will forgive me for not addressing you as 'Your Highness.'"

"Oh, that's all right," said the monarch. "After all, I haven't my crown on and you could not have been expected to recognize me. I always take it off when I go for a swim. The last time I wore it in the water it came off and we had a deuce of a job finding it."

"I'm sorry you had all that trouble, Your Worship," said Pelandok, politely.

"Oh, I didn't mind," answered the king. "I have so many thousands of subjects I knew they would find it sooner or later. It gave them something to do. Subjects become such lazy devils unless you keep 'em busy. More than once I've thought it mightn't be a bad idea to lose something regularly in the water just to keep 'em occupied."

"You speak of having thousands of subjects," said Pelandok, seeing an opening. "How many have you?"

"More than any other ruler in the world," replied the sovereign lord of crocodiledom.

"Impossible, Your Grace!" said Pelandok.

"Why?" asked the king.

"For one thing," said Pelandok, "I'm sure there are more mouse-deer than crocodiles."

The king broke into a laugh. "You know not whereof you speak, Little One," he said. "I will show you."

Clearing his throat, the monarch faced the expanse of water and in a voice that reverberated for miles around, roared out the command: "Show yourselves, O my people!" Instantly thousands of crocodile heads were sticking up out of the water, an endless sea of them that confirmed Pelandok's belief that it would have been fatal to try to swim across that river.

"Are you convinced now?" asked the king.

"I'm afraid not, Your Highness," said Pelandok.

"Do you realize how many crocodiles you are gazing upon?"

asked the sovereign. Then he answered his own question, naming a tremendous sum, and adding, "I'll bet there aren't that many mouse-deer."

"True enough," said the mouse-deer. "But I don't believe there are that many crocodiles either," said Pelandok.

"What!" exclaimed the king, "you doubt my word?"

"Not at all, Your Worship," replied Pelandok with one of his most gracious bows. "I am sure you are a man of honor. Else how could you rule so mighty a kingdom? But I believe you have been misinformed as to the number of your subjects. Have you ever counted them yourself?"

"Of course not!" replied the ruler. "It is not for a ruler to count his subjects. I have more important affairs with which to occupy myself."

"To be sure!" cried Pelandok. "You naturally left the task to one of your cabinet, who seems to have deceived you."

"Do you really think so?" asked the ruler.

"I'm quite sure of it, Your Worship."

"Then, O Little One, satisfy yourself. I wouldn't mind another count myself, now that the subject has come up. I'm sure you're mistaken. But if I should find that a member of my cabinet has deceived me—!"

"You'll find I'm right," said the mouse-deer.

"Heads higher!" commanded the monarch. The crocodiles were beginning to tire of sticking their heads straight out of the water, some of these heads now being barely visible. Up they all bobbed again.

"Now go ahead and count," said the king to Pelandok.

"It is impossible to count them that way, Your Grace," protested the mouse-deer. "It is too confusing. The eye cannot keep track of so many heads."

"What do you suggest?" asked the sovereign.

"I suggest, Your Highness, that you line up your subjects in straight rows, and thus we shall be able to keep an accurate record of the total."

The king agreed to this. He commanded all his subjects to float to the surface and line up in rows. Soon there were several uninterrupted lines of crocodile backs stretching to the other shore.

"I'll start with this row," said Pelandok, selecting one of the lines. "One," he said, jumping on the first crocodile's back. "Two," he counted, as he jumped to the back of the next animal, and so on until he had crossed the stream on the backs of these guileless creatures.

When he had reached a place of safety on the far bank he turned and shouted to the King of the Crocodiles, whom he had outwitted so badly, "I guess you're right, Your Worship. There *are* more crocodiles than mouse-deer. At any rate, I am now willing to concede the point. Good-bye and good luck."

"Wait till I get hold of you!" screamed the infuriated monarch.

"I'm afraid you're going to have a long wait," said Pelandok with a laugh as he scurried off on his way to a section of the jungle where he had an engagement with some of his mouse-deer friends.

I decided, one year, to bring some mouse-deer to America. These charming little creatures had long been favorites of mine and the prospect of bringing back some specimens appealed to me tremendously.

As I made my preparations I still found myself thinking of these pigmy deer in terms of the unreal,—as animated dolls of the animal world rather than as living creatures. I was escorting a group of vitalized toys from the mythical realms of Malay legendry to a less romantic sphere that I hoped they would like as well. After all, there were no tigers and leopards and pythons (and worshipful but hungry natives) to prey upon them in the United States and perhaps they would enjoy the change.

I assembled a group of nine, putting them in two boxes. They were very carefully selected, with the result that I had as hardy and healthy a collection of mouse-deer as could have been rounded up anywhere.

I took great pains with my little Pelandoks all the way across the Pacific, feeding them and looking after them myself. At first it was difficult to get them to eat. I was unable, on board ship, to give them the menu to which they were accustomed in their wild state. I managed, however, to gather together, before sailing, some of the green plants they were fond of (and on which, along with rootcrops and jungle fruits, they mainly subsisted in the thicket). I kept these plants in the ship's ice-box, using them to tempt the little creatures; and once I got these lovely miniatures used to the idea of eating in captivity, I fed them two other dishes which they learned to like, apple and sweet potato, both finely chopped.

It doesn't take women passengers long to discover interesting freight aboard a vessel. As soon as those that were making the crossing on the ship that carried my mouse-deer (along with hundreds of other specimens) found out about my nine little Pelandoks they made a bee-line for the deck on which I was carrying these beauties. Once they got acquainted with the mouse-deer, these women made a regular practice of visiting the boxes that housed the little things. They were entranced with these idols of Malay mythology, declaring that there wasn't a member of their sex that wouldn't want a mouse-deer having once looked at one. Wild prophecies were made as to the amount of money I could make by introducing the species as pets in the United States.

The ecstasy of the ladies on board reached new heights when a baby was born to one of the female Pelandoks. Never have I seen a lovelier bit of living daintiness. So tiny that I was able to place it on the palm of my hand, it was even more a creature out of a legend than the other nine. Imagine a deer small enough to slip into your vest pocket and you have the picture.

After we were about ten days out, my little Pelandoks were very tame, responding to the greetings of visitors by running eagerly to the openings in the front of the boxes. Only the nursing mother remained aloof, she being too busy with her child to pay any attention to the amenities.

When we arrived in San Francisco I took steps to secure a permit that would enable me to land my mouse-deer. These being ruminating animals, it was necessary to have special permission to get them into the country.

The Bureau of Animal Industry of the Department of Agriculture maintains one of the most essential of governmental departments. Under Dr. Mohler it has done important work in checking the importation of animals that might be carriers of bovine diseases, particularly rinderpest and foot and mouth disease.

In the past when I had an order for an animal in the ruminating group (all of which are subject to foot and mouth disease and other bovine ailments) I would secure in advance a permit to bring it into the country. It was by virtue of such permits that I was able to enter with such ruminants as the wild goats and sheep, the deer and antelope, the camels and the Celebes anoas (pigmy water buffaloes) that I have brought to America.

Not having known in advance that I was going to return with a collection of mouse-deer, I had not applied for a permit to bring them in. In fact, it had only vaguely occurred to me to think of these diminutive creatures as members of a banned class.

Not until we were nearing San Francisco did I find myself actively remembering that, as small as these animals were, they were ruminants none the less, and that I would need the permission of the authorities to land them.

Dr. Hicks, the local representative of the Bureau of Animal Industry, placed his O.K. on all of my shipment except the mouse-deer, holding them out as true ruminants and ordering the little animals back to the ship from the place on the dock where they were with my other specimens.

Dr. Hicks was not being unduly severe with me. For years he had inspected animals I had brought into San Francisco and I had always found him fair. It was my misfortune that, at the time I arrived with my little Pelandoks, there was an epidemic of foot and mouth disease in the West, much of this, as usual, being blamed on animals brought into this country from abroad. The Department of Agriculture had issued ironclad orders to the effect that a more careful watch than ever was to be kept in the matter of ruminants and that, regardless of the circumstances, no animal coming under this classification be granted a "special permit" without an O.K. from Washington.

On account of the fact that my nine mouse-deer—no, there were now ten, with the baby—were in excellent condition, with no sign of disease of any kind, I felt confident that there would be a favorable reply to the telegram Dr. Hicks courteously sent to Washington outlining the circumstances and asking whether he could let the little creatures pass.

To my astonishment there came a reply to the effect that the mouse-deer could not be allowed to land. Victims of the strict enforcement of the law that always applies in epidemic times,— when such things as "special permits" cease to be—my lovely ten were doomed. They would have to be destroyed. This was the official pronouncement.

Never have I had a more painful task. One by one I chloroformed them. This was the easiest death I could contrive for the poor little devils. Ten quick applications of a wad of surgical cotton soaked in the death-dealing fluid and ten little Pelandoks were no more. They seemed to die the second the fumes reached their nostrils. Killing the baby was the toughest part of the assignment. I hope I'll never again have such a job. When the bodies were burned the law was satisfied.

Thus ended my one and only attempt to get mouse-deer into the United States. I didn't have the heart to attempt it again.

Some day I hope for a modification of the law so that Americans may have a chance to gaze upon the lovely little heroes of Malay legendry that have never been seen in this country.

Tiger on Horseback

I HAD just arrived in San Francisco after crossing the Pacific with a big shipment of animals, birds and reptiles. There is nothing more wearing than looking after the needs of hundreds of live specimens on a long ocean voyage and I was glad when the trip was over.

With the various members of my collection on the way to their different destinations, my work was finished till the next trip. I stepped out into the streets of San Francisco for a breath of air, finding myself relaxing for the first time in weeks. One of the first things that met my eye was a gaudy circus poster that conveyed the good news that the Al G. Barnes show was in town.

Al G. Barnes, owner of the show, had been a friend and customer of mine for years. I had sold him dozens of wild animals and had grown to admire him for the remarkable results he had obtained with them. No animal was too ferocious for him and his associates to handle.

What impressed me was the fact that Barnes was a real student of animals, displaying a knowledge of their habits and peculiarities that one finds more frequently in a trained zoologist than in a circus man.

The showman's knowledge of wild creatures usually is a superficial one. Humanly enough, he does not bother to learn more about the animals he handles than is needed to put them through their paces. Al Barnes was an exception. He had an expert's knowledge of his wild wards that went far beyond what was needed to make them perform.

I always got a kick out of looking up Al G., Charlie Cook who acted as his manager, and Louis Roth, the head trainer. They were all good friends of mine, and, eager to stage a reunion, I headed for the lot where the show was installed.

My circus cronies were very glad to see me. We sat around for an hour in the dining tent drinking black coffee and swapping stories.

Patrons of his show—(which was a big money-maker, second only to the Ringling Brothers-Barnum and Bailey as a drawing card)—may recall Al G. Barnes. Tall, handsome, picturesque, he was probably the most impressive-looking figure ever seen in a circus ring. When this super-ringmaster would enter the ring,— usually making a spectacular entrance, perfectly timed, on a handsome horse—the hearts of the young ladies in the audience would beat faster and the adolescent young men would gaze in awe and admiration at the Big Boss himself, democratically appearing with the help. It was as if, at a performance of The Greatest Show on Earth, Mr. Barnum or Mr. Bailey had suddenly dashed in on a milk-white charger,—only, of course, neither of those gentlemen could have cut the figure Barnes did.

Barnes and I, after trying to figure out what it was that drove him back to the ring year after year, after his annual renunciation, and what it was that drove me back to Asia for more animals after swearing that each trip was the last, decided that perhaps we'd better be philosophic about our love of action and make up our minds that despite these recurrent yearnings for a life of greater ease, we probably wouldn't settle down for another sixty or seventy years. We shook hands on that and had another swallow of black coffee.

The boss got up to go, his parting shot being that he had put aside a pair of seats for me in front of the center ring and if I didn't show up he'd never again buy so much as a rabbit from me. I needed no coaxing. I always had a lot of fun seeing that show, since it was an all-animal circus. It differed from other circuses in that there were no acrobats and none of the other tedious bores that usually put me to sleep.

Another inducement was that the trainers, in putting the animals through their paces, would "play up" to me. They would wave to me as they came by in the ring,—(if you're seated in front of the center ring, where I always sat, you can be quite chummy with the performers)—salute me, and greet me in other ways. This always aroused the curiosity of the spectators near me who would devote themselves to trying to figure out who this world-famous personage was that drew all this attention. I would sit back in my seat quietly chuckling as the various guesses as to my identity were made. It was almost as much fun as watching the show. Once an enthusiastic lady in a near-by seat decided that I was— But perhaps we'd better let that go. She had got it into her head that I was that "simply divine" Mr. So-and-so, naming a gentleman whom I considered the worst actor, bar none, I had ever seen. Another time I was taken by a kindlier soul for the author of one of my favorite adventure stories. On still another occasion an obliging policeman, called upon to identify me, let it be known, in a whisper you could hear a mile off, that I was the great Mr. ——, naming a notorious politician who wound up in jail not long afterwards.

Every year Barnes featured some one act on his program. One year, for instance, he starred Joe Martin, the famous movie orang-utan. This year the big sensation, dramatically portrayed on the bill-boards, was a tiger riding a horse. I've never seen a circus poster with more of a wallop. Wherever I went along the streets of San Francisco I encountered it and usually there were potential patrons standing by drinking in its drama. Al Barnes was a showman of showmen. When he got out a poster it was a poster; and when you passed one of 'em, you looked. You just had to. Compelling, that's what an Al G. Barnes poster was. It walked you right over to where it was and made you look and look and look.

A treat that I never overlooked when visiting the Barnes show was a long talk with Louis Roth, the head trainer, one of the most skilled men his difficult and little understood field has ever known. Starting as a "punk" (a boy who cleans animal cages, carries water and does all kinds of rough work around the lot) Louis worked at practically every task the circus knows, his love of animals proving the deciding factor in his decision to become a trainer. After working in practically every circus in America, Louis wound up as boss trainer with Barnes, a job he held until the Ringling Brothers bought out the Barnes Show in the fall of 1929. Today he is head trainer at the Luna Park Zoo in Los Angeles which supplies most of the animals used as performers in the movies.

Louis is not the big overpowering type most people picture in visualizing an animal trainer. Rather short of stature and quiet, he is the very antithesis of the thundering giant I once saw in a play in which an animal trainer was depicted.

No one in his field has had more narrow escapes than Louis Roth. On several occasions he has been badly clawed but he has always managed to save himself. Utterly without fear, he has been known to continue working on an animal, without taking time out after the creature had attacked him, just by way of making it clear to the beast that one Louis Roth was still the boss.

A staggering knowledge of the habits and characteristics of animals, plus the greatest amount of patience I've ever seen in a human being, was the answer to Louis's success in making his jungle charges do practically anything at all. I've seen him turn a wild tiger loose in the arena,—(an animal fresh from the jungle) —and spend three hours, without once losing his temper, struggling to get the beast used to the idea of getting up on a pedestal.

"How long will it be, Louis," I asked him after this gruelling session, in the course of which the tiger addressed him several times with teeth and claws bared, "before he'll be getting up on that pedestal without any coaxing?"

"Not very long," said Louis calmly as he mopped his dripping forehead. "I can do it easy in ten or twelve sessions like this."

There's patience for you! All that work just to accomplish a preliminary step in the animal's education!

That night I went to the show with a friend. The best act was one in which Louis Roth worked in the center ring with eight tigers. The star tiger of the group was an amazingly tame and intelligent beast,—one of the most remarkable I had ever seen. Louis would lie down and this great cat would walk over him while the audience gasped. Then, while faint-hearted ladies reached for their smelling salts, the animal would open its cavernous mouth and Louis would calmly stick his head in. A lady in back of me grew hysterical during this part of the act and almost had to be carried out.

Then came the big climax of the act and the show. A property man came out with a big flaming hoop which he held up over his head. Toward him dashed a handsome horse with a tiger on its back. Under the hoop went the horse, a fraction of a second earlier the tiger leaving its perch and shooting through the circle of flame, landing on the horse's back again as the audience thundered its applause. It was one of the most sensational circus stunts I had ever seen. Knowing what tigers are like when they are turned over raw to a trainer I found myself marvelling at the tremendous amount of work that Louis Roth must have had to do before he could take the risk of putting on that stunt before an audience.

When the show was over I went back to Roth's dressing room to congratulate him on his wonderful work. With characteristic modesty Louis said, "Oh, that's nothing."

"There's something I want to know, Louis," I said. "That tiger you worked with in the group of eight,—the one that lets you stick your head down its throat—is that the same one that jumps through the flaming hoop? It looked like the same animal to me."

"Sure," replied Louis, "that's the same tiger."

"Well, all I can say, Louis, is that you've got the smartest tiger in the world in that one. Where the devil did you get it?"

Louis started to laugh. "You ain't kidding me, Frank, are you?"

"No. What do you mean?"

Louis was now having a good laugh. "Hell! You sold us that tiger six years ago. You remember, don't you? It was that shipment when you brought back only one tiger. Mr. Barnes and I met you at the dock to look it over."

With this to serve as a reminder I recalled the circumstances perfectly. There was nothing unusual about identifying an animal in the Barnes Show as one that I had brought back, since I had sold them most of their animals, but somehow as I watched this tiger of the flaming hoop go through its various stunts it never occurred to me to think of it as one of the wild creatures, fresh from the jungle, that I had picked up in Asia.

The story got better and better as I recalled the strange circumstances under which I acquired that wonderful animal.

"Do you want to hear how I got that tiger, Louis?"

"You bet."

I told him the story.

Whenever I am in the vicinity of Kuala Lumpur, the capital of the Federated Malay States, my friend McCarthy, general manager of an American mining company operating in the tin-mining districts of the Malay Peninsula, feels slighted if I do not spend a few days at his bungalow in the company's compound on the outskirts of the city.

With Ali—(I believe I've told you about him, Louis; he's my No. 1 boy on Malayan trips)—I came down from Ipoh where I picked up a pair of black leopards which a Chinese trader had secured for me. Once these were on their way by rail to Singapore, I found myself with some free time on my hands. I thought of Mac at once. The prospect of seeing this old friend again was a most appealing one.

Ali and I wound up at Mac's place at Kuala Lumpur Saturday afternoon. Mac and I had a grand reunion in the early stages of which he told me that if I had not stopped off to see him and he had heard that I had been so close to his headquarters, he'd have brought some awful curse down on my head.

Mac was scheduled to work Sunday morning. I announced to Ali that while Mac was at the tin dredges he and I were going to go down to the market-place by rickshaw to see what was stirring there. In the center of all Malay cities there is a big open market-place to which native produce is brought from the surrounding country. A collector of wild animals gets some of his best tips in these public markets which, among other things, are clearing houses for information about live animals caught in near-by districts.

Shortly after we got into the thick of the market-place crowds, a native came pattering up to Ali and asked him if he thought his *tuan* would like to buy a tiger skin. A series of questions brought out the information that the tiger whose skin was being peddled had been trapped near Klang and had not yet been killed. Failing to find a purchaser for the live animal, the Malays who had caught it were now offering the skin for sale.

Klang is not more than a dozen miles from Kuala Lumpur, so I decided we might as well make the trip right away. I was curious to see what these natives had to offer. At Klang we learned that the *dato,* or headman, of an adjacent village was proprietor of the tiger. We looked him up and he led us four miles into the jungle to a spot where a fine full-grown tiger was trapped in a heavy log cage with two compartments and a deadfall door. The inner compartment had been baited with a baby goat. This infant, bleating loudly for its mamma, attracted the big cat, which, in its haste to pick up an easy meal, soon found itself a prisoner.

It seems incredible, Louis, that that snarling beast,—(you should have heard the howls of rage that went with the useless efforts to escape)—was the same animal that you sent through the blazing hoop tonight. . . .

I didn't feel like bargaining that day, the principal reason being that I was anxious to be on hand at Mac's bungalow when he returned from the dredges. It takes time to bargain with these Malays, and there wouldn't have been any haggling if Ali had not reported to me that he had heard the *dato* say to the native who originally approached us in the market-place, "How much money do you think we can get out of this fool?"

This remark put me in my best bargaining mood. We haggled back and forth over the price of the tiger skin, finally agreeing on twenty Straits dollars, or about $11.60 gold.

The price fixed, the *dato* called for a *parang,* the local curved sword that has ended the career of countless animals of different species, including the human.

I protested. What was the idea of running a blade through my tiger skin?

The headman was puzzled. What else was there to do?

"Take your money and leave the rest to me. I'll take him out of the cage and skin him myself."

The *tuan* meant to shoot the tiger, then? Was that his plan?

No, that wasn't the *tuan's* plan at all. The *tuan* wanted no hole of any kind in his tiger rug. He'd have a perfect rug or none at all.

But surely the *tuan* would have to kill the tiger in some fashion. How did he plan to bring about this savage *harimu's* death?

"*Tidak apa*" [It doesn't matter], was my reply.

The headman, unable to get any satisfaction from me, turned to Ali telling him that I evidently did not know tigers. He asked the boy to explain to me a number of elementary details about the ferocity of these animals. Did I know how vicious they were—that they had been known to kill and eat people? One does not lead them home, these lords of the jungle, as one does a milk-goat. All these things Ali was to make clear to me since the *dato*, it seemed, could not get me to understand.

In the face of these many discouragements I insisted that I knew how to handle the tiger—and would the *dato* please let me handle the situation and take a walk for himself?

This chap was beginning to grow suspicious. He pulled one of his cronies to him and started buzzing in his ear.

What probably happened was that the *dato*, suddenly remembering that a live tiger was worth anywhere from $100 to $200, was confiding to his comrade that perhaps this *tuan* wasn't a fool after all. Could he by any chance—(O horrible thought!)—be slipping one over?

By way of reminding me that the deal was not yet closed, the *dato* said something to the effect that the *tuan* was acting strangely for a man who was buying a tiger skin. He even ventured to say that he did not like the way things were going.

I instructed Ali to tell him that I always acted strangely,— that, in fact, I was the strangest *tuan* in the world, and if this chap wasn't willing to let me buy the "tiger skin" in my own strange way, he could keep it.

That settled matters. The *dato* decided to accept his money and let me handle things my own way. His eyes popping, this fellow stood by watching me get the tiger ready so that I could take it home and "skin" it. The idea even drew a smile,—a faint one, I'll admit—from the laconic Ali.

As soon as the Malay I had sent into Klang for rope returned, Ali and I began the ticklish business of running a noose around one foot of the tiger and lashing it tight against the side of the cage. This took considerable patience. We made several efforts before we were successful, finally managing to get a loop around a front foot by reaching in between the logs of the trap, a not unhazardous proceeding. Then we caught and lashed the near-side back leg in the same manner. It was slow, tedious work. More than an hour elapsed before we had all four legs tied up to one wall of the cage. Next we passed lines between the logs higher up, over and around the big cat's body, securely lashing its forequarters and hindquarters, and finally its head. This done, we knocked away the rest of the framework, leaving the side with the tiger lashed to it standing in place. It was held firm by the corner posts that were imbedded in the earth.

When I secured some carrying poles, we were ready for the march to Klang with our strange piece of baggage.

By now many natives had crowded round and it was an easy matter to recruit four of them to wield the carrying poles at a dollar apiece (more than most of them made in a month).

It was doubtless the first and only time that a tiger, sewed like a trout fly on a sample card in a sports goods shop, was ever carried into the village of Klang,—or for that matter, into any other village, town or city anywhere else. It was a bit awkward, Louis, but quite original.

You should have seen the villagers surround us and gape in wonder at our odd package. We made quite a sensation. You know, Louis, for a man who for years has been called modest I get a curious kick out of being followed around by an awe-struck mob, even when they're only a gang of Malays. . . .

Before leaving San Francisco I re-visited the Al G. Barnes Show to see some other old friends, including a group of wanderoo monkeys I had brought back for this circus in 1919. It was good seeing these odd black simians again with their manes and tufted tails like lions. Then I had a look at some rhesus monkeys with babes that I had shipped Barnes at the beginning of the season.

One by one I greeted various other friends I had brought back from the wilds, including a Malayan tapir that failed to reciprocate my enthusiastic how-de-do. Truth compels the admission that he looked quite bored as I said hello, turning his back on me without much loss of time, by way of good-bye.

Each of these creatures that I had sold to Al Barnes had a separate history, sometimes an interesting and exciting one. I quickly recalled an elephant that I had brought out of Siam, in the early days of my career as a collector. When I delivered her she was only four and a half feet high. As she stood before me now she was a big lady measuring nine or ten feet in height. Unmistakable marks on her ears make her identification simple.

I saluted a pair of black leopards one of which, shortly after I brought it into Singapore and installed it in a new cage, had reached out playfully and torn my coat off my back.

I bowed before the cage of another old friend, a tiger that had two claws gone from one foot. I recalled how when I bought this animal its wounded foot harbored thousands of maggots that I drove out by the use of an antiseptic solution in a squirt-gun; and how the big cat snarled its rage when I worked on this injured member. This animal, now a fine performer, gave me a haughty stare as I stood before it trying to renew old ties. I may have known her in those days,—but not now. She yawned and looked away. . . . Where was that boy with supper, anyhow?

Then there was a spotted leopard with part of one ear gone. I had picked him up as a half-grown cub in northern India. A good-natured creature, with no signs of treachery in his make-up, I had been able to raise him by hand all the way home. Perhaps because I had once been very fond of this likeable beast, I kidded myself into believing that he remembered me. At any rate, he came to the bars of his cage and let me scratch his head.

After visiting several other animals I had brought back for this biggest of all-animal shows, I paid my respects to the Kat from Klang, the celebrated tiger on horseback. Once again publicity had taken its toll. The creature snubbed me utterly. If I had been So Much Dirt I couldn't have been more completely ignored. Words designed to bring the creature to the bars had the effect of driving it to the back of the cage. . . .

Though perhaps it is unfair to accuse the beast of the aloofness in dealing with old associates that famous characters sometimes develop. Perhaps I was just being re-paid for the undignified manner in which I brought this animal into Klang. After all, no tiger likes to be publicly humiliated.

King Cobra

"WE want a king cobra,—a big one." Several times, I had heard those words from Dr. Ditmars of the New York Zoological Park. For a long time I had been on the look-out for a specimen that would fill the bill but without success. The task of bringing back what was wanted by the man who is considered America's greatest reptile authority was as worth-while an assignment as I could ask for; made doubly so by the fact that I looked upon Dr. Ditmars as one who took a friendly interest in my operations.

The difficulties involved in landing a big king cobra are many. Most of the Asiatic traders and trappers that supply me with specimens of other kinds, including dangerous animals and reptiles, have a fear of cobras that makes the disquiet that all other jungle terrors arouse in them seem mild by comparison. Usually when a sizeable king cobra is available for purchase it is the result of an accident or a freakish set of circumstances; there being no regular trade in these reptiles that there is, say, in tigers and leopards.

The reason for this is that of all the creatures that dwell in the jungles of Asia it is the most vicious, being the only one that will attack without provocation. Nowhere in the world is there an animal or reptile that can quite match its unfailing determination to wipe out anything that crosses its path. This lust to kill invests the king cobra with a quality of fiendishness that puts it in a class by itself, almost making of it a jungle synonym for death.

One is always thinking of it in terms of loss of life. I find myself recalling a hundred and one instances of its destructiveness. I think of the many natives, within my own experience, that have succumbed to it, of animals that suffered the same fate. I can't get out of mind, for instance, the picture of a big water

272

buffalo, a fine robust specimen weighing about 1,500 pounds, that, walking through a rice *padi,* had the misfortune to step too close to a ridge where a six-foot king cobra lay coiled up. The uncompromising reptile struck and the buffalo was dead in less than an hour. Then there is a whole series of memories of bullocks and other work animals wiped out by cobras, of the many planters I've known whose dogs suffered the horrible death that follows when His Royal Highness, King Cobra, gets his fangs into play.

It is not a more terrible venom that makes the king cobra the most dangerous of reptiles. In fact, I believe that the poisonous secretions of the Russell's viper of India and the green mamba of Africa are deadlier. The king cobra, however, is a much bigger snake and its poison sacs contain considerably more venom. Then there is another point to consider. The ordinary poisonous reptile makes a quick strike and injects what venom it can in a fraction of a second. When the king cobra strikes it holds its victim fast in its jaw until it has completely emptied its poison sacs. The result is an injection from which recovery is impossible, the system being too saturated with the killing fluid. No other snake injects so much poison and no other snake does so thorough a job of destroying its victim. Swiftly and agonizingly death comes, no more certain or painful death having ever been visited upon man or beast.

Nine times out of ten the mere smell of a human being will send a tiger scurrying off into the jungle. The same is true of the leopard. Even the savage sladung (wild jungle buffalo), considered by many the most formidable of all animals, has no desire to pit himself against man unless wounded or cornered. The presence of mankind is the signal for a hasty retreat. The sudden appearance of a native child has been known to stampede a whole herd of wild elephants. The cobra alone refuses to admit that man is anything to worry about. Cross his path anywhere at any time and he'll raise two or three feet of his body off the ground, stretch out his great hood and go for you. There is a kind of horrible glamour about the unwillingness of this king of reptiles to make his peace with anyone or anything. He's a

fighter always. Bump into him and be prepared to defend yourself.

The only king cobras in this country when Dr. Ditmars was
prodding me to locate a sizeable one for him were specimens four
and five feet long. I had had opportunities to pick up such
cobras but they did not interest me. I was on the look-out for
one that measured at least nine or ten feet. Nothing less would
have satisfied the Reptile Curator of the Bronx Zoo. And I
hoped to do even better than that. (Though I hadn't the faintest
idea how I was going to do it.)

I had brought back many of the spectacled cobras of India
and the black cobras of the Malay Archipelago but I had yet to
enter the United States with a king cobra. I wanted a specimen
that would make zoologists throw their hats in the air, there
being nothing more depressing to me than the spectacle of a
scientist who can only get mildly excited about a specimen I
shove under his nose. Give me joyfully dancing zoologists
every time.

Wherever I went on the collecting trips that kept me bouncing
all over the map of Asia I looked around to see if there wasn't
a chance of picking up the kind of king cobra that was wanted
in New York. If there was anything I could do to put a reptile
in the Bronx Zoo that would make even one spectator forget himself sufficiently to shout, "Lookit the size of that damned thing!"
I wanted to do it.

For some time my efforts were unrewarded. Traders kept
showing me king cobras that looked like shoe-strings till I almost
decided that the species was going back.

Then one day I had a stroke of luck. I was up on the north-
eastern border of Johore looking over some tigers. At the
height of the bargaining—(just as I was saying that while these
were good tigers I could not agree with the trader who was giving
me a line of high pressure Asiatic sales-talk that they were the
finest pair ever caught)—an old Malay Sakai, looking like an
octogenarian monkey, came by with a box on his head. He
spewed up a lot of sentences in a Malay dialect that was a bit

beyond me. Only two of his many words meant anything to me: *"Ular,"* which means "snake," and *"ringgit,"* which means "dollars." Two words out of about two hundred isn't much of a percentage but they told me all I needed to know. If I would part with some of my dollars I could have the snake that this apelike Sakai was carrying on his head. (Sakais,—quite a few of them, at any rate—look so much like monkeys I've been tempted more than once to bring back some specimens and exhibit them.)

The offer of a snake wasn't any cause for excitement. Most reptiles made me yawn. I had looked at so many for weeks that meant absolutely nothing to me that when I asked the old man to take the box off his head and let me have a look at the contents I was merely operating on the principle that there's no harm in looking.

It didn't take me long to see that the old baboon had something remarkable to offer,—the largest king cobra I had ever seen. In fact, it later proved to be the biggest in the world. The record had been held for years by a specimen twelve feet six inches long, preserved in alcohol in the Raffles Museum at Singapore. It developed that the monster I found myself looking at that day in northern Johore was almost a foot longer. Four years later my record was broken by a fourteen-foot specimen that was killed on a rubber estate near Ipoh. This amazing reptile was mounted and is also on exhibit today in the Raffles Museum.

I was overjoyed. So was Ali who accompanied me on this trip. But we saved our handsprings till later. Show too much pleasure over a specimen a native offers you for sale and you let yourself in for hours of trying to convince the wretch that he's mistaken in his suddenly acquired belief that what he is selling is the most precious thing in the world.

I asked the Sakai how much he wanted. *"Sa-puloh ringgit* [Ten dollars, Straits money]," came the reply.

I gave him the ten dollars and the giant king cobra was mine.

The old man interested me. His being a Sakai was enough to accomplish that, for there is no stranger people anywhere in the world than these descendants of the aboriginal possessors of the Malay Peninsula. They hardly ever come out of the jungle where they live with a classic unconcern about such benefits of civilization as clothes. Among the mature men and women there are those who conceal their procreative parts; but the younger generation (perhaps causing the old folks to say there were no such goings-on when *they* were young men and women) spurn such concealments. Serene in their nakedness, it doesn't occur to them to think of the need for clothes any more than such thoughts would enter the heads of the birds and beasts around them.

To the Malays, the Sakais are a lost people, barbarous and unenlightened, which is by way of showing that even in jungle country there is a class system. This is understandable, of course; for the Malays are a civilized lot compared with the primitive Sakais.

The Malays are not above trading with the Sakais but their method of dealing with these wild tribesmen, whom they seek out in their camps, tells the whole story of the superiority they feel. If a Sakai has anything to offer he is told to deposit it at an appointed place and withdraw. The Malay trader then places alongside the Sakai's offering the merchandise he is willing to give in exchange. They bargain back and forth with at least twenty feet separating them until the deal is closed.

In fairness to the Malays it is necessary to point out that they shun the Sakais not merely because they consider them an inferior people but for the practical reason that most of these monkey-like jungle-folk suffer from skin diseases. They are forever scratching themselves like the simians they resemble, industriously working their fingers over the queer, shiny, and sometimes scaly, skin that is so common among them.

The average Malay considers the Sakais worse than pigs but business is business; and if a Malay trader hears that a tribe of Sakais have something to offer that can be converted into profits he loses no time in heading for their camp.

I was curious to hear from the old Sakai how he had come by the tremendous cobra he had sold me. One of the Asiatic jungle's strangest products, he stood before me hugging his ten

Straits dollars to his chest, greatly pleased with his bargain and smiling that I might get a good look at the hideous black stumps that once were teeth. A sack of bones encased in a dark brown skin—(the Sakais are darker than the Malays)—he looked half-starved, though this was no indication that he was. For at least fifty of the seventy or more years of his life—(he might have been eighty, for all anyone could tell)—he probably had had that same emaciated look. There are freakish examples of longevity everywhere in Asia,—old men who all their lives look as if they can't possibly live another minute and who succeed in outliving by many years thousands of their huskier-looking brethren.

The old man was all dressed up and I couldn't help wondering how many years he had owned these habiliments he had donned for his appearance in the village where we met. On those rare occasions when a Sakai ventures out of his camp it is necessary for him to put on some clothes or the Malays will not permit him to enter their villages.

The old man's gala attire—(darned gala for a Sakai)—consisted of a greasy old *sarong* and a dirty rag wrapped turban-fashion around his head. With one hand he scratched himself, with the other he continued to hug to his chest his ten dollars.

I asked Ali to get from him the story of how he had come into possession of the king cobra. The old man, accustomed to being shunned, was pleased when he learned that I wanted to hear his story and he spoke freely, rattling on so rapidly when he became excited that I marvelled at Ali's ability to follow him. Never have I heard a weirder jumble of sounds than came from his lips in those overwrought moments. Authentic Malay isn't especially easy to understand; and, when you hear a strange version of it—a local dialect—spoken by a stimulated old man who is probably getting his first chance to talk in years, the result is unlike anything else that ever reached human ears.

The *tuan* would never regret asking how he (the old Sakai) had acquired that tremendous *ular*. Perhaps the *tuan* would never again hear such a tale. Before he launched his story he repeated over and over again, Ali later told me, that I had done well to seek his story. It was as if, Ali said, he was trying to prolong the novelty of having an audience.

One night when the jungle was a bit chill and damp, he and his comrades started a fire. Sakais have a habit of rolling in the warm ashes on such occasions. One of the men was going through these strange gymnastics when he felt something strike him in the chest. Instinctively he reached out and grabbed it, yelling for all he was worth as he did. Curled up in the ashes, some of them half asleep, were other Sakais. When they heard their fellow tribesman cry out they jumped up to see what was wrong. They found him holding an enormous king cobra. (It would not have been difficult for him to do this as the cobra has no great power in its body like constrictor snakes.) Seeking a warm place the reptile had come into the Sakai camp. Lying directly in the path of the poor devil who was warming himself, it had raised up and struck when he came rolling along to violate the privacy of its resting place.

As the victim kept shrieking away that he had been bitten by a *ular*, one of the Sakais who had scrambled up out of the ashes got a firm hold on the snake behind the head and took it away from his doomed comrade.

Only a Sakai would have had the nerve to do that. Among these wild people is found a knowledge of animals and reptiles that is equalled only by their courage in dealing with them. Only a Malay, with his capacity for making these queer junglefolk feel like so much dirt, can frighten them.

The man with the snake yelled for a kris. He would cut the creature's head off. Our skinny old man, who had shaken himself out of his slumbers and joined the group, ruled no. He was the chief of the tribe (we hadn't realized that we were in the presence of a tribal leader) and what he said was law. He ordered the snake taken alive. Why kill it when it could be sold to the next Malay trader that came along? In all the time he had lived in the jungle—he was sure it must be close to 900 moons—he had never seen so big a cobra and he felt sure it would fetch a good price.

The Sakai who was holding the snake had a very good grip

on it. With the old man directing the operations, a long pole and strips of rattan were quickly produced and the cobra was stretched out and lashed to the pole. Later it was transferred to an old wooden box that a Malay trader had left behind.

Meanwhile the women of the camp were making a great to-do. One of them—the official healer who, we were told, had many miraculous cures to her credit—was working over the moaning victim. First she tried to suck the devils out of the man's chest, then she made a poultice of herbs and applied it. These measures, the old man assured us, were effective in treating many kinds of bites; but this *ular* was too full of devils. So many of them had been transferred to his unfortunate comrade when the poor chap was bitten that they had no trouble killing him long before daylight set in.

For weeks the Sakais waited for a Malay trader to appear. None came—(their visits were irregular)—and the old man decided to dress up and take the cobra to the nearest village, feeling sure that he could find a trader who would want to buy so big a *ular*. The box had started to rot and he was anxious to dispose of his prize before the problem of providing new quarters for it arose.

The first thing I did when I got back to Singapore with my record-breaking king cobra was to order of Hin Mong a fine teakwood box with a heavy plate-glass top sliding in a groove. I wanted to get Dr. Ditmars's future boarder into its new box as soon as possible and then go about the business of putting it in good condition. Cobras are hardy rascals but neglect can harm the toughest of creatures. This one was suffering from too long a stay in that vile-smelling box, a crude affair that couldn't be cleaned, and hardly the right quarters for my thirteen-foot cobra.

When Hin Mong delivered the new box we prepared to transfer the snake by placing the old box over the new and knocking the decaying bottom out of the old. The snake would drop through and with one quick slide of the plate-glass top I would finish the job of installing him in his new and more comfortable home.

I didn't have Ali with me that day. But I had two Chinese boys and two Malay boys working with me in the compound, which gave me more help than I needed for the simple task to be done. The scene of our operations was a nipa-thatched shed in my compound, inclosed on three sides, open in front and partly filled with empty tiger cages and other boxes stacked to the roof.

I sent one of the Chinese boys for the old box. With the rear wall of the shed at my back, I was standing beside the new box which was in readiness for its tenant. As the boy approached he stumbled over some object on the ground, jarring the box sufficiently to cause the rotten bottom to fall out. The snake fell with it, landing on the cement in front of me, belly up.

In a fraction of a second my four boys were frantically scrambling to places of safety. One of the Malay boys, developing a speed that was little short of miraculous in one so lazy, got to the top of the stacked-up tiger cages in record time. If he had been pursued by a whole army of demons he could not have got there more quickly.

I'm not criticizing the boys for running. I was debating whether to do the same thing myself. It was really the sensible thing to do. After all, who wants to fight a cobra? It's all right in case you're interested in the idea of suicide but if you're as keen about life as I am, there's no strategy equal to running while there's still time when you're in a situation like the one that confronted me as I stood in that blind alley. The piled-up tiger boxes formed a wall on my left, the solid side-wall of the shed was at my right and behind me was the back of the shed.

I hesitated long enough to give the snake a chance to right itself. It reared its head three feet and spread its greenish brown hood. Then it saw me.

Instinctively I jumped backward. There wasn't far to go. Another four or five feet and I'd hit the back of the shed. As I made my brief retreat the snake struck, missing my leg by only an inch or two.

I was trapped. I suffered more from plain ordinary fright at that moment—and I'm not ashamed to admit it—than at any time in all my long career of adventure. Through my mind flashed a quick picture of what had happened to the Sakai that this terrible reptile had bitten. It made me pretty sick.

I flattened myself against the back of the shed, grimly eyeing the killer that lay almost at my feet. The expressionless eyes calmly looking back at me gave me a cold and clammy feeling. I didn't want to die this way. It was not my notion of a decent death. Surely there must be some way out. Desperately I ran my eyes around for something to bring down over the enemy's head. I wasn't particular. Anything would do, anything that could be converted into a club,—a stick of wood, a . . .

The cobra was poising itself for another strike. The hideous head rose slightly and stretched forward a bit. I got the impression of a calculating foe gauging its distance before launching another attack.

I had passed the point where fear was any longer a definite emotion. It had disappeared, along with all other emotions, and all I was aware of was a numbness of mind and body.

Staring hard ahead I poised myself too . . . for a fight to a finish, though just how I was going to fight I didn't know. I had nothing to fight with, nothing with which to fend off the attack.

My hands, with which I had successfully defended myself in the past against animals of many species, including the human, now seemed ridiculous. Hands, without something to wield, aren't much good in a scrap with a cobra. They might be strong enough to strangle two such enemies—and they were—but if my grisly antagonist punctured one of them with his fangs the fight would be over. And he had so many other targets . . . legs, arms, body . . .

Mechanically I found myself going through some motions. I don't recall that they were part of a plan. They represented, rather, the final idea of a paralyzed brain, stirred into action by the second assault of the enemy. As it struck I went through those motions to which I refer. Frantically slipping over my head the white duck coat which I was wearing over a bare skin,— (quaint custom of the tropics)—I held it in front of me, and as the snake came on I lunged forward and threw myself upon it. I hit the ground with a bang, the cobra under me. I could feel the wriggling body under mine, and with each wriggle I pressed down harder, hopeful of keeping the reptile so weighted down that it would not be able to do anything with those murderous fangs.

I screamed like a lunatic for those boys of mine. A picture of them roasting in hell flashed through my mind and it seemed too kind a fate for them.

The cobra continued to squirm and wriggle. With a crazy kind of desperation I kept pressing down with my body, cursing the pavement for not having handles that would enable me to get a grip and bear down harder. Picture a man trying to dig his fingers into a cement floor and you have a fair idea of how demented I was at that moment.

Part of the snake got loose and kept hitting against my hip. In my unhinged condition I decided that the part that was free was the head and every time it struck I imagined myself being bitten. Knowing how cobra bite affects the human system, I quickly developed all the symptoms and in the next few minutes managed to die a dozen times.

My shrieks finally accomplished something. One of the Malay boys appeared.

. . . The *tuan* was mistaken. . . . That was the snake's tail that was loose, not his head. . . . Of course, it was the tail! Who said it was the head? The head was under my chest. Couldn't I feel it? Didn't I know the difference between the tail of a snake and its head? I called that boy everything under the sun. . . .

And now that he had reassured me, my hysteria vanished and I no longer felt the cobra's tail biting me. How I could ever have taken that flapping end for the head I'll never be able to explain, for plainly the head was under my chest. It was as obvious now as if I could see it.

I barked out some orders. The gist of them was that the boy was to slide his hand under my chest and wad the coat around the head. With my weight pressing down on it, the snake was unable to strike. It was a ticklish job but it was one that could be done. I would slowly raise up and . . .

The boy backed off. He would have none of it. He wanted to help the *tuan* but . . .

I started yelling like mad for one of the other boys. One of the Chinese lads appeared. He was game. And intelligent. As I cautiously raised up a bit, not sufficient to allow the reptile to lift its head high enough for a striking position, he slid his hand underneath me and made a quick grab for the snake behind the head; and as I slowly raised up higher and higher he began the process of tightly twisting the white duck coat over the cobra's mouth, head and neck until it was helpless.

Less than ten minutes later the king cobra that had almost succeeded in killing me was dropped into his new box. I never ceased to be grateful to the courageous little Chinese boy that came to my rescue when the Malay walked out on me. You'd have thought I was handing him a million dollars when I presented him with the wrist watch I bought for him at de Silva's in Singapore. Strangely enough, when I also tried to give him some money he refused it. The watch was sufficient, he insisted. It was one of the few instances in my many years in the East of an Oriental declining money.

When I was ready to start my king cobra on its trip to America I directed one of my boys to round up a supply of food for it. This meant gathering up some small snakes, for the king cobra, one of the cannibal reptiles, eats nothing but other snakes. He belongs to a species that can go for weeks without food but when I tested his appetite with a two-foot brown snake he made it disappear so fast it was obvious he was hungry and would be in the mood for eating on board ship.

My boy had no luck in his quest for small snakes. Few native traders handle them (there being a very limited market for them) and it looked as if the cobra was in for a long fast. I knew I could find plenty of small snakes to feed the villain in America but I didn't feel like letting him go that long without a meal. I was anxious to deliver this record-breaker in the finest condition possible and I made up my mind to consult every source in Singapore until I located some snakes for him to bolt.

Failing to find what I wanted, the day before I was due to sail I bought two small pythons of Chop Joo Soon, the Chinese dealer with whom I frequently traded. Each of these reptiles measured about six feet,—small enough for pythons but powerful reptiles. Normally I would not have considered such formidable specimens as food for my cobra but I had no choice. They were better than nothing.

The main thing that worried me about these pythons when I considered them as cobra food was that, being constrictors, they might give the hooded chap more of a squeezing than was good for him before consenting to be food. The cobra, having no constricting powers, would have to confine himself in the skirmish that would ensue to striving for a quick head-lock that would enable him to swallow the enemy. This I felt confident he would be able to do. The cobra's poison sacs meant no advantage over the venomless constrictor for snakes are unaffected by the deadliest poisons of other snakes.

When our ship, the *Granite State,* was well out and all of my specimens were stowed away where they belonged, I decided to give the cobra its first meal. I had told Captain Harry Wallis that the operation would probably be worth watching and he had made me promise not to go ahead without giving him a chance to be on hand.

When I was ready to proceed, I went to the bridge and called the captain. As we walked forward the mate joined us, followed by the boatswain and a couple of sailors.

In all there were about a dozen members of the ship's personnel standing around when I reached into the box where it lay thinking things over and grabbed a python by the back of the head. If a twenty foot python had been involved this would have been a dangerous operation for a constrictor that size is capable of crushing a man to death. The little fellow I was handling possessed no such powers, of course, but he had to be carefully watched just the same. A python about this size once wound himself around my wrist and by the time I got him unwound he had done so good a job of squeezing that my whole arm felt as if paralysis had suddenly set in.

As I pulled the python out of the box I had a boy (Ali's nephew, who accompanied me) straighten him out and stretch him out taut. I opened the slide door of the king cobra's box and quickly stuck the python's head in, working him in as if I were handling so much heavy rope. I pushed the constrictor in as fast as I could, increasing the opening of the adjustable door as the body grew thicker. (At its thickest point the python was almost as big around as the cobra was at a corresponding point.)

As the python made his forced entrance the cobra spread his hood, raised up a few inches, and prepared to strike. When about a foot of the constrictor was inside the box, the cobra made a side-swipe for him, his jaws gripping the enemy's head at about the midway mark.

When I had worked in about two-thirds of that living rope, the python required no further handling, fairly flying in to get at the thing inside that had that terrible grip on his head. In a series of lightning-fast whirls the python got three coils around the cobra, one around the hood, another about six inches further down and a third about six inches below that. Madly shaking his head and squeezing the cobra for all he was worth, the python struggled to break that first vicious hold that had put him at a disadvantage.

As the reptiles tumbled over and over in a tangled ball my gallery, as pop-eyed an audience as I've ever seen, shouted and cheered like spectators at a big sporting contest. They would never see another contest like it, a struggle that would not cease until one of the antagonists was dead. The silent fury of the snakes and the total lack of expression in their artificial-seeming eyes added a note of ghastliness that gave the struggle a kind of unearthly fascination.

I began to grow worried about my cobra.

I kept my eyes glued on his jaws, knowing that if they relaxed and let go, it meant that the python was squeezing him to death. Once, after the python had put him through a series of terrific whirls in the course of which those coils tightened like vises that are being clamped closer and closer together I thought the cobra was going to let go. Quickly I slid back the glass top of the box, and, with a heavy stick that I kept in my hand, I made ready to swat the constrictor and break his hold. I had no intention of losing that giant cobra.

The straining and tugging continued, the cobra still retaining that awful head-lock. The python seemed to tire from his convulsive struggle to whirl himself free, confining himself for half a minute or so to an attempt to squash the enemy by squeezing hard in those three places around which he lay coiled. As I looked down I noticed that the cobra was cleverly working his head around. Slowly but surely he shifted his jaws until he had improved his side hold to a front hold. (It will be remembered that originally he side-swiped the python, retaining the same grip till now.)

Instead of trying to draw the python to him the cobra was working his jaws over his antagonist's head, until he had it almost entirely in his mouth. This roused the python to a new series of violent whirls, the resultant tumbling, twisting and squirming working up the audience to a pitch of excitement that I've never seen equalled in a small group.

The cobra kept drawing his head over the python and when the constrictor's head started disappearing I slid the glass top back in place, knowing that the fight was over. The python continued furiously struggling but with each deft forward movement of the cobra's head there was less and less python.

When a whole foot of the constrictor was down the cobra's throat their bodies were as much of a tangle as ever, with the disappearing victim still struggling hard.

Even when he was half swallowed, the python continued to fight, squeezing with a fury that would have burst the sides of a less hardy opponent.

There was something horrible about the methodical way in which the cobra kept working his head over the defeated foe, a soundless, steady, unemotional process that seemed the work of a machine rather than the efforts of a living creature. Not a drop of blood was shed, which gave the battle a further note of unreality.

An hour after I had started feeding the cobra, the last bit of the python's tail, wriggling hard, by way of letting the world know that he hadn't given up yet, disappeared down the cobra's throat.

Dr. Ditmars was delighted with his giant cobra when it was delivered to the Bronx Zoo three or four weeks later. It was the prize exhibit of the Reptile House there until 1929 when, tired, perhaps, of being stared at, or eager to see what the snake-hereafter was like, it died. This, however, did not halt its earthly career. Mounted, and tagged with the details of its reptilian importance, it may be seen in the American Museum of Natural History.

A NOTE ABOUT THE AUTHOR

FRANK BUCK was born in Gainesville, Texas, the son of pioneer parents who are still hale and hearty. While still a boy, he was removed to Dallas. The Buck home, on the outskirts of the town, was not far from a densely wooded area through which ran Turtle Creek. In these woods and on the borders of this creek Frank Buck made his first acquaintance with animals. It was to develop into a lifelong friendship, and was later to make him internationally famous as a zoological collector and one of the world's leading authorities on wild animal, bird and reptile life.

From Texas he went to Chicago and from there to South America in search of rare birds. Upon returning from his second South American trip, he decided to sell half of his private collection of birds and found the deal so profitable that he resolved to go in for animal collecting on a wholesale scale. Although he has been all over the world, he has specialized in the fauna of Asia and maintains his headquarters at Singapore, the capital of the Straits Settlements.

He has crossed the Pacific forty times, circumnavigated the world five times, knocked out an orang-utan in a fair fight, walked practically the entire width of the island of Borneo, contracted to deliver (and delivered) to the city of Dallas one complete zoo, including 500 specimens of birds, mammals and reptiles; and assembled in his Singapore compound the biggest assortment of live animals ever collected in one place (with the possible exceptions of the big zoos in New York, Philadelphia, London and Hamburg).

He is internationally famous for having brought back to this country an amazingly large number of "firsts" or unique specimens. These include the only authentic man-eating tiger ever seen in this country, captured on a rubber plantation in Johore, Malaya, by Buck and his native helpers after it had killed and partly eaten a coolie; the biggest king cobra ever captured alive (delivered to Dr. Raymond L. Ditmars, Curator of the New York Zoological Park); two rare Indian rhinos which he transported from the jungles of Nepal where no white man is allowed, 16,000 miles to Dr. Hornaday and Dr. Penrose of the New York and Philadelphia zoos; and a whole group of utterly exotic specimens never before seen here alive, such as the anoa or pigmy water buffalo of Celebes, the babirussa, rarest of wild swine, the long-nosed or proboscis monkey of Borneo, the siamang gibbon, largest of the gibbon apes, the great black cockatoo of New Guinea, the fairy blue bird of Borneo, the red-crested greenwood partridge of Malaya, and many others.